CLEP-24 COLLEGE-LEVEL EXAMINATION
PROGRAM SERIES

This is your
PASSBOOK for...

Introductory Sociology

Test Preparation Study Guide
Questions & Answers

NATIONAL LEARNING CORPORATION®

COPYRIGHT NOTICE

This book is SOLELY intended for, is sold ONLY to, and its use is RESTRICTED to individual, bona fide applicants or candidates who qualify by virtue of having seriously filed applications for appropriate license, certificate, professional and/or promotional advancement, higher school matriculation, scholarship, or other legitimate requirements of education and/or governmental authorities.

This book is NOT intended for use, class instruction, tutoring, training, duplication, copying, reprinting, excerption, or adaptation, etc., by:

1) Other publishers
2) Proprietors and/or Instructors of "Coaching" and/or Preparatory Courses
3) Personnel and/or Training Divisions of commercial, industrial, and governmental organizations
4) Schools, colleges, or universities and/or their departments and staffs, including teachers and other personnel
5) Testing Agencies or Bureaus
6) Study groups which seek by the purchase of a single volume to copy and/or duplicate and/or adapt this material for use by the group as a whole without having purchased individual volumes for each of the members of the group
7) Et al.

Such persons would be in violation of appropriate Federal and State statutes.

PROVISION OF LICENSING AGREEMENTS – Recognized educational, commercial, industrial, and governmental institutions and organizations, and others legitimately engaged in educational pursuits, including training, testing, and measurement activities, may address request for a licensing agreement to the copyright owners, who will determine whether, and under what conditions, including fees and charges, the materials in this book may be used them. In other words, a licensing facility exists for the legitimate use of the material in this book on other than an individual basis. However, it is asseverated and affirmed here that the material in this book CANNOT be used without the receipt of the express permission of such a licensing agreement from the Publishers. Inquiries re licensing should be addressed to the company, attention rights and permissions department.

All rights reserved, including the right of reproduction in whole or in part, in any form or by any means, electronic or mechanical, including photocopying, recording, or by any information storage and retrieval system, without permission in writing from the Publisher.

Copyright © 2025 by
National Learning Corporation

212 Michael Drive, Syosset, NY 11791
(516) 921-8888 • www.passbooks.com
E-mail: info@passbooks.com

PASSBOOK® SERIES

THE *PASSBOOK® SERIES* has been created to prepare applicants and candidates for the ultimate academic battlefield – the examination room.

At some time in our lives, each and every one of us may be required to take an examination – for validation, matriculation, admission, qualification, registration, certification, or licensure.

Based on the assumption that every applicant or candidate has met the basic formal educational standards, has taken the required number of courses, and read the necessary texts, the *PASSBOOK® SERIES* furnishes the one special preparation which may assure passing with confidence, instead of failing with insecurity. Examination questions – together with answers – are furnished as the basic vehicle for study so that the mysteries of the examination and its compounding difficulties may be eliminated or diminished by a sure method.

This book is meant to help you pass your examination provided that you qualify and are serious in your objective.

The entire field is reviewed through the huge store of content information which is succinctly presented through a provocative and challenging approach – the question-and-answer method.

A climate of success is established by furnishing the correct answers at the end of each test.

You soon learn to recognize types of questions, forms of questions, and patterns of questioning. You may even begin to anticipate expected outcomes.

You perceive that many questions are repeated or adapted so that you can gain acute insights, which may enable you to score many sure points.

You learn how to confront new questions, or types of questions, and to attack them confidently and work out the correct answers.

You note objectives and emphases, and recognize pitfalls and dangers, so that you may make positive educational adjustments.

Moreover, you are kept fully informed in relation to new concepts, methods, practices, and directions in the field.

You discover that you are actually taking the examination all the time: you are preparing for the examination by "taking" an examination, not by reading extraneous and/or supererogatory textbooks.

In short, this PASSBOOK®, used directedly, should be an important factor in helping you to pass your test.

NONTRADITIONAL EDUCATION

Students returning to school as adults bring more varied experience to their studies than do the teenagers who begin college shortly after graduating from high school. As a result, there are numerous programs for students with nontraditional learning curves. Hundreds of colleges and universities grant degrees to people who cannot attend classes at a regular campus or have already learned what the college is supposed to teach.

You can earn nontraditional education credits in many ways:
- Passing standardized exams
- Demonstrating knowledge gained through experience
- Completing campus-based coursework, and
- Taking courses off campus

Some methods of assessing learning for credit are objective, such as standardized tests. Others are more subjective, such as a review of life experiences.

With some help from four hypothetical characters – Alice, Vin, Lynette, and Jorge – this article describes nontraditional ways of earning educational credit. It begins by describing programs in which you can earn a high school diploma without spending 4 years in a classroom. The college picture is more complicated, so it is presented in two parts: one on gaining credit for what you know through course work or experience, and a second on college degree programs. The final section lists resources for locating more information.

Earning High School Credit

People who were prevented from finishing high school as teenagers have several options if they want to do so as adults. Some major cities have back-to-school programs that allow adults to attend high school classes with current students. But the more practical alternatives for most adults are to take the General Educational Development (GED) tests or to earn a high school diploma by demonstrating their skills or taking correspondence classes.

Of course, these options do not match the experience of staying in high school and graduating with one's friends. But they are viable alternatives for adult learners committed to meeting and, often, continuing their educational goals.

GED Program

Alice quit high school her sophomore year and took a job to help support herself, her younger brother, and their newly widowed mother. Now an adult, she wants to earn her high school diploma – and then go on to college. Because her job as head cook and her family responsibilities keep her busy during the day, she plans to get a high school equivalency diploma. She will study for, and take, the GED tests. Every year, about half a million adults earn their high school credentials this way. A GED diploma is accepted in lieu of a high school one by more than 90 percent of employers, colleges, and universities, so it is a good choice for someone like Alice.

The GED testing program is sponsored by the American Council on Education and State and local education departments. It consists of examinations in five subject areas: Writing, science, mathematics, social studies, and literature and the arts. The tests also measure skills such as analytical ability, problem solving, reading comprehension, and ability to understand and apply information. Most of the questions are multiple choice; the writing test includes an essay section on a topic of general interest.

Eligibility rules for taking the exams vary, but some states require that you must be at least 18. Tests are given in English, Spanish, and French. In addition to standard print, versions in large print, Braille, and audiocassette are also available. Total time allotted for the tests is 7 1/2 hours.

The GED tests are not easy. About one-fourth of those who complete the exams every year do not pass. Passing scores are established by administering the tests to a sample of graduating high school seniors. The minimum standard score is set so that about one-third of graduating seniors would not pass the tests if they took them.

Because of the difficulty of the tests, people need to prepare themselves to take them. Often, they start by taking the Official GED Practice Tests, usually available through a local adult education center. Centers are listed in your phone book's blue pages under "Adult Education," "Continuing Education," or "GED." Adult education centers also have information about GED preparation classes and self-study materials. Classes are generally arranged to accommodate adults' work schedules. National Learning Corporation publishes several study guides that aim to thoroughly prepare test-takers for the GED.

School districts, colleges, adult education centers, and community organizations have information about GED testing schedules and practice tests. For more information, contact them, your nearest GED testing center, or:

GED Testing Service
One Dupont Circle, NW, Suite 250
Washington, DC 20036-1163
1(800) 62-MY GED (626-9433)
(202) 939-9490

Skills Demonstration

Adults who have acquired high school level skills through experience might be eligible for the National External Diploma Program. This alternative to the GED does not involve any direct instruction. Instead, adults seeking a high school diploma must demonstrate mastery of 65 competencies in 8 general areas: Communication; computation; occupational preparedness; and self, social, consumer, scientific, and technological awareness.

Mastery is shown through the completion of the tasks. For example, a participant could prove competency in computation by measuring a room for carpeting, figuring out the amount of carpet needed, and computing the cost.

Before being accepted for the program, adults undergo an evaluation. Tests taken at one of the program's offices measure reading, writing, and mathematics abilities. A take-home segment includes a self-assessment of current skills, an individual skill evaluation, and an occupational interest and aptitude test.

Adults accepted for the program have weekly meetings with an assessor. At the meeting, the assessor reviews the participant's work from the previous week. If the task has not been completed properly, the assessor explains the mistake. Participants continue to correct their errors until they master each competency. A high school diploma is awarded upon proven mastery of all 65 competencies.

Fourteen States and the District of Columbia now offer the External Diploma Program. For more information, contact:

External Diploma Program
One Dupont Circle, NW, Suite 250
Washington, DC 20036-1193
(202) 939-9475

Correspondence and Distance Study

Vin dropped out of high school during his junior year because his family's frequent moves made it difficult for him to continue his studies. He promised himself at the time he dropped out that he would someday finish the courses needed for his diploma. For people like Vin, who prefer to earn a traditional diploma in a nontraditional way, there are about a dozen accredited courses of study for earning a high school diploma by correspondence, or distance study. The programs are either privately run, affiliated with a university, or administered by a State education department.

Distance study diploma programs have no residency requirements, allowing students to continue their studies from almost any location. Depending on the course of study, students need not be enrolled full time and usually have more flexible schedules for finishing their work. Selection of courses ranges from vo-tech to college prep, and some programs place different emphasis on the types of diplomas offered. University affiliated schools, for example, allow qualified students to take college courses along with their high school ones. Students can then apply the college credits toward a degree at that university or transfer them to another institution.

Taking courses by distance study is often more challenging and time consuming than attending classes, especially for adults who have other obligations. Success depends on each student's motivation. Students usually do reading assignments on their own. Written exercises, which they complete and send to an instructor for grading, supplement their reading material.

A list of some accredited high schools that offer diplomas by distance study is available free from the Distance Education and Training Council, formerly known as the National Home Study Council. Request the "DETC Directory of Accredited Institutions" from:

The Distance Education and Training Council
1601 18th Street, NW.
Washington, DC 20009-2529
(202) 234-5100

Some publications profiling nontraditional college programs include addresses and descriptions of several high school correspondence ones. See the Resources section at the end of this article for more information.

Getting College Credit For What You Know

Adults can receive college credit for prior coursework, by passing examinations, and documenting experiential learning. With help from a college advisor, nontraditional students should assess their skills, establish their educational goals, and determine the number of college credits they might be eligible for.

Even before you meet with a college advisor, you should collect all your school and training records. Then, make a list of all knowledge and abilities acquired through experience, no matter how irrelevant they seem to your chosen field. Next, determine your educational goals: What specific field do you wish to study? What kind of a degree do you want? Finally, determine how your past work fits into the field of study. Later on, you will evaluate educational programs to find one that's right for you.

People who have complex educational or experiential learning histories might want to have their learning evaluated by the Regents Credit Bank. The Credit Bank, operated by Regents College of the University of the State of New York, allows people to consolidate credits earned through college, experience, or other methods. Special assessments are available for Regents College enrollees whose knowledge in a specific field cannot be adequately evaluated by standardized exams. For more information, contact the Regents Credit Bank at:

Regents College
7 Columbia Circle
Albany, NY 12203-5159
(518) 464-8500

Credit For Prior College Coursework

When Lynette was in college during the 1970s, she attended several different schools and took a variety of courses. She did well in some classes and poorly in others. Now that she is a successful business owner and has more focus, Lynette thinks she should forget about her previous coursework and start from scratch. Instead, she should start from where she is.

Lynette should have all her transcripts sent to the colleges or universities of her choice and let an admissions officer determine which classes are applicable toward a degree. A few credits here and there may not seem like much, but they add up. Even if the subjects do not seem relevant to any major, they might be counted as elective credits toward a degree. And comparing the cost of transcripts with the cost of college courses, it makes sense to spend a few dollars per transcript for a chance to save hundreds, and perhaps thousands, of dollars in books and tuition.

Rules for transferring credits apply to all prior coursework at accredited colleges and universities, whether done on campus or off. Courses completed off campus, often called extended learning, include those available to students through independent study and correspondence. Many schools have extended learning programs; Brigham Young University, for example, offers more than 300 courses through its Department of Independent Study. One type of extended learning is distance learning, a form of correspondence study by technological means such as television, video and audio, CD-ROM, electronic mail, and computer tutorials. See the Resources section at the end of this article for more information about publications available from the National University Continuing Education Association.

Any previously earned college credits should be considered for transfer, no matter what the subject or the grade received. Many schools do not accept the transfer of courses graded below a C or ones taken more than a designated number of years ago. Some colleges and universities also have limits on the number of credits that can be transferred and applied toward a degree. But not all do. For example, Thomas Edison State College, New Jersey's State college for adults, accepts the transfer of all 120 hours of credit required for a baccalaureate degree – provided all the credits are transferred from regionally accredited schools, no more than 80 are at the junior college level, and the student's grades overall and in the field of study average out to C.

To assign credit for prior coursework, most schools require original transcripts. This means you must complete a form or send a written, signed request to have your transcripts released directly to a college or university. Once you have chosen the schools you want to apply to, contact the schools you attended before. Find out how much each transcript costs, and ask them to send your transcripts to the ones you are applying to. Write a letter that includes your name (and names used during attendance, if different) and dates of attendance, along with the names and addresses of the schools to which your transcripts should be sent. Include payment and mail to the registrar at the schools you have attended. The registrar's office will process your request and send an official transcript of your coursework to the colleges or universities you have designated.

Credit For Noncollege Courses

Colleges and universities are not the only ones that offer classes. Volunteer organizations and employers often provide formal training worth college credit. The American Council on Education has two programs that assess thousands of specific courses and make recommendations on the amount of college credit they are worth. Colleges and universities accept the recommendations or use them as guidelines.

One program evaluates educational courses sponsored by government agencies, business and industry, labor unions, and professional and voluntary organizations. It is the Program on Noncollegiate Sponsored Instruction (PONSI). Some of the training seminars Alice has participated in covered topics such as food preparation, kitchen safety, and nutrition. Although she has not yet earned her GED, Alice can earn college credit because of her completion of these formal job-training seminars. The number of credits each seminar is worth does not hinge on Alice's current eligibility for college enrollment.

The other program evaluates courses offered by the Army, Navy, Air Force, Marines, Coast Guard, and Department of Defense. It is the Military Evaluations Program. Jorge has never attended college, but the engineering technology classes he completed as part of his military training are worth college credit. And as an Army veteran, Jorge is eligible for a service that takes the evaluations one step further. The Army/American Council on Education Registry Transcript System (AARTS) will provide Jorge with an individualized transcript of American Council on Education credit recommendations for all courses he completed, the military occupational specialties (MOS's) he held, and examinations he passed while in the Army. All Army and National Guard enlisted personnel and veterans who enlisted after October 1981 are eligible for the transcript. Similar services are being considered by the Navy and Marine Corps.

To obtain a free transcript, see your Army Education Center for a 5454R transcript request form. Include your name, Social Security number, basic active service date, and complete address where you want the transcript sent. Mail your request to:
AARTS Operations Center
415 McPherson Ave.
Fort Leavenworth, KS 66027-1373

Recommendations for PONSI are published in *The National Guide to Educational Credit for Training Programs;* military program recommendations are in *The Guide to the Evaluation of Educational Experiences in the Armed Forces.* See the Resources section at the end of this article for more information about these publications.

Former military personnel who took a foreign language course through the Defense Language Institute may request course transcripts by sending their name, Social Security number, course title, duration of the course, and graduation date to:

> Commandant, Defense Language Institute
> Attn: ATFL-DAA-AR
> Transcripts
> Presidio of Monterey
> Monterey, CA 93944-5006

Not all of Jorge's and Alice's courses have been assessed by the American Council on Education. Training courses that have no Council credit recommendation should still be assessed by an advisor at the schools they want to attend. Course descriptions, class notes, test scores, and other documentation may be helpful for comparing training courses to their college equivalents. An oral examination or other demonstration of competency might also be required.

There is no guarantee you will receive all the credits you are seeking – but you certainly won't if you make no attempt.

Credit By Examination

Standardized tests are the best-known method of receiving college credit without taking courses. These exams are often taken by high school students seeking advanced placement for college, but they are also available to adult learners. Testing programs and colleges and universities offer exams in a number of subjects. Two U.S. Government institutes have foreign language exams for employees that also may be worth college credit.

It is important to understand that receiving a passing score on these exams does not mean you get college credit automatically. Each school determines which test results it will accept, minimum scores required, how scores are converted for credit, and the amount of credit, if any, to be assigned. Most colleges and universities accept the American Council on Education credit recommendations, published every other year in the 250-page *Guide to Educational Credit by Examination*. For more information, contact:

> The American Council on Education
> Credit by Examination Program
> One Dupont Circle, Suite 250
> Washington, DC 20036-1193
> (202) 939-9434

Testing programs:

You might know some of the five national testing programs by their acronyms or initials: CLEP, ACT PEP: RCE, DANTES, AP, and NOCTI. (The meanings of these initialisms are explained below.) There is some overlap among programs; for example, four of them have introductory accounting exams. Since you will not be awarded credit more than once for a specific subject, you should carefully evaluate each program for the subject exams you wish to take. And before taking an exam, make sure you will be awarded credit by the college or university you plan to attend.

CLEP (College-Level Examination Program), administered by the College Board, is the most widely accepted of the national testing programs; more than 2,800 accredited schools award credit for passing exam scores. Each test covers material taught in basic undergraduate courses. There are five general exams – English composition, humanities, college mathematics, natural sciences, and social sciences and history – and many subject exams. Most exams are entirely multiple-choice, but English composition exams may include an essay section. For more information, contact:

    CLEP
    P.O. Box 6600
    Princeton, NJ 08541-6600
    (609) 771-7865

ACT PEP: RCE (American College Testing Proficiency Exam Program: Regents College Examinations) tests are given in 38 subjects within arts and sciences, business, education, and nursing. Each exam is recommended for either lower- or upper-level credit. Exams contain either objective or extended response questions, and are graded according to a standard score, letter grade, or pass/fail. Fees vary, depending on the subject and type of exam. For more information or to request free study guides, contact:

    ACT PEP: Regents College Examinations
    P.O. Box 4014
    Iowa City, IA 52243
    (319) 337-1387
    (New York State residents must contact Regents College directly.)

DANTES (Defense Activity for Nontraditional Education Support) standardized tests are developed by the Educational Testing Service for the Department of Defense. Originally administered only to military personnel, the exams have been available to the public since 1983. About 50 subject tests cover business, mathematics, social science, physical science, humanities, foreign languages, and applied technology. Most of the tests consist entirely of multiple-choice questions. Schools determine their own administering fees and testing schedules. For more information or to request free study sheets, contact:

    DANTES Program Office
    Mail Stop 31-X
    Educational Testing Service
    Princeton, NJ 08541
    1(800) 257-9484

The AP (Advanced Placement) Program is a cooperative effort between secondary schools and colleges and universities. AP exams are developed each year by committees of college and high school faculty appointed by the College Board and assisted by consultants from the Educational Testing Service. Subjects include arts and languages, natural sciences, computer science, social sciences, history, and mathematics. Most tests are 2 or 3 hours long and include both multiple-choice and essay questions. AP courses are available to help students prepare for exams, which are offered in the spring. For more information about the Advanced Placement Program, contact:

    Advanced Placement Services
    P.O. Box 6671
    Princeton, NJ 08541-6671
    (609) 771-7300

NOCTI (National Occupational Competency Testing Institute) assessments are designed for people like Alice, who have vocational-technical skills that cannot be evaluated by other tests. NOCTI assesses competency at two levels: Student/job ready and teacher/experienced worker. Standardized evaluations are available for occupations such as auto-body repair, electronics, mechanical drafting, quantity food preparation, and upholstering. The tests consist of multiple-choice questions and a performance component. Other services include workshops, customized assessments, and pre-testing. For more information, contact:

NOCTI
500 N. Bronson Ave.
Ferris State University
Big Rapids, MI 49307
(616) 796-4699

Colleges and universities:

Many colleges and universities have credit-by-exam programs, through which students earn credit by passing a comprehensive exam for a course offered by the institution. Among the most widely recognized are the programs at Ohio University, the University of North Carolina, Thomas Edison State College, and New York University.

Ohio University offers about 150 examinations for credit. In addition, you may sometimes arrange to take special examinations in non-laboratory courses offered at Ohio University. To take a test for credit, you must enroll in the course. If you plan to transfer the credit earned, you also need written permission from an official at your school. Books and study materials are available, for a cost, through the university. Exams must be taken within 6 months of the enrollment date; most last 3 hours. You may arrange to take the exam off campus if you do not live near the university.

Ohio University is on the quarter-hour system; most courses are worth 4 quarter hours, the equivalent of 3 semester hours. For more information, contact:

Independent Study
Tupper Hall 302
Ohio University
Athens, OH 45701-2979
1(800) 444-2910
(614) 593-2910

The University of North Carolina offers a credit-by-examination option for 140 independent study (correspondence) courses in foreign languages, humanities, social sciences, mathematics, business administration, education, electrical and computer engineering, health administration, and natural sciences. To take an exam, you must request and receive approval from both the course instructor and the independent studies department. Exams must be taken within six months of enrollment, and you may register for no more than two at a time. If you are not near the University's Chapel Hill campus, you may take your exam under supervision at an accredited college, university, community college, or technical institute. For more information, contact:

Independent Studies
CB #1020, The Friday Center
UNC-Chapel Hill
Chapel Hill, NC 27599-1020
1(800) 862-5669 / (919) 962-1134

The Thomas Edison College Examination Program offers more than 50 exams in liberal arts, business, and professional areas. Thomas Edison State College administers tests twice a month in Trenton, New Jersey; however, students may arrange to take their tests with a proctor at any accredited American college or university or U.S. military base. Most of the tests are multiple choice; some also include short answer or essay questions. Time limits range from 90 minutes to 4 hours, depending on the exam. For more information, contact:

Thomas Edison State College
TECEP, Office of Testing and Assessment
101 W. State Street
Trenton, NJ 08608-1176
(609) 633-2844

New York University's Foreign Language Program offers proficiency exams in more than 40 languages, from Albanian to Yiddish. Two exams are available in each language: The 12-point test is equivalent to 4 undergraduate semesters, and the 16-point exam may lead to upper level credit. The tests are given at the university's Foreign Language Department throughout the year.

Proof of foreign language proficiency does not guarantee college credit. Some colleges and universities accept transcripts only for languages commonly taught, such as French and Spanish. Nontraditional programs are more likely than traditional ones to grant credit for proficiency in other languages.

For an informational brochure and registration form for NYU's foreign language proficiency exams, contact:

New York University
Foreign Language Department
48 Cooper Square, Room 107
New York, NY 10003
(212) 998-7030

Government institutes:

The Defense Language Institute and Foreign Service Institute administer foreign language proficiency exams for personnel stationed abroad. Usually, the tests are given at the end of intensive language courses or upon completion of service overseas. But some people – like Jorge, who knows Spanish – speak another language fluently and may be allowed to take a proficiency exam in that language before completing their tour of duty. Contact one of the offices listed below to obtain transcripts of those scores. Proof of proficiency does not guarantee college credit, however, as discussed above.

To request score reports from the Defense Language Institute for Defense Language Proficiency Tests, send your name, Social Security number, language for which you were tested, and, most importantly, when and where you took the exam to:

Commandant, Defense Language Institute
Attn: ATFL-ES-T
DLPT Score Report Request
Presidio of Monterey
Monterey, CA 93944-5006

To request transcripts of scores for Foreign Service Institute exams, send your name, Social Security number, language for which you were tested, and dates or year of exams to:

Foreign Service Institute
Arlington Hall
4020 Arlington Boulevard
Rosslyn, VA 22204-1500
Attn: Testing Office (Send your request to the attention of the testing office of the foreign language in which you were tested)

Credit For Experience

Experiential learning credit may be given for knowledge gained through job responsibilities, personal hobbies, volunteer opportunities, homemaking, and other experiences. Colleges and universities base credit awards on the knowledge you have attained, not for the experience alone. In addition, the knowledge must be college level; not just any learning will do. Throwing horseshoes as a hobby is not likely to be worth college credit. But if you've done research on how and where the sport originated, visited blacksmiths, organized tournaments, and written a column for a trade journal – well, that's a horseshoe of a different color.

Adults attempting to get credit for their experience should be forewarned: Having your experience evaluated for college credit is time-consuming, tedious work – not an easy shortcut for people who want quick-fix college credits. And not all experience, no matter how valuable, is the equivalent of college courses.

Requesting college credit for your experiential learning can be tricky. You should get assistance from a credit evaluations officer at the school you plan to attend, but you should also have a general idea of what your knowledge is worth. A common method for converting knowledge into credit is to use a college catalog. Find course titles and descriptions that match what you have learned through experience, and request the number of credits offered for those courses.

Once you know what credit to ask for, you must usually present your case in writing to officials at the college you plan to attend. The most common form of presenting experiential learning for credit is the portfolio. A portfolio is a written record of your knowledge along with a request for equivalent college credit. It includes an identification and description of the knowledge for which you are requesting credit, an explanatory essay of how the knowledge was gained and how it fits into your educational plans, documentation that you have acquired such knowledge, and a request for college credit. Required elements of a portfolio vary by schools but generally follow those guidelines.

In identifying knowledge you have gained, be specific about exactly what you have learned. For example, it is not enough for Lynette to say she runs a business. She must identify the knowledge she has gained from running it, such as personnel management, tax law, marketing strategy, and inventory review. She must also include brief descriptions about her knowledge of each to support her claims of having those skills.

The essay gives you a chance to relay something about who you are. It should address your educational goals, include relevant autobiographical details, and be well organized, neat, and convey confidence. In his essay, Jorge might first state his goal of becoming an engineer. Then he would explain why he joined the Army, where he got hands-on training and experience in developing and servicing electronic equipment.

This, he would say, led to his hobby of creating remote-controlled model cars, of which he has built 20. His conclusion would highlight his accomplishments and tie them to his desire to become an electronic engineer.

Documentation is evidence that you've learned what you claim to have learned. You can show proof of knowledge in a variety of ways, including audio or video recordings, letters from current or former employers describing your specific duties and job performance, blueprints, photographs or artwork, and transcripts of certifying exams for professional licenses and certification – such as Alice's certification from the American Culinary Federation. Although documentation can take many forms, written proof alone is not always enough. If it is impossible to document your knowledge in writing, find out if your experiential learning can be assessed through supplemental oral exams by a faculty expert.

Earning a College Degree

Nontraditional students often have work, family, and financial obligations that prevent them from quitting their jobs to attend school full time. Can they still meet their educational goals? Yes.

More than 150 accredited colleges and universities have nontraditional bachelor's degree programs that require students to spend little or no time on campus; over 300 others have nontraditional campus-based degree programs. Some of those schools, as well as most junior and community colleges, offer associate's degrees nontraditionally. Each school with a nontraditional course of study determines its own rules for awarding credit for prior coursework, exams, or experience, as discussed previously. Most have charges on top of tuition for providing these special services.

Several publications profile nontraditional degree programs; see the Resources section at the end of this article for more information. To determine which school best fits your academic profile and educational goals, first list your criteria. Then, evaluate nontraditional programs based on their accreditation, features, residency requirements, and expenses. Once you have chosen several schools to explore further, write to them for more information. Detailed explanations of school policies should help you decide which ones you want to apply to.

Get beyond the printed word – especially the glowing words each school writes about itself. Check out the schools you are considering with higher education authorities, alumni, employers, family members, and friends. If possible, visit the campus to talk to students and instructors and sit in on a few classes, even if you will be completing most or all of your work off campus. Ask school officials questions about such things as enrollment numbers, graduation rate, faculty qualifications, and confusing details about the application process or academic policies. After you have thoroughly investigated each prospective college or university, you can make an informed decision about which is right for you.

Accreditation

Accreditation is a process colleges and universities submit to voluntarily for getting their credentials. An accredited school has been investigated and visited by teams of observers and has periodic inspections by a private accrediting agency. The initial review can take two years or more.

Regional agencies accredit entire schools, and professional agencies accredit either specialized schools or departments within schools. Although there are no national accrediting standards, not just any accreditation will do. Countless "accreditation associations" have been invented by schools, many of which have no academic programs and sell phony degrees, to accredit themselves. But 6 regional and about 80 professional accrediting associations in the United States are recognized by the U.S. Department of Education or the Commission on Recognition of Postsecondary Accreditation. When checking accreditation, these are the names to look for. For more information about accreditation and accrediting agencies, contact:

> Institutional Participation Oversight Service Accreditation and State Liaison Division
> U.S. Department of Education
> ROB 3, Room 3915
> 600 Independence Ave., SW
> Washington, DC 20202-5244
> (202) 708-7417

Because accreditation is not mandatory, lack of accreditation does not necessarily mean a school or program is bad. Some schools choose not to apply for accreditation, are in the process of applying, or have educational methods too unconventional for an accrediting association's standards. For the nontraditional student, however, earning a degree from a college or university with recognized accreditation is an especially important consideration. Although nontraditional education is becoming more widely accepted, it is not yet mainstream. Employers skeptical of a degree earned in a nontraditional manner are likely to be even less accepting of one from an unaccredited school.

Program Features

Because nontraditional students have diverse educational objectives, nontraditional schools are diverse in what they offer. Some programs are geared toward helping students organize their scattered educational credits to get a degree as quickly as possible. Others cater to those who may have specific credits or experience but need assistance in completing requirements. Whatever your educational profile, you should look for a program that works with you in obtaining your educational goals.

A few nontraditional programs have special admissions policies for adult learners like Alice, who plan to earn their GEDs but want to enroll in college in the meantime. Other features of nontraditional programs include individualized learning agreements, intensive academic counseling, cooperative learning and internship placement, and waiver of some prerequisites or other requirements – as well as college credit for prior coursework, examinations, and experiential learning, all discussed previously.

Lynette, whose primary goal is to finish her degree, wants to earn maximum credits for her business experience. She will look for programs that do not limit the number of credits awarded for equivalency exams and experiential learning. And since well-documented proof of knowledge is essential for earning experiential learning credits, Lynette should make sure the program she chooses provides assistance to students submitting a portfolio.

Jorge, on the other hand, has more credits than he needs in certain areas and is willing to forego some. To become an engineer, he must have a bachelor's degree; but because he is accustomed to hands-on learning, Jorge is interested in getting experience as he gains more technical skills. He will concentrate on finding schools with strong cooperative education, supervised fieldwork, or internship programs.

Residency Requirements

Programs are sometimes deemed nontraditional because of their residency requirements. Many people think of residency for colleges and universities in terms of tuition, with in-state students paying less than out-of-state ones. Residency also may refer to where a student lives, either on or off campus, while attending school.

But in nontraditional education, residency usually refers to how much time students must spend on campus, regardless of whether they attend classes there. In some nontraditional programs, students need not ever step foot on campus. Others require only a very short residency, such as one day or a few weeks. Many schools have standard residency requirements of several semesters but schedule classes for evenings or weekends to accommodate working adults.

Lynette, who previously took courses by independent study, prefers to earn credits by distance study. She will focus on schools that have no residency requirement. Several colleges and universities have nonresident degree completion programs for adults with some college credit. Under the direction of a faculty advisor, students devise a plan for earning their remaining credits. Methods for earning credits include independent study, distance learning, seminars, supervised fieldwork, and group study at arranged sites. Students may have to earn a certain number of credits through the degree-granting institution. But many programs allow students to take courses at accredited schools of their choice for transfer toward their degree.

Alice wants to attend lectures but has an unpredictable schedule. Her best course of action will be to seek out short residency programs that require students to attend seminars once or twice a semester. She can take courses that are televised and videotape them to watch when her schedule permits, with the seminars helping to ensure that she properly completes her coursework. Many colleges and universities with short residency requirements also permit students to earn some credits elsewhere, by whatever means the student chooses.

Some fields of study require classroom instruction. As Jorge will discover, few colleges and universities allow students to earn a bachelor's degree in engineering entirely through independent study. Nontraditional residency programs are designed to accommodate adults' daytime work schedules. Jorge should look for programs offering evening, weekend, summer, and accelerated courses.

Tuition and Other Expenses

The final decisions about which schools Alice, Jorge, and Lynette attend may hinge in large part on a single issue: Cost. And rising tuition is only part of the equation. Beginning with application fees and continuing through graduation fees, college expenses add up.

Traditional and nontraditional students have some expenses in common, such as the cost of books and other materials. Tuition might even be the same for some courses, especially for colleges and universities offering standard ones at unusual times. But for nontraditional programs, students may also pay fees for services such as credit or transcript review, evaluation, advisement, and portfolio assessment.

Students are also responsible for postage and handling or setup expenses for independent study courses, as well as for all examination and transcript fees for transferring credits. Usually, the more nontraditional the program, the more detailed the fees. Some schools charge a yearly enrollment fee rather than tuition for degree completion candidates who want their files to remain active.

Although tuition and fees might seem expensive, most educators tell you not to let money come between you and your educational goals. Talk to someone in the financial aid department of the school you plan to attend or check your library for publications about financial aid sources. The U.S. Department of Education publishes a guide to Federal aid programs such as Pell Grants, student loans, and work-study. To order the free 74-page booklet, *The Student Guide: Financial Aid from the U.S. Department of Education,* contact:

Federal Student Aid Information Center
P.O. Box 84
Washington, DC 20044
1 (800) 4FED-AID (433-3243)

Resources

Information on how to earn a high school diploma or college degree without following the usual routes is available from several organizations and in numerous publications. Information on nontraditional graduate degree programs, available for master's through doctoral level, though not discussed in this article, can usually be obtained from the same resources that detail bachelor's degree programs.

National Learning Corporation publishes study guides for all of these exams, for both general examinations and tests in specific subject areas. To order study guides, or to browse their catalog featuring more than 5,000 titles, visit NLC online at www.passbooks.com, or contact them by phone at (800) 632-8888.

Organizations

Adult learners should always contact their local school system, community college, or university to learn about programs that are readily available. The following national organizations can also supply information:

American Council on Education
One Dupont Circle
Washington, DC 20036-1193
(202) 939-9300

Within the American Council on Education, the Center for Adult Learning and Educational Credentials administers the National External Diploma Program, the GED Program, the Program on Noncollegiate Sponsored Instruction, the Credit by Examination Program, and the Military Evaluations Program.

College-Level Examination Program (CLEP)

1. WHAT IS CLEP?

CLEP stands for the College-Level Examination Program, sponsored by the College Board. It is a national program of credit-by-examination that offers you the opportunity to obtain recognition for college-level achievement. No matter when, where, or how you have learned – by means of formal or informal study – you can take CLEP tests. If the results are acceptable to your college, you can receive credit.

You may not realize it, but you probably know more than your academic record reveals. Each day you, like most people, have an opportunity to learn. In private industry and business, as well as at all levels of government, learning opportunities continually occur. If you read widely or intensively in a particular field, think about what you read, discuss it with your family and friends, you are learning. Or you may be learning on a more formal basis by taking a correspondence course, a television or radio course, a course recorded on tape or cassettes, a course assembled into programmed tests, or a course taught in your community adult school or high school.

No matter how, where, or when you gained your knowledge, you may have the opportunity to receive academic credit for your achievement that can be counted toward an undergraduate degree. The College-Level Examination Program (CLEP) enables colleges to evaluate your achievement and give you credit. A wide range of college-level examinations are offered by CLEP to anyone who wishes to take them. Scores on the tests are reported to you and, if you wish, to a college, employer, or individual.

2. WHAT ARE THE PURPOSES OF THE COLLEGE-LEVEL EXAMINATION PROGRAM?

The basic purpose of the College-Level Examination Program is to enable individuals who have acquired their education in nontraditional ways to demonstrate their academic achievement. It is also intended for use by those in higher education, business, industry, government, and other fields who need a reliable method of assessing a person's educational level.

Recognizing that the real issue is not how a person has acquired his education but what education he has, the College Level Examination Program has been designed to serve a variety of purposes. The basic purpose, as listed above, is to enable those who have reached the college level of education in nontraditional ways to assess the level of their achievement and to use the test results in seeking college credit or placement.

In addition, scores on the tests can be used to validate educational experience obtained at a nonaccredited institution or through noncredit college courses.

Some colleges and universities may use the tests to measure the level of educational achievement of their students, and for various institutional research purposes.

Other colleges and universities may wish to use the tests in the admission, placement, and guidance of students who wish to transfer from one institution to another.

Businesses, industries, governmental agencies, and professional groups now accept the results of these tests as a basis for advancement, eligibility for further training, or professional or semi-professional certification.

Many people are interested in the examination simply to assess their own educational progress and attainment.

The college, university, business, industry, or government agency that adopts the tests in the College-Level Examination Program makes its own decision about how it will use and interpret the test scores. The College Board will provide the tests, score them, and report the results either to the individuals who took the tests or the college or agency that administered them. It does NOT, and cannot, award college credit, certify college equivalency, or make recommendations regarding the standards these institutions should establish for the use of the test results.

Therefore, if you are taking the tests to secure credit from an institution, you should FIRST ascertain whether the college or agency involved will accept the scores. Each institution determines which CLEP tests it will accept for credit and the amount of credit it will award. If you want to take tests for college credit, first call, write, or visit the college you wish to attend to inquire about its policy on CLEP scores, as well as its other admission requirements.

The services of the program are also available to people who have been requested to take the tests by an employer, a professional licensing agency, a certifying agency, or by other groups that recognize college equivalency on the basis of satisfactory CLEP scores. You may, of course, take the tests SOLELY for your own information. If you do, your scores will be reported only to you.

While neither CLEP nor the College Board can evaluate previous credentials or award college credit, you will receive, with your scores, basic information to help you interpret your performance on the tests you have taken.

3. WHAT ARE THE COLLEGE-LEVEL EXAMINATIONS?

In order to meet different kinds of curricular organization and testing needs at colleges and universities, the College-Level Examination Program offers 35 different subject tests falling under five separate general categories: Composition and Literature, Foreign Languages, History and Social Sciences, Science and Mathematics, and Business.

4. WHAT ARE THE SUBJECT EXAMINATIONS?

The 35 CLEP tests offered by the College Board are listed below:

COMPOSITION AND LITERATURE:
- American Literature
- Analyzing and Interpreting Literature
- English Composition
- English Composition with Essay
- English Literature
- Freshman College Composition
- Humanities

FOREIGN LANGUAGES
- French
- German
- Spanish

HISTORY AND SOCIAL SCIENCES
- American Government
- Introduction to Educational Psychology
- History of the United States I: Early Colonization to 1877
- History of the United States II: 1865 to the Present
- Human Growth and Development
- Principles of Macroeconomics
- Principles of Microeconomics
- Introductory Psychology
- Social Sciences and History
- Introductory Sociology
- Western Civilization I: Ancient Near East to 1648
- Western Civilization II: 1648 to the Present

SCIENCE AND MATHEMATICS
- College Algebra
- College Algebra-Trigonometry
- Biology
- Calculus
- Chemistry
- College Mathematics
- Natural Sciences
- Trigonometry
- Precalculus

BUSINESS
- Financial Accounting
- Introductory Business Law
- Information Systems and Computer Applications
- Principles of Management
- Principles of Marketing

CLEP Examinations cover material taught in courses that most students take as requirements in the first two years of college. A college usually grants the same amount of credit to students earning satisfactory scores on the CLEP examination as it grants to students successfully completing the equivalent course.

Many examinations are designed to correspond to one-semester courses; some, however, correspond to full-year or two-year courses.

Each exam is 90 minutes long and, except for English Composition with Essay, is made up primarily of multiple-choice questions. Some tests have several other types of questions besides multiple choice. To see a more detailed description of a particular CLEP exam, visit www.collegeboard.com/clep.

The English Composition with Essay exam is the only exam that includes a required essay. This essay is scored by college English faculty designated by CLEP and does not require an additional fee. However, other Composition and Literature tests offer optional essays, which some college and universities require and some do not. These essays are graded by faculty at the individual institutions that require them and require an additional $10 fee. Contact the particular institution to ask about essay requirements, and check with your test center for further details.

All 35 CLEP examinations are administered on computer. If you are unfamiliar with taking a test on a computer, consult the CLEP Sampler online at www.collegeboard.com/clep. The Sampler contains the same tutorials as the actual exams and helps familiarize you with navigation and how to answer different types of questions.

Points are not deducted for wrong or skipped answers – you receive one point for every correct answer. Therefore it is best that an answer is supplied for each exam question, whether it is a guess or not. The number of correct answers is then converted to a formula score. This formula, or "scaled," score is determined by a statistical process called *equating*, which adjusts for slight differences in difficulty between test forms and ensures that your score does not depend on the specific test form you took or how well others did on the same form. The scaled scores range from 20 to 80 – this is the number that will appear on your score report.

To ensure that you complete all questions in the time allotted, you would probably be wise to skip the more difficult or perplexing questions and return to them later. Although the multiple-choice items in these tests are carefully designed so as not to be tricky, misleading, or ambiguous, on the other hand, they are not all direct questions of factual information. They attempt, in their way, to elicit a response that indicates your knowledge or lack of knowledge of the material in question or your ability or inability to use or interpret a fact or idea. Thus, you should concentrate on answering the questions as they appear to be without attempting to out-guess the testmakers.

5. WHAT ARE THE FEES?

The fee for all CLEP examinations is $55. Optional essays required by some institutions are an additional $10.

6. WHEN ARE THE TESTS GIVEN?

CLEP tests are administered year-round. Consult the CLEP website (www.collegeboard.com/clep) and individual test centers for specific information.

7. WHERE ARE THE TESTS GIVEN?

More than 1,300 test centers are located on college and university campuses throughout the country, and additional centers are being established to meet increased needs. Any accredited collegiate institution with an explicit and publicly available policy of credit by examination can become a CLEP test center. To obtain a list of these centers, visit the CLEP website at www.collegeboard.com/clep.

8. HOW DO I REGISTER FOR THE COLLEGE-LEVEL EXAMINATION PROGRAM?

Contact an individual test center for information regarding registration, scheduling and fees. Registration/admission forms can also be obtained on the CLEP website.

9. MAY I REPEAT THE COLLEGE-LEVEL EXAMINATIONS?

You may repeat any examination providing at least six months have passed since you were last administered this test. If you repeat a test within a period of time less than six months, your scores will be cancelled and your fees forfeited. To repeat a test, check the appropriate space on the registration form.

10. WHEN MAY I EXPECT MY SCORE REPORTS?

With the exception of the English Composition with Essay exam, you should receive your score report instantly once the test is complete.

11. HOW SHOULD I PREPARE FOR THE COLLEGE-LEVEL EXAMINATIONS?

This book has been specifically designed to prepare candidates for these examinations. It will help you to consider, study, and review important content, principles, practices, procedures, problems, and techniques in the form of varied and concrete applications.

12. QUESTIONS AND ANSWERS APPEARING IN THIS PUBLICATION

The College-Level Examinations are offered by the College Board. Since copies of past examinations have not been made available, we have used equivalent materials, including questions and answers, which are highly recommended by us as an appropriate means of preparing for these examinations.

If you need additional information about CLEP Examinations, visit www.collegeboard.com/clep.

THE COLLEGE-LEVEL EXAMINATION PROGRAM

How The Program Works

CLEP examinations are administered at many colleges and universities across the country, and most institutions award college credit to those who do well on them. The examinations provide people who have acquired knowledge outside the usual educational settings the opportunity to show that they have learned college-level material without taking certain college courses.

The CLEP examinations cover material that is taught in introductory-level courses at many colleges and universities. Faculties at individual colleges review the tests to ensure that they cover the important material taught in their courses. Colleges differ in the examinations they accept; some colleges accept only two or three of the examinations while others accept nearly all of them.

Although CLEP is sponsored by the College Board and the examinations are scored by Educational Testing Service (ETS), neither of these organizations can award college credit. Only accredited colleges may grant credit toward a degree. When you take a CLEP examination, you may request that a copy of your score report be sent to the college you are attending or plan to attend. After evaluating your scores, the college will decide whether or not to award you credit for a certain course or courses, or to exempt you from them. If the college gives you credit, it will record the number of credits on your permanent record, thereby indicating that you have completed work equivalent to a course in that subject. If the college decides to grant exemption without giving you credit for a course, you will be permitted to omit a course that would normally be required of you and to take a course of your choice instead.

What the Examinations Are Like

The examinations consist mostly of multiple-choice questions to be answered within a 90-minute time limit. Additional information about each CLEP examination is given in the examination guide and on the CLEP website.

Where To Take the Examinations

CLEP examinations are administered throughout the year at the test centers of approximately 1,300 colleges and universities. On the CLEP website, you will find a list of institutions that award credit for satisfactory scores on CLEP examinations. Some colleges administer CLEP examinations to their own students only. Other institutions administer the tests to anyone who registers to take them. If your college does not administer the tests, contact the test centers in your area for information about its testing schedule.

Once you have been tested, your score report will be available instantly. CLEP scores are kept on file at ETS for 20 years; and during this period, for a small fee, you may have your transcript sent to another college or to anyone else you specify. (Your scores will never be sent to anyone without your approval.)

APPROACHING A COLLEGE ABOUT CLEP

The following sections provide a step-by-step approach to learning about the CLEP policy at a particular college or university. The person or office that can best assist students desiring CLEP credit may have a different title at each institution, but the following guidelines will lead you to information about CLEP at any institution.

Adults returning to college often benefit from special assistance when they approach a college. Opportunities for adults to return to formal learning in the classroom are now widespread, and colleges and universities have worked hard to make this a smooth process for older students. Many colleges have established special service offices that are staffed with trained professionals who understand the kinds of problems facing adults returning to college. If you think you might benefit from such assistance, be sure to find out whether these services are available at your college.

How to Apply for College Credit

STEP 1. Obtain the General Information Catalog and a copy of the CLEP policy from the colleges you are considering. If you have not yet applied for admission, ask for an admissions application form too.

Information about admissions and CLEP policies can be obtained by contacting college admissions offices or finding admissions information on the school websites. Tell the admissions officer that you are a prospective student and that you are interested in applying for admission and CLEP credit. Ask for a copy of the publication in which the college's complete CLEP policy is explained. Also get the name and the telephone number of the person to contact in case you have further questions about CLEP.

At this step, you may wish to obtain information from external degree colleges. Many adults find that such colleges suit their needs exceptionally well.

STEP 2. If you have not already been admitted to the college you are considering, look at its admission requirements for undergraduate students to see if you can qualify.

This is an important step because if you can't get into college, you can't get college credit for CLEP. Nearly all colleges require students to be admitted and to enroll in one or more courses before granting the students CLEP credit.

Virtually all public community colleges and a number of four-year state colleges have open admission policies for in-state students. This usually means that they admit anyone who has graduated from high school or has earned a high school equivalency diploma.

If you think you do not meet the admission requirements, contact the admissions office for an interview with a counselor. Colleges do sometimes make exceptions, particularly for adult applicants. State why you want the interview and ask what documents you should bring with you or send in advance. (These materials may include a high school transcript, transcript of previous college work, completed application for admission, etc.) Make an extra effort to have all the information requested in time for the interview.

During the interview, relax and be yourself. Be prepared to state honestly why you think you are ready and able to do college work. If you have already taken CLEP examinations and scored high enough to earn credit, you have shown that you are able to do college work. Mention this achievement to the admissions counselor because it may increase your chances of being accepted. If you have not taken a CLEP examination, you can still improve your chances of being accepted by describing how your job training or independent study has helped prepare you for college-level work. Tell the counselor what you have learned from your work and personal experiences.

STEP 3. Evaluate the college's CLEP policy.

Typically, a college lists all its academic policies, including CLEP policies, in its general catalog. You will probably find the CLEP policy statement under a heading such as Credit-by-Examination, Advanced Standing, Advanced Placement, or External Degree Program. These sections can usually be found in the front of the catalog.

Many colleges publish their credit-by-examination policies in a separate brochure, which is distributed through the campus testing office, counseling center, admissions office, or registrar's office. If you find a very general policy statement in the college catalog, seek clarification from one of these offices.

Review the material in the section of this guide entitled Questions to Ask About a College's CLEP Policy. Use these guidelines to evaluate the college's CLEP policy. If you have not yet taken a CLEP examination, this evaluation will help you decide which examinations to take and whether or not to take the free-response or essay portion. Because individual colleges have different CLEP policies, a review of several policies may help you decide which college to attend.

STEP 4. If you have not yet applied for admission, do so early.

Most colleges expect you to apply for admission several months before you enroll, and it is essential that you meet the published application deadlines. It takes time to process your application for admission; and if you have yet to take a CLEP examination, it will be some time before the college receives and reviews your score report. You will probably want to take some, if not all, of the CLEP examinations you are interested in before you enroll so you know which courses you need not register for. In fact, some colleges require that all CLEP scores be submitted before a student registers.

Complete all forms and include all documents requested with your application(s) for admission. Normally, an admissions decision cannot be reached until all documents have been submitted and evaluated. Unless told to do so, do not send your CLEP scores until you have been officially admitted.

STEP 5. Arrange to take CLEP examination(s) or to submit your CLEP score(s).

You may want to wait to take your CLEP examinations until you know definitely which college you will be attending. Then you can make sure you are taking tests your college will accept for credit. You will also be able to request that your scores be sent to the college, free of charge, when you take the tests.

If you have already taken CLEP examinations, but did not have a copy of your score report sent to your college, you may request the College Board to send an official transcript at any time for a small fee. Use the Transcript Request Form that was sent to you with your score report. If you do not have the form, you may find it online at www.collegeboard.com/clep.

Your CLEP scores will be evaluated, probably by someone in the admissions office, and sent to the registrar's office to be posted on your permanent record once you are enrolled. Procedures vary from college to college, but the process usually begins in the admissions office.

STEP 6. Ask to receive a written notice of the credit you receive for your CLEP score(s).

A written notice may save you problems later, when you submit your degree plan or file for graduation. In the event that there is a question about whether or not you earned CLEP credit, you will have an official record of what credit was awarded. You may also need this verification of course credit if you go for academic counseling before the credit is posted on your permanent record.

STEP 7. Before you register for courses, seek academic counseling.

A discussion with your academic advisor can prevent you from taking unnecessary courses and can tell you specifically what your CLEP credit will mean to you. This step may be accomplished at the time you enroll. Most colleges have orientation sessions for new students prior to each enrollment period. During orientation, students are usually assigned an academic advisor who then gives them individual help in developing long-range plans and a course schedule for the next semester. In conjunction with this counseling, you may be asked to take some additional tests so that you can be placed at the proper course level.

External Degree Programs

If you have acquired a considerable amount of college-level knowledge through job experience, reading, or noncredit courses, if you have accumulated college credits at a variety of colleges over a period of years, or if you prefer studying on your own rather than in a classroom setting, you may want to investigate the possibility of enrolling in an external degree program. Many colleges offer external degree programs that allow you to earn a degree by passing examinations (including CLEP), transferring credit from other colleges, and demonstrating in other ways that you have satisfied the educational requirements. No classroom attendance is required, and the programs are open to out-of-state candidates as well as residents. Thomas A. Edison State College in New Jersey and Charter Oaks College in Connecticut are fully accredited independent state colleges; the New York program is part of the state university system and is also fully accredited. If you are interested in exploring an external degree, you can write for more information to:

Charter Oak College
The Exchange, Suite 171
270 Farmington Avenue
Farmington, CT 06032-1909

Regents External Degree Program
Cultural Education Center
Empire State Plaza
Albany, New York 12230

Thomas A. Edison State College
101 West State Street
Trenton, New Jersey 08608

Many other colleges also have external degree or weekend programs. While they often require that a number of courses be taken on campus, the external degree programs tend to be more flexible in transferring credit, granting credit-by-examination, and allowing independent study than other traditional programs. When applying to a college, you may wish to ask whether it has an external degree or weekend program.

Questions to Ask About a College's CLEP Policy

Before taking CLEP examinations for the purpose of earning college credit, try to find the answers to these questions:

1. Which CLEP examinations are accepted by this college?

A college may accept some CLEP examinations for credit and not others - possibly not the one you are considering. The English faculty may decide to grant college English credit based on the CLEP English Composition examination, but not on the Freshman College Composition examination. Or, the mathematics faculty may decide to grant credit based on the College Mathematics to non-mathematics majors only, requiring majors to take an examination in algebra, trigonometry, or calculus to earn credit. For these reasons, it is important that you know the specific CLEP tests for which you can receive credit.

2. Does the college require the optional free-response (essay) section as well as the objective portion of the CLEP examination you are considering?

Knowing the answer to this question ahead of time will permit you to schedule the optional essay examination when you register to take your CLEP examination.

3. Is credit granted for specific courses? If so, which ones?

You are likely to find that credit will be granted for specific courses and the course titles will be designated in the college's CLEP policy. It is not necessary, however, that credit be granted for a specific course in order for you to benefit from your CLEP credit. For instance, at many liberal arts colleges, all students must take certain types of courses; these courses may be labeled the core curriculum, general education requirements, distribution requirements, or liberal arts requirements. The requirements are often expressed in terms of credit hours. For example, all students may be required to take at least six hours of humanities, six hours of English, three hours of mathematics, six hours of natural science, and six hours of social science, with no particular courses in these disciplines specified. In these instances, CLEP credit may be given as 6 hrs. English credit or 3 hrs. Math credit without specifying for which English or mathematics courses credit has been awarded. In order to avoid possible disappointment, you should know before taking a CLEP examination what type of credit you can receive and whether you will only be exempted from a required course but receive no credit.

4. How much credit is granted for each examination you are considering, and does the college place a limit on the total amount of CLEP credit you can earn toward your degree?

Not all colleges that grant CLEP credit award the same amount for individual tests. Furthermore, some colleges place a limit on the total amount of credit you can earn through CLEP or other examinations. Other colleges may grant you exemption but no credit toward your degree. Knowing several colleges' policies concerning these issues may help you decide which college you will attend. If you think you are capable of passing a number of CLEP examinations, you may want to attend a college that will allow you to earn credit for all or most of them. For example, the state external degree programs grant credit for most CLEP examinations (and other tests as well).

5. What is the required score for earning CLEP credit for each test you are considering?

Most colleges publish the required scores or percentile ranks for earning CLEP credit in their general catalog or in a brochure. The required score may vary from test to test, so find out the required score for each test you are considering.

6. What is the college's policy regarding prior course work in the subject in which you are considering taking a CLEP test?

Some colleges will not grant credit for a CLEP test if the student has already attempted a college-level course closely aligned with that test. For example, if you successfully completed English 101 or a comparable course on another campus, you will probably not be permitted to receive CLEP credit in that subject, too. Some colleges will not permit you to earn CLEP credit for a course that you failed.

7. Does the college make additional stipulations before credit will be granted?

It is common practice for colleges to award CLEP credit only to their enrolled students. There are other stipulations, however, that vary from college to college. For example, does the college require you to formally apply for or accept CLEP credit by completing and signing a form? Or does the college require you to validate your CLEP score by successfully completing a more advanced course in the subject? Answers to these and other questions will help to smooth the process of earning college credit through CLEP.

The above questions and the discussions that follow them indicate some of the ways in which colleges' CLEP policies can vary. Find out as much as possible about the CLEP policies at the colleges you are interested in so you can choose a college with a policy that is compatible with your educational goals. Once you have selected the college you will attend, you can find out which CLEP examinations your college recognizes and the requirements for earning CLEP credit.

DECIDING WHICH EXAMINATIONS TO TAKE

If You're Taking the Examinations for College Credit or Career Advancement:

Most people who take CLEP examinations do so in order to earn credit for college courses. Others take the examinations in order to qualify for job promotions or for professional certification or licensing. It is vital to most candidates who are taking the tests for any of these reasons that they be well prepared for the tests they are taking so that they can advance as rapidly as possible toward their educational or career goals.

It is usually advisable that those who have limited knowledge in the subjects covered by the tests they are considering enroll in the college courses in which that material is taught. Those who are uncertain about whether or not they know enough about a subject to do well on a particular CLEP test will find the following guidelines helpful.

There is no way to predict if you will pass a particular CLEP examination, but answers to the questions under the seven headings below should give you an indication of whether or not you are likely to succeed.

1. Test Descriptions

Read the description of the test provided. Are you familiar with most of the topics and terminology in the outline?

2. Textbooks

Examine the suggested textbooks and other resource materials following the test descriptions in this guide. Have you recently read one or more of these books, or have you read similar college-level books on this subject? If you have not, read through one or more of the textbooks listed, or through the textbook used for this course at your college. Are you familiar with most of the topics and terminology in the book?

3. Sample Questions

The sample questions provided are intended to be typical of the content and difficulty of the questions on the test. Although they are not an exact miniature of the test, the proportion of the sample questions you can answer correctly should be a rough estimate of the proportion of questions you will be able to answer correctly on the test.

Answer as many of the sample questions for this test as you can. Check your answers against the correct answers. Did you answer more than half the questions correctly?

Because of variations in course content at different institutions, and because questions on CLEP tests vary from easy to difficult - with most being of moderate difficulty - the average student who passes a course in a subject can usually answer correctly about half the questions on the corresponding CLEP examination. Most colleges set their passing scores near this level, but some set them higher. If your college has set its required score above the level required by most colleges, you may need to answer a larger proportion of questions on the test correctly.

4. Previous Study

Have you taken noncredit courses in this subject offered by an adult school or a private school, through correspondence, or in connection with your job? Did you do exceptionally well in this subject in high school, or did you take an honors course in this subject?

5. Experience

Have you learned or used the knowledge or skills included in this test in your job or life experience? For example, if you lived in a Spanish-speaking country and spoke the language for a year or more, you might consider taking the Spanish examination. Or, if you have worked at a job in which you used accounting and finance skills, Principles of Accounting would be a likely test for you to take. Or, if you have read a considerable amount of literature and attended many art exhibits, concerts, and plays, you might expect to do well on the Humanities exam.

6. Other Examinations

Have you done well on other standardized tests in subjects related to the one you want to take? For example, did you score well above average on a portion of a college entrance examination covering similar skills, or did you obtain an exceptionally high score on a high school equivalency test or a licensing examination in this subject? Although such tests do not cover exactly the same material as the CLEP examinations and may be easier, persons who do well on these tests often do well on CLEP examinations, too.

7. Advice

Has a college counselor, professor, or some other professional person familiar with your ability advised you to take a CLEP examination?

If your answer was yes to questions under several of the above headings, you probably have a good chance of passing the CLEP examination you are considering. It is unlikely that you would have acquired sufficient background from experience alone. Learning gained through reading and study is essential, and you will probably find some additional study helpful before taking a CLEP examination.

<u>If You're Taking the Examinations to Prepare for College</u>

Many people entering college, particularly adults returning to college after several years away from formal education, are uncertain about their ability to compete with other college students. They wonder whether they have sufficient background for college study, and those who have been away from formal study for some time wonder whether they have forgotten how to study, how to take tests, and how to write papers. Such people may wish to improve their test-taking and study skills prior to enrolling in courses.

One way to assess your ability to perform at the college level and to improve your test-taking and study skills at the same time is to prepare for and take one or more CLEP examinations. You need not be enrolled in a college to take a CLEP examination, and you may have your scores sent only to yourself and later request that a transcript be sent to a college if you then decide to apply for credit. By reviewing the test descriptions and sample questions, you may find one or several subject areas in which you think you have substantial knowledge. Select one examination, or more if you like, and carefully read at least one of the textbooks listed in the bibliography for the test. By doing this, you will get a better idea of how much you know of what is usually taught in a college-level course in that subject. Study as much material as you can, until you think you have a good grasp of the subject matter. Then take the test at a college in your area. It will be several weeks before you receive your results, and you may wish to begin reviewing for another test in the meantime.

To find out if you are eligible for credit for your CLEP score, you must compare your score with the score required by the college you plan to attend. If you are not yet sure which college you will attend, or whether you will enroll in college at all, you should begin to follow the steps outlined. It is best that you do this before taking a CLEP test, but if you are taking the test only for the experience and to familiarize yourself with college-level material and requirements, you might take the test before you approach a college. Even if the college you decide to attend does not accept the test you took, the experience of taking such a test will enable you to meet with greater confidence the requirements of courses you will take.

You will find information about how to interpret your scores in WHAT YOUR SCORES MEAN, which you will receive with your score report, and which can also be found online at the CLEP website. Many colleges follow the recommendations of the American Council on Education (ACE) for setting their required scores, so you can use this information as a guide in determining how well you did. The ACE recommendations are included in the booklet.

If you do not do well enough on the test to earn college credit, don't be discouraged. Usually, it is the best college students who are exempted from courses or receive credit-by-examination. The fact that you cannot get credit for your score means that you should probably enroll in a college course to learn the material. However, if your score was close to the required score, or if you feel you could do better on a second try or after some additional study, you may retake the test after six months. Do not take it sooner or your score will not be reported and your fee will be forfeited.

If you do earn the score required to earn credit, you will have demonstrated that you already have some college-level knowledge. You will also have a better idea whether you should take additional CLEP examinations. And, what is most important, you can enroll in college with confidence, knowing that you do have the ability to succeed.

PREPARING TO TAKE CLEP EXAMINATIONS

Having made the decision to take one or more CLEP examinations, most people then want to know if it is worthwhile to prepare for them - how much, how long, when, and how should they go about it? The precise answers to these questions vary greatly from individual to individual. However, most candidates find that some type of test preparation is helpful.

Most people who take CLEP examinations do so to show that they have already learned the important material that is taught in a college course. Many of them need only a quick review to assure themselves that they have not forgotten some of what they once studied, and to fill in some of the gaps in their knowledge of the subject. Others feel that they need a thorough review and spend several weeks studying for a test. A few wish to take a CLEP examination as a kind of final examination for independent study of a subject instead of the college course. This last group requires significantly more study than those who only need to review, and they may need some guidance from professors of the subjects they are studying.

The key to how you prepare for CLEP examinations often lies in locating those skills and areas of prior learning in which you are strong and deciding where to focus your energies. Some people may know a great deal about a certain subject area, but may not test well. These individuals would probably be just as concerned about strengthening their test-taking skills as they are about studying for a specific test. Many mental and physical skills are used in preparing for a test. It is important not only to review or study for the examinations, but to make certain that you are alert, relatively free of anxiety, and aware of how to approach standardized tests. Suggestions on developing test-taking skills and preparing psychologically and physically for a test are given. The following section suggests ways of assessing your knowledge of the content of a test and then reviewing and studying the material.

Using This Study Guide

Begin by carefully reading the test description and outline of knowledge and skills required for the examination, if given. As you read through the topics listed there, ask yourself how much you know about each one. Also note the terms, names, and symbols that are mentioned, and ask yourself whether you are familiar with them. This will give you a quick overview of how much you know about the subject. If you are familiar with nearly all the material, you will probably need a minimum of review; however, if less than half of it is familiar, you will probably require substantial study to do well on the test.

If, after reviewing the test description, you find that you need extensive review, delay answering the sample question until you have done some reading in the subject. If you complete them before reviewing the material, you will probably look for the answers as you study, and then they will not be a good assessment of your ability at a later date.

If you think you are familiar with most of the test material, try to answer the sample questions.

Apply the test-taking strategies given. Keeping within the time limit suggested will give you a rough idea of how quickly you should work in order to complete the actual test.

Check your answers against the answer key. If you answered nearly all the questions correctly, you probably do not need to study the subject extensively. If you got about half the questions correct, you ought o review at least one textbook or other suggested materials on the subject. If you answered less than half the questions correctly, you will probably benefit from more extensive reading in the subject and thorough study of one or more textbooks. The textbooks listed are used at many colleges but they are not the only good texts. You will find helpful almost any standard text available to you., such as the textbook used at your college, or earlier editions of texts listed. For some examinations, topic outlines and textbooks may not be available. Take the sample tests in this book and check your answers at the end of each test. Check wrong answers.

Suggestions for Studying

The following suggestions have been gathered from people who have prepared for CLEP examinations or other college-level tests.

1. Define your goals and locate study materials

First, determine your study goals. Set aside a block of time to review the material provided in this book, and then decide which test(s) you will take. Using the suggestions, locate suitable resource materials. If a preparation course is offered by an adult school or college in your area, you might find it helpful to enroll.

2. Find a good place to study

To determine what kind of place you need for studying, ask yourself questions such as: Do I need a quiet place? Does the telephone distract me? Do objects I see in this place remind me of things I should do? Is it too warm? Is it well lit? Am I too comfortable here? Do I have space to spread out my materials? You may find the library more conducive to studying than your home. If you decide to study at home, you might prevent interruptions by other household members by putting a sign on the door of your study room to indicate when you will be available.

3. Schedule time to study

To help you determine where studying best fits into your schedule, try this exercise: Make a list of your daily activities (for example, sleeping, working, and eating) and estimate how many hours per day you spend on each activity. Now, rate all the activities on your list in order of their importance and evaluate your use of time. Often people are astonished at how an average day appears from this perspective. They may discover that they were unaware how large portions of time are spent, or they learn their time can be scheduled in alternative ways. For example, they can remove the least important activities from their day and devote that time to studying or another important activity.

4. Establish a study routine and a set of goals

In order to study effectively, you should establish specific goals and a schedule for accomplishing them. Some people find it helpful to write out a weekly schedule and cross out each study period when it is completed. Others maintain their concentration better by writing down the time when they expect to complete a study task. Most people find short periods of intense study more productive than long stretches of time. For example, they may follow a regular schedule of several 20- or 30-minute study periods with short breaks between them. Some people like to allow themselves rewards as they complete each study goal. It is not essential that you accomplish every goal exactly within your schedule; the point is to be committed to your task.

5. Learn how to take an active role in studying.

If you have not done much studying for some time, you may find it difficult to concentrate at first. Try a method of studying, such as the one outlined below, that will help you concentrate on and remember what you read.

    a. First, read the chapter summary and the introduction. Then you will know what to look for in your reading.

    b. Next, convert the section or paragraph headlines into questions. For example, if you are reading a section entitled, The Causes of the American Revolution, ask yourself: *What were the causes of the American Revolution?* Compose the answer as you read the paragraph. Reading and answering questions aloud will help you understand and remember the material.

c. Take notes on key ideas or concepts as you read. Writing will also help you fix concepts more firmly in your mind. Underlining key ideas or writing notes in your book can be helpful and will be useful for review. Underline only important points. If you underline more than a third of each paragraph, you are probably underlining too much.

d. If there are questions or problems at the end of a chapter, answer or solve them on paper as if you were asked to do them for homework. Mathematics textbooks (and some other books) sometimes include answers to some or all of the exercises. If you have such a book, write your answers before looking at the ones given. When problem-solving is involved, work enough problems to master the required methods and concepts. If you have difficulty with problems, review any sample problems or explanations in the chapter.

e. To retain knowledge, most people have to review the material periodically. If you are preparing for a test over an extended period of time, review key concepts and notes each week or so. Do not wait for weeks to review the material or you will need to relearn much of it.

Psychological and Physical Preparation

Most people feel at least some nervousness before taking a test. Adults who are returning to college may not have taken a test in many years or they may have had little experience with standardized tests. Some younger students, as well, are uncomfortable with testing situations. People who received their education in countries outside the United States may find that many tests given in this country are quite different from the ones they are accustomed to taking.

Not only might candidates find the types of tests and the kinds of questions on them unfamiliar, but other aspects of the testing environment may be strange as well. The physical and mental stress that results from meeting this new experience can hinder a candidate's ability to demonstrate his or her true degree of knowledge in the subject area being tested. For this reason, it is important to go to the test center well prepared, both mentally and physically, for taking the test. You may find the following suggestions helpful.

1. Familiarize yourself, as much as possible, with the test and the test situation before the day of the examination. It will be helpful for you to know ahead of time:

a. How much time will be allowed for the test and whether there are timed subsections.

b. What types of questions and directions appear on the examination.

c. How your test score will be computed.

d. How to properly answer the questions on the computer (See the CLEP Sample on the CLEP website)

e. In which building and room the examination will be administered. If you don't know where the building is, locate it or get directions ahead of time.

f. The time of the test administration. You might wish to confirm this information a day or two before the examination and find out what time the building and room will be open so that you can plan to arrive early.

g. Where to park your car or, if you wish to take public transportation, which bus or train to take and the location of the nearest stop.

h. Whether smoking will be permitted during the test.

i. Whether there will be a break between examinations (if you will be taking more than one on the same day), and whether there is a place nearby where you can get something to eat or drink.

2. Go to the test situation relaxed and alert. In order to prepare for the test:

a. Get a good night's sleep. Last minute cramming, particularly late the night before, is usually counterproductive.

b. Eat normally. It is usually not wise to skip breakfast or lunch on the day of the test or to eat a big meal just before the test.

c. Avoid tranquilizers and stimulants. If you follow the other directions in this book, you won't need artificial aids. It's better to be a little tense than to be drowsy, but stimulants such as coffee and cola can make you nervous and interfere with your concentration.

d. Don't drink a lot of liquids before the test. Having to leave the room during the test will disturb your concentration and take valuable time away from the test.

e. If you are inclined to be nervous or tense, learn some relaxation exercises and use them before and perhaps during the test.

3. Arrive for the test early and prepared. Be sure to:

a. Arrive early enough so that you can find a parking place, locate the test center, and get settled comfortably before testing begins. Allow some extra time in case you are delayed unexpectedly.

b. Take the following with you:

- Your completed Registration/Admission Form
- Two forms of identification – one being a government-issued photo ID with signature, such as a driver's license or passport
- Non-mechanical pencil
- A watch so that you can time your progress (digital watches are prohibited)
- Your glasses if you need them for reading or seeing the chalkboard or wall clock

c. Leave all books, papers, and notes outside the test center. You will not be permitted to use your own scratch paper; it will be provided. Also prohibited are calculators, cell phones, beepers, pagers, photo/copy devices, radios, headphones, food, beverages, and several other items.

d. Be prepared for any temperature in the testing room. Wear layers of clothing that can be removed if the room is too hot but will keep you warm if it is too cold.

4. When you enter the test room:

a. Sit in a seat that provides a maximum of comfort and freedom from distraction.

b. Read directions carefully, and listen to all instructions given by the test administrator. If you don't understand the directions, ask for help before test timing begins. If you must ask a question after the test has begun, raise your hand and a proctor will assist you. The proctor can answer certain kinds of questions but cannot help you with the test.

c. Know your rights as a test taker. You can expect to be given the full working time allowed for the test(s) and a reasonably quiet and comfortable place in which to work. If a poor test situation is preventing you from doing your best, ask if the situation can be remedied. If bad test conditions cannot be remedied, ask the person in charge to report the problem in the Irregularity Report that will be sent to ETS with the answer sheets. You may also wish to contact CLEP. Describe the exact circumstances as completely as you can. Be sure to include the test date and name(s) of the test(s) you took. ETS will investigate the problem to make sure it does not happen again, and, if the problem is serious enough, may arrange for you to retake the test without charge.

TAKING THE EXAMINATIONS

A person may know a great deal about the subject being tested, but not do as well as he or she is capable of on the test. Knowing how to approach a test is an important part of the testing process. While a command of test-taking skills cannot substitute for knowledge of the subject matter, it can be a significant factor in successful testing.

Test-taking skills enable a person to use all available information to earn a score that truly reflects his or her ability. There are different strategies for approaching different kinds of test questions. For example, free-response questions require a very different tack than do multiple-choice questions. Other factors, such as how the test will be graded, may also influence your approach to the test and your use of test time. Thus, your preparation for a test should include finding out all you can about the test so that you can use the most effective test-taking strategies.

Before taking a test, you should know approximately how many questions are on the test, how much time you will be allowed, how the test will be scored or graded, what types of questions and directions are on the test, and how you will be required to record your answers.

Taking Multiple-Choice Tests

1. Listen carefully to the instructions given by the test administrator and read carefully all directions before you begin to answer the questions.

2. Note the time that the test administrator starts timing the test. As you proceed, make sure that you are not working too slowly. You should have answered at least half the questions in a section when half the time for that section has passed. If you have not reached that point in the section, speed up your pace on the remaining questions.

3. Before answering a question, read the entire question, including all the answer choices. Don't think that because the first or second answer choice looks good to you, it isn't necessary to read the remaining options. Instructions usually tell you to select the best answer. Sometimes one answer choice is partially correct, but another option is better; therefore, it is usually a good idea to read all the answers before you choose one.

4. Read and consider every question. Questions that look complicated at first glance may not actually be so difficult once you have read them carefully.

5. Do not puzzle too long over any one question. If you don't know the answer after you've considered it briefly, go on to the next question. Make sure you return to the question later.

6. Make sure you record your response properly.

7. In trying to determine the correct answer, you may find it helpful to cross out those options that you know are incorrect, and to make marks next to those you think might be correct. If you decide to skip the question and come back to it later, you will save yourself the time of reconsidering all the options.

8. Watch for the following key words in test questions:

all	generally	never	perhaps
always	however	none	rarely
but	may	not	seldom
except	must	often	sometimes
every	necessary	only	usually

When a question or answer option contains words such as always, every, only, never, and none, there can be no exceptions to the answer you choose. Use of words such as often, rarely, sometimes, and generally indicates that there may be some exceptions to the answer.

9. Do not waste your time looking for clues to right answers based on flaws in question wording or patterns in correct answers. Professionals at the College Board and ETS put

a great deal of effort into developing valid, reliable, fair tests. CLEP test development committees are composed of college faculty who are experts in the subject covered by the test and are appointed by the College Board to write test questions and to scrutinize each question that is included on a CLEP test. Committee members make every effort to ensure that the questions are not ambiguous, that they have only one correct answer, and that they cover college-level topics. These committees do not intentionally include trick questions. If you think a question is flawed, ask the test administrator to report it, or contact CLEP immediately.

Taking Free-Response or Essay Tests

If your college requires the optional free-response or essay portion of a CLEP Composition and Literature exams, you should do some additional preparation for your CLEP test. Taking an essay test is very different from taking a multiple-choice test, so you will need to use some other strategies.

The essay written as part of the English Composition and Essay exam is graded by English professors from a variety of colleges and universities. A process called holistic scoring is used to rate your writing ability.

The optional free-response essays, on the other hand, are graded by the faculty of the college you designate as a score recipient. Guidelines and criteria for grading essays are not specified by the College Board or ETS. You may find it helpful, therefore, to talk with someone at your college to find out what criteria will be used to determine whether you will get credit. If the test requires essay responses, ask how much emphasis will be placed on your writing ability and your ability to organize your thoughts as opposed to your knowledge of subject matter. Find out how much weight will be given to your multiple-choice test score in comparison with your free-response grade in determining whether you will get credit. This will give you an idea where you should expend the greatest effort in preparing for and taking the test.

Here are some strategies you will find useful in taking any essay test:

1. Before you begin to write, read all questions carefully and take a few minutes to jot down some ideas you might include in each answer.

2. If you are given a choice of questions to answer, choose the questions you think you can answer most clearly and knowledgeably.

3. Determine in what order you will answer the questions. Answer those you find the easiest first so that any extra time can be spent on the more difficult questions.

4. When you know which questions you will answer and in what order, determine how much testing time remains and estimate how many minutes you will devote to each question. Unless suggested times are given for the questions or one question appears to require more or less time than the others, allot an equal amount of time to each question.

5. Before answering each question, indicate the number of the question as it is given in the test book. You need not copy the entire question from the question sheet, but it will be helpful to you and to the person grading your test if you indicate briefly the topic you are addressing – particularly if you are not answering the questions in the order in which they appear on the test.

6. Before answering each question, read it again carefully to make sure you are interpreting it correctly. Underline key words, such as those listed below, that often appear in free-response questions. Be sure you know the exact meaning of these words before taking the test.

analyze	demonstrate	enumerate	list
apply	derive	explain	outline
assess	describe	generalize	prove
compare	determine	illustrate	rank
contrast	discuss	interpret	show
define	distinguish	justify	summarize

If a question asks you to outline, define, or summarize, do not write a detailed explanation; if a question asks you to analyze, explain, illustrate, interpret, or show, you must do more than briefly describe the topic.

For a current listing of CLEP Colleges

where you can get credit and be tested, write:

CLEP, P.O. Box 6600, Princeton, NJ 08541-6600

Or e-mail: clep@ets.org, or call: (609) 771-7865

INTRODUCTORY SOCIOLOGY

Description of the Examination

The Introductory Sociology examination is designed to assess an individual's knowledge of the material typically presented in a one-semester introductory sociology course at most colleges and universities. The examination emphasizes basic facts and concepts as well as general theoretical approaches used by sociologists. Highly specialized knowledge of the subject and the methodology of the discipline is not required or measured by the test content.

The examination contains approximately 100 questions to be answered in 90 minutes. Some of these are pretest questions that will not be scored. Any time candidates spend on tutorials and providing personal information is in addition to the actual testing time.

Knowledge and Skills Required

Questions on the Introductory Sociology examination require candidates to demonstrate one or more of the following abilities. Some questions may require more than one of these abilities.

- Identification of specific names, facts, and concepts from sociological literature
- Understanding of relationships between concepts, empirical generalizations, and theoretical propositions of sociology
- Understanding of the methods by which sociological relationships are established
- Application of concepts, propositions, and methods to hypothetical situations
- Interpretation of tables and charts

The subject matter of the Introductory Sociology examination is drawn from the following topics. The percentages next to the main topics indicate the approximate percentage of exam questions on that topic.

20% Institutions
- Economic
- Educational
- Family
- Medical
- Political
- Religious

15% Social Patterns
- Community
- Demography
- Human ecology
- Rural/urban patterns

20% Social Processes
- Collective behavior and social movements
- Culture
- Deviance and social control
- Groups and organizations
- Social change
- Social interaction
- Socialization

30% Social Stratification (Process and Structure)
- Aging
- Power and social inequality
- Professions and occupations
- Race and ethnic relations
- Sex and gender roles
- Social class
- Social mobility

15% The Sociological Perspective
- History of sociology
- Methods
- Sociological theory

HOW TO TAKE A TEST

You have studied long, hard and conscientiously.

With your official admission card in hand, and your heart pounding, you have been admitted to the examination room.

You note that there are several hundred other applicants in the examination room waiting to take the same test.

They all appear to be equally well prepared.

You know that nothing but your best effort will suffice. The "moment of truth" is at hand: you now have to demonstrate objectively, in writing, your knowledge of content and your understanding of subject matter.

You are fighting the most important battle of your life—to pass and/or score high on an examination which will determine your career and provide the economic basis for your livelihood.

What extra, special things should you know and should you do in taking the examination?

I. YOU MUST PASS AN EXAMINATION

A. WHAT EVERY CANDIDATE SHOULD KNOW
Examination applicants often ask us for help in preparing for the written test. What can I study in advance? What kinds of questions will be asked? How will the test be given? How will the papers be graded?

B. HOW ARE EXAMS DEVELOPED?
Examinations are carefully written by trained technicians who are specialists in the field known as "psychological measurement," in consultation with recognized authorities in the field of work that the test will cover. These experts recommend the subject matter areas or skills to be tested; only those knowledges or skills important to your success on the job are included. The most reliable books and source materials available are used as references. Together, the experts and technicians judge the difficulty level of the questions.
Test technicians know how to phrase questions so that the problem is clearly stated. Their ethics do not permit "trick" or "catch" questions. Questions may have been tried out on sample groups, or subjected to statistical analysis, to determine their usefulness.
Written tests are often used in combination with performance tests, ratings of training and experience, and oral interviews. All of these measures combine to form the best-known means of finding the right person for the right job.

II. HOW TO PASS THE WRITTEN TEST

A. BASIC STEPS

1) Study the announcement

How, then, can you know what subjects to study? Our best answer is: "Learn as much as possible about the class of positions for which you've applied." The exam will test the knowledge, skills and abilities needed to do the work.

Your most valuable source of information about the position you want is the official exam announcement. This announcement lists the training and experience qualifications. Check these standards and apply only if you come reasonably close to meeting them. Many jurisdictions preview the written test in the exam announcement by including a section called "Knowledge and Abilities Required," "Scope of the Examination," or some similar heading. Here you will find out specifically what fields will be tested.

2) Choose appropriate study materials

If the position for which you are applying is technical or advanced, you will read more advanced, specialized material. If you are already familiar with the basic principles of your field, elementary textbooks would waste your time. Concentrate on advanced textbooks and technical periodicals. Think through the concepts and review difficult problems in your field.

These are all general sources. You can get more ideas on your own initiative, following these leads. For example, training manuals and publications of the government agency which employs workers in your field can be useful, particularly for technical and professional positions. A letter or visit to the government department involved may result in more specific study suggestions, and certainly will provide you with a more definite idea of the exact nature of the position you are seeking.

3) Study this book!

III. KINDS OF TESTS

Tests are used for purposes other than measuring knowledge and ability to perform specified duties. For some positions, it is equally important to test ability to make adjustments to new situations or to profit from training. In others, basic mental abilities not dependent on information are essential. Questions which test these things may not appear as pertinent to the duties of the position as those which test for knowledge and information. Yet they are often highly important parts of a fair examination. For very general questions, it is almost impossible to help you direct your study efforts. What we can do is to point out some of the more common of these general abilities needed in public service positions and describe some typical questions.

1) General information

Broad, general information has been found useful for predicting job success in some kinds of work. This is tested in a variety of ways, from vocabulary lists to questions about current events. Basic background in some field of work, such as sociology or economics, may be sampled in a group of questions. Often these are principles which have become familiar to most persons through exposure rather than through formal training. It is difficult to advise you how to study for these questions; being alert to the world around you is our best suggestion.

2) Verbal ability

An example of an ability needed in many positions is verbal or language ability. Verbal ability is, in brief, the ability to use and understand words. Vocabulary and grammar tests are typical measures of this ability. Reading comprehension or paragraph interpretation questions are common in many kinds of civil service tests. You are given a paragraph of written material and asked to find its central meaning.

IV. KINDS OF QUESTIONS

1. Multiple-choice Questions

Most popular of the short-answer questions is the "multiple choice" or "best answer" question. It can be used, for example, to test for factual knowledge, ability to solve problems or judgment in meeting situations found at work.

A multiple-choice question is normally one of three types:
- It can begin with an incomplete statement followed by several possible endings. You are to find the one ending which best completes the statement, although some of the others may not be entirely wrong.
- It can also be a complete statement in the form of a question which is answered by choosing one of the statements listed.
- It can be in the form of a problem – again you select the best answer.

Here is an example of a multiple-choice question with a discussion which should give you some clues as to the method for choosing the right answer:

When an employee has a complaint about his assignment, the action which will best help him overcome his difficulty is to
    A. discuss his difficulty with his coworkers
    B. take the problem to the head of the organization
    C. take the problem to the person who gave him the assignment
    D. say nothing to anyone about his complaint

In answering this question, you should study each of the choices to find which is best. Consider choice "A" – Certainly an employee may discuss his complaint with fellow employees, but no change or improvement can result, and the complaint remains unresolved. Choice "B" is a poor choice since the head of the organization probably does not know what assignment you have been given, and taking your problem to him is known as "going over the head" of the supervisor. The supervisor, or person who made the assignment, is the person who can clarify it or correct any injustice. Choice "C" is, therefore, correct. To say nothing, as in choice "D," is unwise. Supervisors have and interest in knowing the problems employees are facing, and the employee is seeking a solution to his problem.

2. True/False

3. Matching Questions

Matching an answer from a column of choices within another column.

V. RECORDING YOUR ANSWERS

Computer terminals are used more and more today for many different kinds of exams.

For an examination with very few applicants, you may be told to record your answers in the test booklet itself. Separate answer sheets are much more common. If this separate answer sheet is to be scored by machine – and this is often the case – it is highly important that you mark your answers correctly in order to get credit.

VI. BEFORE THE TEST

YOUR PHYSICAL CONDITION IS IMPORTANT

If you are not well, you can't do your best work on tests. If you are half asleep, you can't do your best either. Here are some tips:

1) Get about the same amount of sleep you usually get. Don't stay up all night before the test, either partying or worrying—DON'T DO IT!
2) If you wear glasses, be sure to wear them when you go to take the test. This goes for hearing aids, too.
3) If you have any physical problems that may keep you from doing your best, be sure to tell the person giving the test. If you are sick or in poor health, you relay cannot do your best on any test. You can always come back and take the test some other time.

Common sense will help you find procedures to follow to get ready for an examination. Too many of us, however, overlook these sensible measures. Indeed, nervousness and fatigue have been found to be the most serious reasons why applicants fail to do their best on civil service tests. Here is a list of reminders:

- Begin your preparation early – Don't wait until the last minute to go scurrying around for books and materials or to find out what the position is all about.
- Prepare continuously – An hour a night for a week is better than an all-night cram session. This has been definitely established. What is more, a night a week for a month will return better dividends than crowding your study into a shorter period of time.
- Locate the place of the exam – You have been sent a notice telling you when and where to report for the examination. If the location is in a different town or otherwise unfamiliar to you, it would be well to inquire the best route and learn something about the building.
- Relax the night before the test – Allow your mind to rest. Do not study at all that night. Plan some mild recreation or diversion; then go to bed early and get a good night's sleep.
- Get up early enough to make a leisurely trip to the place for the test – This way unforeseen events, traffic snarls, unfamiliar buildings, etc. will not upset you.
- Dress comfortably – A written test is not a fashion show. You will be known by number and not by name, so wear something comfortable.
- Leave excess paraphernalia at home – Shopping bags and odd bundles will get in your way. You need bring only the items mentioned in the official notice you received; usually everything you need is provided. Do not bring reference books to the exam. They will only confuse those last minutes and be taken away from you when in the test room.

- Arrive somewhat ahead of time – If because of transportation schedules you must get there very early, bring a newspaper or magazine to take your mind off yourself while waiting.
- Locate the examination room – When you have found the proper room, you will be directed to the seat or part of the room where you will sit. Sometimes you are given a sheet of instructions to read while you are waiting. Do not fill out any forms until you are told to do so; just read them and be prepared.
- Relax and prepare to listen to the instructions
- If you have any physical problem that may keep you from doing your best, be sure to tell the test administrator. If you are sick or in poor health, you really cannot do your best on the exam. You can come back and take the test some other time.

VII. AT THE TEST

The day of the test is here and you have the test booklet in your hand. The temptation to get going is very strong. Caution! There is more to success than knowing the right answers. You must know how to identify your papers and understand variations in the type of short-answer question used in this particular examination. Follow these suggestions for maximum results from your efforts:

1) Cooperate with the monitor

The test administrator has a duty to create a situation in which you can be as much at ease as possible. He will give instructions, tell you when to begin, check to see that you are marking your answer sheet correctly, and so on. He is not there to guard you, although he will see that your competitors do not take unfair advantage. He wants to help you do your best.

2) Listen to all instructions

Don't jump the gun! Wait until you understand all directions. In most civil service tests you get more time than you need to answer the questions. So don't be in a hurry. Read each word of instructions until you clearly understand the meaning. Study the examples, listen to all announcements and follow directions. Ask questions if you do not understand what to do.

3) Identify your papers

Civil service exams are usually identified by number only. You will be assigned a number; you must not put your name on your test papers. Be sure to copy your number correctly. Since more than one exam may be given, copy your exact examination title.

4) Plan your time

Unless you are told that a test is a "speed" or "rate of work" test, speed itself is usually not important. Time enough to answer all the questions will be provided, but this does not mean that you have all day. An overall time limit has been set. Divide the total time (in minutes) by the number of questions to determine the approximate time you have for each question.

5) Do not linger over difficult questions

If you come across a difficult question, mark it with a paper clip (useful to have along) and come back to it when you have been through the booklet. One caution if you do this – be sure to skip a number on your answer sheet as well. Check often to be sure that you have not lost your place and that you are marking in the row numbered the same as the question you are answering.

6) Read the questions

Be sure you know what the question asks! Many capable people are unsuccessful because they failed to read the questions correctly.

7) Answer all questions

Unless you have been instructed that a penalty will be deducted for incorrect answers, it is better to guess than to omit a question.

8) Speed tests

It is often better NOT to guess on speed tests. It has been found that on timed tests people are tempted to spend the last few seconds before time is called in marking answers at random – without even reading them – in the hope of picking up a few extra points. To discourage this practice, the instructions may warn you that your score will be "corrected" for guessing. That is, a penalty will be applied. The incorrect answers will be deducted from the correct ones, or some other penalty formula will be used.

9) Review your answers

If you finish before time is called, go back to the questions you guessed or omitted to give them further thought. Review other answers if you have time.

10) Return your test materials

If you are ready to leave before others have finished or time is called, take ALL your materials to the monitor and leave quietly. Never take any test material with you. The monitor can discover whose papers are not complete, and taking a test booklet may be grounds for disqualification.

VIII. EXAMINATION TECHNIQUES

1) Read the general instructions carefully. These are usually printed on the first page of the exam booklet. As a rule, these instructions refer to the timing of the examination; the fact that you should not start work until the signal and must stop work at a signal, etc. If there are any special instructions, such as a choice of questions to be answered, make sure that you note this instruction carefully.

2) When you are ready to start work on the examination, that is as soon as the signal has been given, read the instructions to each question booklet, underline any key words or phrases, such as least, best, outline, describe and the like. In this way you will tend to answer as requested rather than discover on reviewing your paper that you listed without describing, that you selected the worst choice rather than the best choice, etc.

3) If the examination is of the objective or multiple-choice type – that is, each question will also give a series of possible answers: A, B, C or D, and you are called upon to select the best answer and write the letter next to that answer on your answer paper – it is advisable to start answering each question in turn. There may be anywhere from 50 to 100 such questions in the three or four hours allotted and you can see how much time would be taken if you read through all the questions before beginning to answer any. Furthermore, if you

come across a question or group of questions which you know would be difficult to answer, it would undoubtedly affect your handling of all the other questions.

4) If the examination is of the essay type and contains but a few questions, it is a moot point as to whether you should read all the questions before starting to answer any one. Of course, if you are given a choice – say five out of seven and the like – then it is essential to read all the questions so you can eliminate the two that are most difficult. If, however, you are asked to answer all the questions, there may be danger in trying to answer the easiest one first because you may find that you will spend too much time on it. The best technique is to answer the first question, then proceed to the second, etc.

5) Time your answers. Before the exam begins, write down the time it started, then add the time allowed for the examination and write down the time it must be completed, then divide the time available somewhat as follows:
    - If 3-1/2 hours are allowed, that would be 210 minutes. If you have 80 objective-type questions, that would be an average of 2-1/2 minutes per question. Allow yourself no more than 2 minutes per question, or a total of 160 minutes, which will permit about 50 minutes to review.
    - If for the time allotment of 210 minutes there are 7 essay questions to answer, that would average about 30 minutes a question. Give yourself only 25 minutes per question so that you have about 35 minutes to review.

6) The most important instruction is to read each question and make sure you know what is wanted. The second most important instruction is to time yourself properly so that you answer every question. The third most important instruction is to answer every question. Guess if you have to but include something for each question. Remember that you will receive no credit for a blank and will probably receive some credit if you write something in answer to an essay question. If you guess a letter – say "B" for a multiple-choice question – you may have guessed right. If you leave a blank as an answer to a multiple-choice question, the examiners may respect your feelings but it will not add a point to your score. Some exams may penalize you for wrong answers, so in such cases only, you may not want to guess unless you have some basis for your answer.

7) Suggestions
    a. Objective-type questions
        1. Examine the question booklet for proper sequence of pages and questions
        2. Read all instructions carefully
        3. Skip any question which seems too difficult; return to it after all other questions have been answered
        4. Apportion your time properly; do not spend too much time on any single question or group of questions
        5. Note and underline key words – all, most, fewest, least, best, worst, same, opposite, etc.
        6. Pay particular attention to negatives
        7. Note unusual option, e.g., unduly long, short, complex, different or similar in content to the body of the question
        8. Observe the use of "hedging" words – probably, may, most likely, etc.

9. Make sure that your answer is put next to the same number as the question
10. Do not second-guess unless you have good reason to believe the second answer is definitely more correct
11. Cross out original answer if you decide another answer is more accurate; do not erase until you are ready to hand your paper in
12. Answer all questions; guess unless instructed otherwise
13. Leave time for review

b. Essay questions
1. Read each question carefully
2. Determine exactly what is wanted. Underline key words or phrases.
3. Decide on outline or paragraph answer
4. Include many different points and elements unless asked to develop any one or two points or elements
5. Show impartiality by giving pros and cons unless directed to select one side only
6. Make and write down any assumptions you find necessary to answer the questions
7. Watch your English, grammar, punctuation and choice of words
8. Time your answers; don't crowd material

8) Answering the essay question

Most essay questions can be answered by framing the specific response around several key words or ideas. Here are a few such key words or ideas:

M's: manpower, materials, methods, money, management
P's: purpose, program, policy, plan, procedure, practice, problems, pitfalls, personnel, public relations

a. Six basic steps in handling problems:
1. Preliminary plan and background development
2. Collect information, data and facts
3. Analyze and interpret information, data and facts
4. Analyze and develop solutions as well as make recommendations
5. Prepare report and sell recommendations
6. Install recommendations and follow up effectiveness

b. Pitfalls to avoid
1. Taking things for granted – A statement of the situation does not necessarily imply that each of the elements is necessarily true; for example, a complaint may be invalid and biased so that all that can be taken for granted is that a complaint has been registered
2. Considering only one side of a situation – Wherever possible, indicate several alternatives and then point out the reasons you selected the best one
3. Failing to indicate follow up – Whenever your answer indicates action on your part, make certain that you will take proper follow-up action to see how successful your recommendations, procedures or actions turn out to be
4. Taking too long in answering any single question – Remember to time your answers properly

EXAMINATION SECTION

EXAMINATION SECTION
TEST 1

DIRECTIONS: Each question or incomplete statement is followed by several suggested answers or completions. Select the one that BEST answers the question or completes the statement. *PRINT THE LETTER OF THE CORRECT ANSWER IN THE SPACE AT THE RIGHT.*

1. It is generally agreed that stratification in a society is a result of the allocation of three distinct resources.
   Which of the following is NOT one of these resources?
   - A. Class
   - B. Ownership
   - C. Power
   - D. Status

   1.____

2. What is the term for a social collectivity whose members occupy the same place at the same time?
   - A. Group
   - B. Aggregate
   - C. Crowd
   - D. Amalgamation

   2.____

3. What is the term widely used to describe the breakdown of societal rules and norms that regulate human behaviors?
   - A. Anomie
   - B. Ennui
   - C. Relapse
   - D. Angst

   3.____

4. Which of the following is NOT included in the concept of culture?
   - A. Biological heredity
   - B. Languages
   - C. Religious beliefs
   - D. Morals and customs

   4.____

5. Each of the following is an important reason for the great social significance of institutions EXCEPT
   - A. they have powerful ordering effects on a society
   - B. institutions initiate social change processes within societies
   - C. within institutional structures, people have the expectation of stable value and normative systems
   - D. they develop and transmit the deeply held values of a society

   5.____

6. The *hidden* values of the middle class, revealed in leisure activities, are known as _____ values.
   - A. Hawthorne
   - B. subterranean
   - C. clandestine
   - D. revelatory

   6.____

7. The socially legitimated right, by virtue of a social status, to control the action of others is known specifically as
   - A. influence
   - B. power
   - C. jurisdiction
   - D. authority

   7.____

8. The term for the scientific study of populations is
   - A. statistics
   - B. compilation
   - C. demography
   - D. differential association

   8.____

9. Historically, American schools have had a harder time than those of other industrialized countries in

   A. uniting the people in a common tradition
   B. preventing revolutionary movements
   C. training people for emerging job types
   D. producing industrial workers

10. According to most research, over half of the unemployed in America blame

    A. the economic system for their problems
    B. fate or bad luck
    C. themselves
    D. their former employers

11. Which of the following is NOT an example of direct institutional discrimination?

    A. South Africa's apartheid system
    B. Corporate America's current inequity in top-level executive positions
    C. The American South's Jim Crow laws
    D. The Nazi holocaust

12. Social stratification assigned to a person at birth is termed

    A. charged   B. fixed   C. attached   D. ascribed

13. The means by which it can sometimes be demonstrated that a particular variable is the cause of a phenomenon is

    A. participant observation   B. field study
    C. experimentation   D. correlation

14. In the simplest societies, the economic institution is embedded within each of the following arrangements EXCEPT

    A. family   B. education   C. polity   D. religion

15. According to Piaget, the need for norms is best understood if they are learned from

    A. religious authorities   B. a peer group
    C. political leaders   D. parents

16. Which method for stratification analysis divides a given population into hierarchies of income and occupational, educational, or other predetermined categories?

    A. Subjective self-placement   B. Subjective reputation
    C. Subjective scaled   D. Objective

17. The sociologist Peter Berger introduced the idea of sociological analysis as

    A. a relativist approach to stratification
    B. a Darwinist study of the struggle for social survival
    C. unmasking apparent social realities
    D. a study of social performance as theater

18. The world's various religions are most alike in

    A. the belief in the continuity of the religious tradition
    B. the shared belief in some form of heaven and hell
    C. belief in a single god
    D. belief in a return to this earthly life in some form

19. The root of all cultural systems is said to be

    A. family   B. religion   C. language   D. economics

20. Prejudice is characterized by each of the following EXCEPT

    A. once established, it persists as a component of the culture
    B. it is something believed about groups rather than individuals
    C. it is behavioral in nature
    D. it involves stereotypes

21. Countries that implement coercive antinatalist measures assume that

    A. governments can control the breeding habits of their people
    B. poor countries will not need international aid
    C. poor countries will be rescued by international intervention
    D. rich countries should suffer as much as poor ones

22. According to current estimates, what percentage of American children will spend some time in a single-parent household before reaching the age of 18?

    A. 10   B. 35   C. 65   D. 90

23. Demographers in the field of sociology are typically interested in each of the following EXCEPT

    A. processes such as mortality and migration
    B. the political composition of a population
    C. the size and spatial distribution of a population
    D. the structure and characteristics of a population

24. What is the term for a stratum of poor persons who are excluded from meaningful participation in the economy and thus experience no upward social mobility?

    A. Underclass   B. Caste
    C. Status community   D. Cognitive minority

25. When a sociological study is to focus on past events, the primary approach to gathering information will most likely be

    A. direct question   B. direct observation
    C. survey   D. indirect question

KEY (CORRECT ANSWERS)

1.	B	11.	B
2.	B	12.	D
3.	A	13.	C
4.	A	14.	B
5.	B	15.	B
6.	B	16.	D
7.	D	17.	C
8.	C	18.	A
9.	A	19.	C
10.	C	20.	C

21. A
22. C
23. B
24. A
25. D

———

TEST 2

DIRECTIONS: Each question or incomplete statement is followed by several suggested answers or completions. Select the one that BEST answers the question or completes the statement. *PRINT THE LETTER OF THE CORRECT ANSWER IN THE SPACE AT THE RIGHT.*

1. In those societies _____, aged members are most likely to be abandoned or killed.   1.____

    A. that have no religious beliefs
    B. with insufficient food
    C. that revile the aged
    D. that think of the afterlife as blissful

2. According to the classifications established by Joseph Gusfield, a burglar would be classified as a(n) _____ deviant.   2.____

    A. sick   B. enemy   C. repentant   D. cynical

3. According to the work of Levi-Strauss, a society's most common reason for minimizing family importance is   3.____

    A. competing military requirements
    B. immorality
    C. a primitive stage of development
    D. economic avarice

4. Which of the following is NOT true of the scientific method?   4.____

    A. Conclusions, once reached, are no longer subject to revision.
    B. Findings are accepted even if they conflict with previous views.
    C. No shortcuts to knowledge are accepted.
    D. Procedures are systematic.

5. What is the sociological term for the inability to maintain physical survival on a long-term basis?   5.____

    A. Absolute poverty   B. Divergence
    C. Incompetence   D. Insufficiency

6. A small business generally differs from a large corporation in that it   6.____

    A. hires better managers because they are less bureaucratic
    B. introduces more new products experimentally
    C. has better bargaining power
    D. receives better treatment from banks and lending agencies

7. If a girl dreams of being a basketball player, watches major college players and tries to imitate them, the basketball players are a _____ group for her.   7.____

    A. primary   B. secondary   C. reference   D. peer

8. If asked to rank their social position on a five-way scale, most Americans would (and do) rate themselves as _____ class. 8.____

    A. upper or upper middle
    B. upper middle or middle
    C. lower middle or working
    D. working class or lower

9. According to the conflict theory of social deviance, 9.____

    A. deviance is primarily a product of conflicting prevailing norms within a society
    B. deviance is a product of the weakening of a societal consensus about fundamental values
    C. deviance is sometimes taught and learned in primary group settings
    D. societal definitions and the treatment of deviance are a consequence of social inequalities

10. Which of the following was NOT a characteristic of the American colonial family? 10.____

    A. Its size was generally limited due to economic considerations.
    B. Extended family systems were an important element in community structures.
    C. The most important social function of the family was economic in nature.
    D. It was largely a nuclear, rather than an extended, family.

11. The MAIN conclusion of the work of Thomas Malthus is that 11.____

    A. preventive controls will solve most population problems
    B. population tends to outrun food supply
    C. food supply increases faster than population
    D. countries should practice pronatalist policies

12. The occurrence of displaced persons typically results from all of the following EXCEPT 12.____

    A. political oppression   B. economic disruption
    C. slavery   D. warfare

13. Which phase of demographic transition is characterized by high birth and death rates? 13.____

    A. First   B. Second   C. Third   D. Fourth

14. According to the multiple hierarchies theory of social stratification, an individual's class position within a larger society is determined by the 14.____

    A. level of prestige or rank accorded by others
    B. level of life chances
    C. ability to mobilize and employ power
    D. ownership of private property

15. Basically, *class* means 15.____

    A. power   B. character
    C. material wealth   D. sphere of influence

16. The *period explanation* for the recent decline in urban growth in America includes each of the following EXCEPT

    A. a growing number of elderly Americans added to the population of nonmetropolitan areas
    B. disinvestment in heavily industrialized *winter* cities was caused by the 1987 stock market scare
    C. smaller cities and towns gained population as light industries and services emerged
    D. it is only a temporary distortion of continuing urban expansion

17. Which of the following would be a characteristic used to determine physical minorities in a society?

    A. Dialect   B. Ethnicity   C. Religion   D. Age

18. Which of the following does NOT describe a *secondary* group?

    A. Formal   B. Diffuse
    C. Instrumental   D. Segmented

19. _____ are relatively permanent structural configurations centered on the tasks of meeting the important material and nonmaterial requirements of a society.

    A. Institutions   B. Norms
    C. Rituals   D. Classes

20. A subculture is

    A. a divergent pattern that rejects the larger culture
    B. a divergent pattern contained within the larger culture
    C. substituted for an actual culture
    D. inferior to the major culture

21. Each of the following is a structural explanation for the existence of American poverty EXCEPT:

    A. Some categories of people have been disadvantaged by well-institutionalized patterns of prejudice and discrimination
    B. Poverty is a consequence of both government policies and specific economic trends
    C. The situation of poverty gives rise to a world view and behavioral patterns that serve to perpetuate the existence of poverty
    D. The presence of poor people has been built into certain economic systems, especially in capitalist societies

22. Which of the following sociologists first became interested in applying some of the principles of biological science to human societies?

    A. Emile Durkheim   B. Lester Frank Ward
    C. Max Weber   D. William Graham Sumner

23. The study and explanation of religion largely as a response to the human desire to discover meanings is MOST typical of the field of

    A. philosophy
    B. sociology
    C. psychology
    D. anthropology

24. According to the concentric-zone model of urbanization, zone 3 contains

    A. commuter residences
    B. stores, offices, and commercial establishments
    C. homes of unskilled laborers
    D. ethnic enclaves

25. In risk taking, the values of orderliness, certainty, and dependability are supplanted by the _____ values of the middle class.

    A. work
    B. normative
    C. reliability
    D. subterranean

KEY (CORRECT ANSWERS)

1.	B	11.	B
2.	D	12.	C
3.	A	13.	A
4.	A	14.	B
5.	A	15.	C
6.	B	16.	B
7.	B	17.	D
8.	B	18.	B
9.	D	19.	A
10.	A	20.	B

21. C
22. B
23. A
24. D
25. D

TEST 3

DIRECTIONS: Each question or incomplete statement is followed by several suggested answers or completions. Select the one that BEST answers the question or completes the statement. *PRINT THE LETTER OF THE CORRECT ANSWER IN THE SPACE AT THE RIGHT.*

Questions 1-2.

DIRECTIONS: Questions 1 and 2 refer to the figure below, a graphic depiction of the Atlantic slave trade.

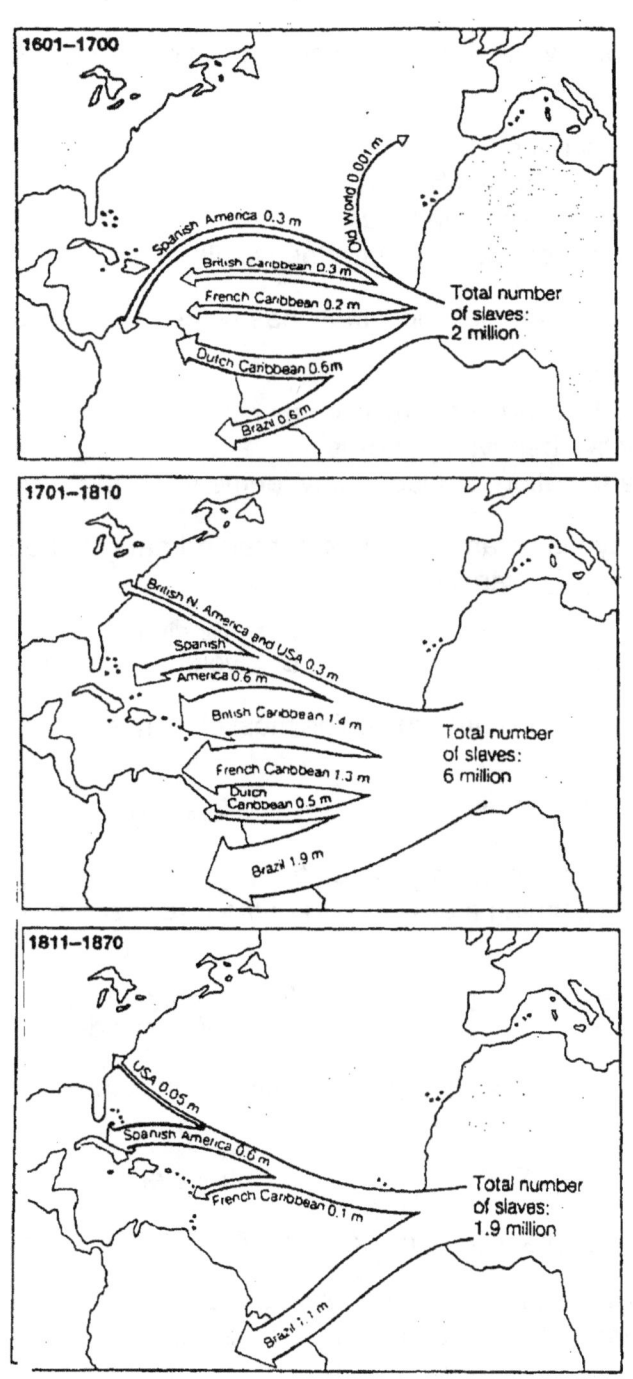

1. Most of the slaves from Africa were captured and exported during the period

   A. 1601-1700
   B. 1701-1810
   C. 1811-1870
   D. it is impossible to tell from the given information

2. Other than Brazil, the largest importer of slaves during the years of 1701-1811 was

   A. the United States
   B. the British Caribbean
   C. the Dutch Caribbean
   D. British North America

3. In most studies, including Warner's, the factor that distinguishes the upper upper class from the lower upper class is

   A. the source of the wealth
   B. whether the amount of wealth is increasing
   C. how long the wealth has been held
   D. the prestige of the work done to earn the wealth

4. Which of the following human biological traits has helped to make culture possible?

   A. Continuous sex drive
   B. Unusually acute hearing and smell senses
   C. Complex instinctive behavior patterns
   D. Total physical adaptation to specific environments

5. Each of the following types of families has emerged primarily in 20th-century American society EXCEPT the _____ family.

   A. blended
   B. abusive
   C. dual-earner
   D. voluntarily childless

6. Which of the following Freudian terminologies most closely approximates the meaning of *conscience*?

   A. Id
   B. Ego
   C. Superego
   D. Anima

7. The yearly income required to provide a nutritionally adequate diet for a typical nonfarm family of four people, assuming that one-third of the total income is used for food, is an index known as the

   A. subsistence level
   B. retention line
   C. poverty line
   D. support index

8. Which of the following is NOT a type of illegal immigrant categorized by the U.S. Census Bureau?

   A. Commuter
   B. Settler
   C. Traveler
   D. Sojourner

9. In American schools, the practice of tracking is MOST defensible on the premise that it

   A. makes mistakes in assigning students less likely
   B. makes slower learners aware of their lower academic status
   C. decreases discipline problems
   D. creates fairer competition

10. Primary relationships can NOT be described as

    A. contractual
    B. durable
    C. small in size
    D. emotionally involved

11. In America, working class women and supporters of the women's movement are in closest agreement on the issue of

    A. spousal abuse
    B. child-care centers
    C. equal pay for equal work
    D. abortion

12. LEAST likely to reduce the world's resources is

    A. nonmechanized farming
    B. industrialization
    C. increasing affluence
    D. petroleum-based agriculture

13. The tendency of religious leaders to seek reform in order to bring society closer to its religious ideals is known as the _____ function.

    A. reformation
    B. eschatological
    C. charismatic
    D. prophetic

14. The use of documentary research in sociological study

    A. is easier for subsequent researchers to repeat than other methods
    B. is often essential when a study is either wholly historical or has a defined historical dimension
    C. usually excludes many aspects of social life
    D. can only be used to study relatively small groups or communities

15. According to most six-class models of the American class structure, the 65% of the population that fuels the economy exist in the _____ strata.

    A. working poor and underclass
    B. working class and working poor
    C. middle and working
    D. upper middle and middle

16. The process of labeling individuals includes each of the following EXCEPT

    A. retrospective interpretation
    B. differential reinforcement
    C. negotiation
    D. stereotyping

17. The most obvious effect of the American two-party political system is

    A. the encouragement of multilateral debate of political issues
    B. the requirement of good standing in either of the parties in order to participate in government
    C. a lopsided distribution of material wealth
    D. an unusually high degree of governmental stability

18. Religious sects differ from denominations in that they involve

    A. a membership that includes community leaders
    B. acceptance of modern science
    C. emotional conversion experiences
    D. clergy trained in seminaries

19. Which of the following is NOT a common criticism of the conflict theory of gender roles in a society?

    A. It fails to take into account the historic economic and political importance of roles filled by women
    B. Its overemphasis on differences
    C. The Marxist assertion that gender oppression is associated exclusively with capitalism
    D. The consistent appearance of hidden agendas in male-female relations

20. Which of the following is not a distinguishing characteristic of wealth resources?

    A. They are extremely fluid resources
    B. They are an object of conflict between individuals and groups
    C. They are more easily acquired than either status or power
    D. The more liquid the resource, the more valuable it becomes

21. In the late 20th century, American metropolitan areas are generally no longer

    A. having serious financial difficulty
    B. showing decay at the urban core
    C. growing at the expense of rural areas
    D. experiencing more crime than rural areas

22. Poor nonwhite families in America are more likely than white middle-class families to be

    A. headed by women   B. stable
    C. headed by men   D. patriarchal

23. If a politician makes a statement about her country's *proud tradition,* her viewpoint would be most like those sociological theorists who use a(n) _____ model.

    A. symbolic-interactionist   B. non-Marxist conflict
    C. unitary   D. conflict

24. The rules in any given society that must be obeyed under any circumstances, and which elicit strong negative sanctions if violated are known sociologically as

    A. mores   B. norms   C. codes   D. laws

25. The *crisis of middle age,* in Erickson's developmental scheme, is one of developing

    A. intimacy   B. identity
    C. generativity   D. autonomy

KEY (CORRECT ANSWERS)

1.	B	11.	C
2.	B	12.	A
3.	C	13.	D
4.	A	14.	B
5.	B	15.	C
6.	C	16.	B
7.	C	17.	D
8.	C	18.	C
9.	D	19.	A
10.	A	20.	D

21. C
22. A
23. C
24. A
25. C

___

TEST 4

DIRECTIONS: Each question or incomplete statement is followed by several suggested answers or completions. Select the one that BEST answers the question or completes the statement. *PRINT THE LETTER OF THE CORRECT ANSWER IN THE SPACE AT THE RIGHT.*

1. In pre-industrial families, the most basic social institution was the

    A. nuclear family
    B. extended family
    C. small community
    D. entire society

2. Which of the following is NOT a distinguishing characteristic of bureaucracy?

    A. Individual bureaus are linked through an established hierarchy
    B. Positions are filled on the basis of talent and ability
    C. Interactions among members are governed by larger societal norms
    D. Clear distinction made between organizational life and personal life

3. The idea that every social structure yields some benefit and fulfills some need for the social system as a whole, and that this need fulfillment is the reason and explanation for the existence of that institutional component, is a basic assumption of the _____ theory of social stratification.

    A. social conflict
    B. structural-functional
    C. natural superiority
    D. self-esteem

4. Competitive social relations in a society include the emergence of each of the following EXCEPT

    A. parallel institutions
    B. split labor markets
    C. middleman minorities
    D. enclaves

5. Tentative explanations that are put to a test by an experiment are called

    A. hypotheses
    B. precepts
    C. dependent variables
    D. theories

6. In American schools, the higher success rate of students of higher socioeconomic status is best explained in terns of

    A. gender
    B. motivation
    C. material resources
    D. family values

7. In which of the following ways is work NOT related to leisure activity in America?

    A. Friendships and group activities
    B. A reaction against the working pattern
    C. Avocational interests
    D. Leisure-time expense

8. In the classification system established by Robert Merton, prejudice in the absence of discrimination is a behavior that typifies a(n)

    A. bigot
    B. timid bigot
    C. fair-weather liberal
    D. all-weather liberal

9. The convergence theory of active crowds is most concerned with the

   A. psychological trait of suggestibility
   B. reasons people become part of a crowd
   C. development of norms within crowds
   D. dangers associated with crowds

10. In most societies, the task of imparting meaning and significance to social arrangements is fulfilled by

    A. education   B. polity
    C. class structure   D. religion

11. Which of the following is NOT an advantage associated with the use of face-to-face interviewing in sociological research?

    A. The need for literate population is eliminated
    B. It permits the researcher to explore more complex topics
    C. Relatively low time consumption
    D. Ability to read nonverbal aspects of communication

12. The idea that stratification is the result of valuing and rewarding our own characteristics, while disvaluing those of others, is a basic assumption of the _____ theory of social stratification.

    A. social conflict   B. structural-functional
    C. natural superiority   D. self-esteem

13. Which of the following is NOT a specific content that is transmitted in socialization processes?

    A. Role-taking skills   B. Spirituality
    C. Self-concept   D. Language

14. What is the term for any human attribute that is deeply discrediting, and thus makes persons different from others, and of a less desirable kind?

    A. Slur   B. Quirk
    C. Stigma   D. Stereotype

15. The extent of an individual's awareness that he/she is performing a social role or presenting a self to others is known as

    A. socialization   B. role distance
    C. dramaturgical analysis   D. self-concept

16. The eastern seaboard of the U.S. from Boston to Virginia is nost clearly an example of a(n)

    A. gemeinschaft   B. blight
    C. SMSA   D. megalopolis

17. In urban environments, the middle and upper classes are more likely than the poor to

    A. purchase products that will improve their personal appearance
    B. interact with neighbors
    C. join associations
    D. maintain ties with relatives

18. Religious cults are characterized, in varying degrees, by each of the following EXCEPT

    A. intense sense of mission
    B. surrender of individual autonomy and decision-making
    C. resocialization techniques
    D. varied stratification into several classes of power-holders

19. According to the classifications established by Joseph Gusfield, the _____ deviant poses the least symbolic threat to a dominant social order.

    A. sick   B. enemy   C. repentant   D. cynical

20. The tendency to view one's own culture as best and to judge other cultures by its own standards is known as

    A. enclavism   B. misanthropy
    C. ethnocentrism   D. bigotry

21. The situation in which diverse religions within a society maintain their autonomy and compete with each other for members is known as religious

    A. consolidation   B. differentiation
    C. pluralism   D. selection

22. Which of the following is the most serious flaw that is typically involved in the conduct of subjective reputational stratification analyses?

    A. Mobility of contemporary societies
    B. Difference in perception of hierarchy by respondents who occupy different levels
    C. Self-obviating responses from members of closed systems
    D. Perception of social class as a matter of prestige

23. The most obvious result of slower population growth is

    A. a larger proportion of middle-aged and elderly people
    B. greater academic achievement of children
    C. an end to pollution
    D. replenishment of fuel resources

24. In modern societies, the task of defending the society from outside encroachment is addressed by

    A. the executive officers of the society's government
    B. linking the society's stability with the will of a supreme being
    C. several overlapping institutional functions
    D. the formation of a subinstitutional set of structures

25. Industrial organizations typically use each of the following methods to lower costs EXCEPT
    A. encouraging collective bargaining
    B. operating overseas in areas of low wages
    C. resorting to automation
    D. operating in areas of weak unionism

KEY (CORRECT ANSWERS)

1. B
2. C
3. B
4. B
5. A

6. B
7. C
8. B
9. B
10. D

11. C
12. D
13. B
14. C
15. B

16. D
17. C
18. D
19. D
20. C

21. C
22. B
23. A
24. D
25. A

EXAMINATION SECTION

TEST 1

DIRECTIONS: Each question or incomplete statement is followed by several suggested answers or completions. Select the one that BEST answers the question or completes the statement. *PRINT THE LETTER OF THE CORRECT ANSWER IN THE SPACE AT THE RIGHT.*

Questions 1-4.

DIRECTIONS: Questions 1 through 4 refer to the figure below, a representation of Southeast Asian economies in 2012.

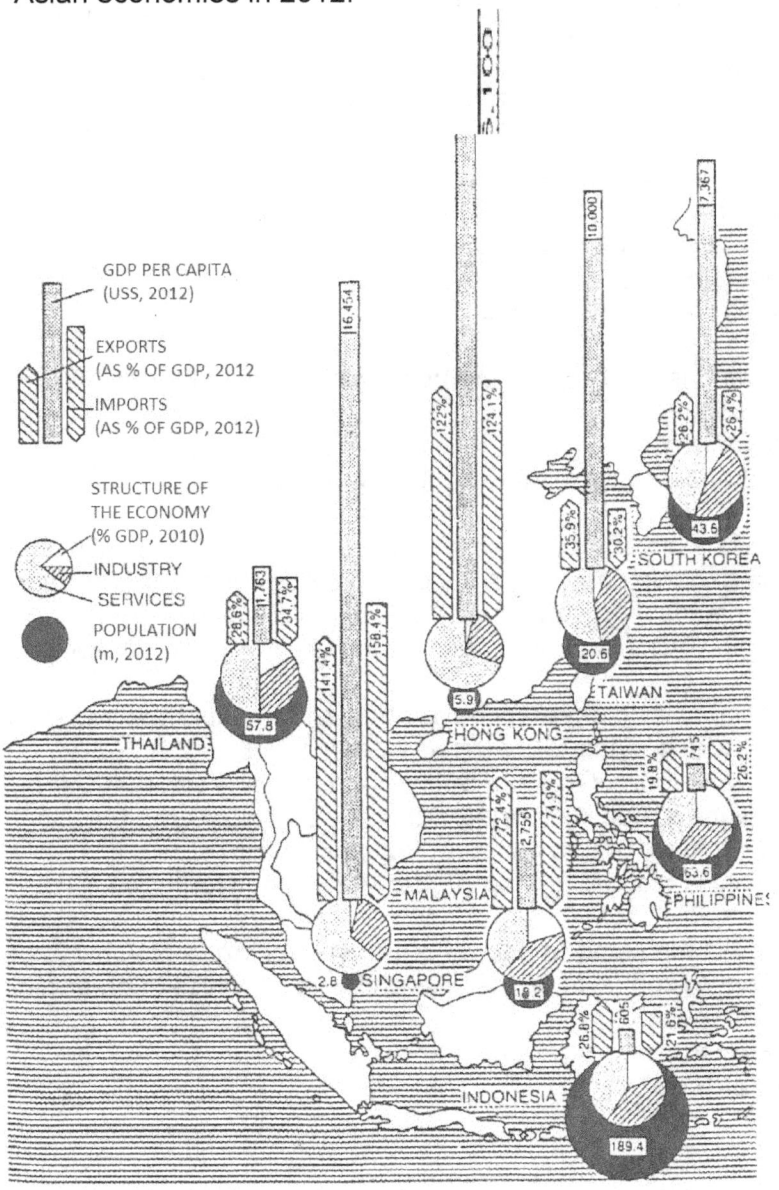

1. In 2012, the country with the LARGEST population in Southeast Asia was
   A. Philippines   B. Indonesia   C. South Korea   D. Thailand

2. The MOST industrial nation in Southeast Asia in 2012 appears to have been
   A. Thailand   B. Singapore   C. South Korea   D. Hong Kong

3. The country with the HIGHEST export proportion in 2012 was
   A. Singapore   B. Malaysia   C. Hong Kong   D. Taiwan

4. Agriculture seems to have been MOST important to the economy of _____ in 2012.
   A. Hong Kong   B. Singapore   C. Philippines   D. Taiwan

5. According to Marx's theory of class conflict, the single most important fact of life for every human population is its
   A. objective classes
   B. superstructure
   C. mode of production
   D. mores

6. Which of the following is a push factor in returning people to an urban area?
   A. Exciting city life
   B. Rising prices of suburban housing
   C. Museums and libraries
   D. Close proximity to city attractions

7. Which of the following is NOT one of the primary functions of a society's educational institution?
   A. Cultural transmission
   B. Occupation allocation
   C. Maintenance of authority relations
   D. Skill training

8. In sociological study, the term for a sample composed of persons, cases, or events exhibiting known characteristics of special relevance for the research question being studied is _____ sample.
   A. stratified   B. random   C. mixed   D. purposive

9. When different racial or ethnic groups have been employed at the same job at different wages, which of the following has been TRUE?
   A. Low-priced workers tend to drive out high-priced workers.
   B. Status groups have quickly formed within the organization.
   C. High-priced workers tend to drive out low-priced workers.
   D. Unemployment is highest among African-American workers.

10. The MAIN criticism of the sector model of urban spatial organization is that it
    A. places too much emphasis on the role of the upper class in determining spatial organization
    B. ignores the topography of an urban area
    C. is overgeneralized
    D. is inaccurate

11. Which of the following is NOT one of the essential aspects of scientific sociological analysis?
    A. Replication
    B. Empirical availability
    C. Explanation
    D. Consistency of results

12. The descent norms of industrialized families tend to be
    A. insignificant
    B. bilineal
    C. patrilineal
    D. matrilineal

13. Which of the following is NOT a way in which the modern personality type differs from the previous one?
    A. Interest in urban and national affairs
    B. Allegiance to elders and small-community leaders
    C. Interest in government, labor, and education
    D. Willingness to accept new ideas

14. In the United States, the _____ is LEAST likely to experience countervailing forces.
    A. Department of Education
    B. Federal Bureau of Investigation
    C. Department of Justice
    D. Central Intelligence Agency

15. School, as an agency of socialization,
    A. finds that lower-class children are indifferent to teacher approval
    B. is more helpful to middle-class than to lower-class children
    C. is usually more influential than the home
    D. invariably reinforces the teachings of the home

16. Exchange relations in societies are expressed in
    A. enclaves
    B. assimilation
    C. coalitions
    D. pluralism

17. Which of the following is NOT a social correlate to mortality in the United States?
    A. People who are married have lower mortality rates than singles.
    B. Non-white mortality is higher than white mortality in every group up to age eighty.
    C. As a group, men live approximately seven years longer than women.
    D. As a group's occupational prestige goes up, death rates go down.

18. Most research on college-educated Americans reveals that they
    A. usually limit their interests to their own vocational field
    B. lag behind popular culture
    C. usually keep up their interest in learning
    D. show no greater knowledge than mere high-school graduates later in life

19. The *regional restructuring* theory concerning the recent de-industrialization of American cities holds that
    A. areas that successfully make the transition to a post-industrial, service-oriented economy will prosper in the future
    B. smaller cities and towns will continue to decline as light industries and services emerge
    C. it is only a temporary distortion of continuing urban expansion
    D. urban populations in the northeast will experience a revitalization

20. In what way is old age worse in modern societies than in earlier agricultural societies?
    A. Greater role loss
    B. Too many activities
    C. Poor health care
    D. Elevated expectations of the elderly

21. The sociological term for an ordering system that classifies individual phenomena into categories based on the basis of distinguishing characteristics is
    A. schema   B. substructure   C. typology   D. matrix

22. In the Marxist view, the GREATEST criticism of spectator sports is that they
    A. lead to gambling   B. are usually corrupted
    C. are given too much significance   D. establish escapism

23. One of the PRIMARY assumptions of the *looking glass* process assumption is that people
    A. are by nature narcissistic
    B. develop their self-image according to how others see them
    C. are highly introspective
    D. see only a faint reflection of the true reality surrounding them

24. Each of the following is a generalized change within the family structure that was brought about by industrialization EXCEPT
    A. a reduction in its social functions
    B. decreased literacy
    C. increasing attention to emotional well-being of members

25. Direct questioning would be the MOST appropriate approach for gathering information during sociological study when the research questions focus on
    A. past events   B. behavioral patterns
    C. theoretical circumstances   D. cognitive or emotional patterns

KEY (CORRECT ANSWERS)

1. B
2. C
3. A
4. C
5. C

6. B
7. C
8. D
9. A
10. A

11. D
12. B
13. B
14. D
15. B

16. C
17. C
18. C
19. A
20. A

21. C
22. D
23. B
24. B
25. D

TEST 2

DIRECTIONS: Each question or incomplete statement is followed by several suggested answers or completions. Select the one that BEST answers the question or completes the statement. *PRINT THE LETTER OF THE CORRECT ANSWER IN THE SPACE AT THE RIGHT.*

1. Socialism CANNOT be described as
   A. a perfect adjustment of the individual to societal demands
   B. the development of an individual personality
   C. a mutual process
   D. a process of internalizing social values

   1.____

2. Current studies reveal that female-headed families account for approximately 17% of all American households. What approximate percentage of *poor* households are made up of female-headed households?
   A. 17   B. 30   C. 55   D. 75

   2.____

3. As a general rule, status inconsistency (but not status decline) is associated with
   A. ethnicity   B. conservatism
   C. liberalism   D. undemocratic viewpoints

   3.____

4. In collective behavior, the actions involved are relatively
   A. organized   B. radical-inspired
   C. spontaneous   D. institutionalized

   4.____

5. What is the MOST likely reason crime rates have risen among American women?
   A. Women are more likely to be frustrated by family considerations than men
   B. An increasing number of women in positions offering the possibility of white-collar crime
   C. They are increasingly occupying the underclass
   D. They simply outnumber men in our society

   5.____

6. In a society that has become stratified, _____ distinctions tend to be the very first stratification designations that are made.
   A. power   B. wealth   C. class   D. prestige

   6.____

7. Studies have shown that police in America are LEAST likely to enforce laws against
   A. drug use   B. social gambling
   C. prostitution   D. petty larceny

   7.____

8. Which of the following is a term that classifies a family structure in terms of *authority*?
   A. Endogamous   B. Matriarchal   C. Patrilineal   D. Extended

   8.____

9. According to the work of Merton, the person MOST respected by society is the
   A. ritualist   B. rebel   C. innovator   D. conformist

10. The primary DISADVANTAGE associated with the use of subjective self-placement as a means of stratification analysis is that it(s)
    A. does not accurately indicate people's beliefs and behaviors
    B. responses are more a function of available options than clearly held opinions
    C. assumes that all people are willing to rank themselves in society
    D. does not instruct respondents in correct terminology

11. According to the work of Durkheim, older societies were held together PRIMARILY by
    A. structural functionalism   B. organic solidarity
    C. mechanical solidarity   D. synthesis

12. Structural-functional theorists would explain a society's gender roles in terms of
    A. self-perpetuating stereotypes
    B. their existence as instruments of oppression in society
    C. subgroup differences
    D. their contributions to societal survival

13. In what way do vagrancy laws in the United States illustrate a conflict perspective on deviance?
    A. Their justification is constantly debated.
    B. They show a clear consensus regarding the law.
    C. They are enforced primarily against lower-class people.
    D. They are employed mainly during times of conflict.

14. American political attitudes can BEST be generalized as
    A. conservative
    B. liberal
    C. operationally liberal but ideologically conservative
    D. operationally conservative but ideologically liberal

15. What is the term for any act of differential treatment of persons that creates a social disadvantage and is based upon the perception of people as members of a group, community, or stratum?
    A. Discrimination   B. Stereotyping   C. Prejudice   D. Bias

16. The sociologist Margaret Mead, who performed extensive field work in other cultures, argued that the specific cultural practices of any society must be understood and interpreted in the context of that society's culture alone. Mead was among the first to establish the concept of
    A. subjectivism   B. differential association
    C. cultural relativism   D. interactionism

17. The economic contrast between a mixed economic system and communism lies in
    A. political dictatorship
    B. opposition to religion
    C. introduction of new experimental products
    D. government ownership of industry

18. Special types of dress or speech that identify members of a group and keep them separate from others are termed _____ mechanisms.
    A. defensive
    B. differential
    C. boundary maintenance
    D. adaptive

19. Each of the following is a feature that is characteristic of a caste system EXCEPT
    A. ranking that includes stigma
    B. membership at birth, and for life
    C. strict avoidance of members of other strata
    D. exogamy

20. According to Malthusian theory, each of the following is a *positive* check on population EXCEPT
    A. celibacy   B. epidemic   C. famine   D. war

21. What is the term for a type of social conflict in which a population or community is subjugated through economic dependency and thus is controlled and exploited by another community or population?
    A. Slavery
    B. Colonialism
    C. Establishmentarianism
    D. Imperialism

22. The PRIMARY reason for using interviews during sociological research, rather than questionnaires, is to
    A. save printing costs
    B. make sure both the questions and the responses are fully understood
    C. prevent the subjects from giving clearly false or outrageous answers
    D. make the research more engaging and enjoyable

23. Which of the following would be LEAST likely to interfere with religion's ability to perform some of its traditional societal roles?
    A. Religious pluralism
    B. Theocracy
    C. Separation of church and state
    D. Secular humanism

24. What is the term for a social collectivity whose members are clustered strategically on the basis of common characteristics?
    A. Faction   B. Group   C. Aggregate   D. Category

25. Social stratification is described as the result of individual differences in strength, intelligence, or some other human trait by the _____ theory.
    A. social conflict
    B. structural-functional
    C. natural superiority
    D. self-esteem

25.____

KEY (CORRECT ANSWERS)

1. A
2. C
3. C
4. C
5. B

6. D
7. B
8. B
9. D
10. B

11. C
12. D
13. C
14. C
15. A

16. C
17. D
18. C
19. D
20. A

21. B
22. B
23. B
24. D
25. C

TEST 3

DIRECTIONS: Each question or incomplete statement is followed by several suggested answers or completions. Select the one that BEST answers the question or completes the statement. *PRINT THE LETTER OF THE CORRECT ANSWER IN THE SPACE AT THE RIGHT.*

Questions 1-2.

DIRECTIONS: Questions 1 and 2 are to be answered on the basis of the figure below, a graph of alternate theories about the world's future.

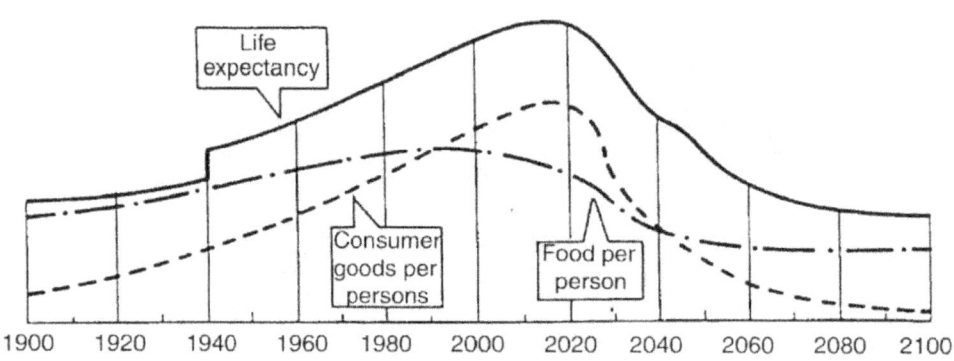
PESSIMISTIC SCENARIO
Continuation of present policies

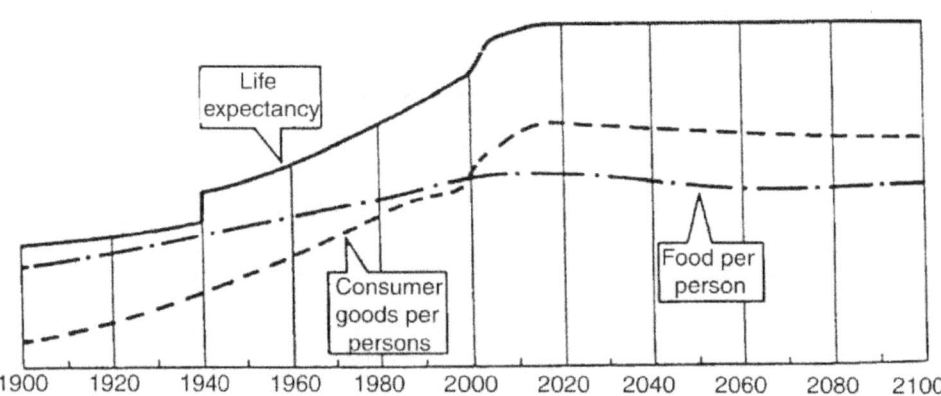
OPTIMISTIC SCENARIO
World population of 7.7 billion: modest growth

1. According to the pessimistic scenario
   A. the decline in a person's life expectancy will be caused by a shortage of consumer goods
   B. the world's population will experience a sharp drop beginning in 2020
   C. the amount of food available in the world will eventually level off
   D. there will be a direct relationship between life expectancy and food availability

1.____

2. The optimistic scenario believes that
   A. the average life expectancy will eventually reach a plateau that will not change as long as food is available
   B. it is not possible for humans to become extinct
   C. the increase in life expectancy will be due in part to the quality of consumer goods
   D. the world's population will increase indefinitely no matter what actions are taken

3. Which of the following is NOT a theory that is used to explain the generalized population shift to U.S. sunbelt cities that began in the 1970's?
   A. Higher wage rates
   B. Transition to post-industrial economy
   C. Tax incentives
   D. Federal expenditure patterns

4. What is considered to be the main DISADVANTAGE associated with the use of social conflict theory to explain stratification?
   A. Does not explain why some equalities are so great
   B. Underestimation of cooperation between apparent adversaries such as management and labor
   C. Focuses on incentive, rather than on dominance and control
   D. Frequent exceptions such as the salaries of film stars or professional athletes

5. For most Americans, a long period spent in college and graduate school generally has the effect of making attitudes toward authority more
   A. personal   B. stable   C. hostile   D. submissive

6. Each of the following statements related to voluntary childlessness in America is true EXCEPT:
   A. Childless marriages increase as the level of education of the marital partners increases.
   B. The decision to remain childless increases as the age at marriage increases.
   C. Childlessness increases as female participation in the labor force increases.
   D. Childlessness increases at the number of siblings of each marital partner decreases.

7. Both riots an mobs are types of _____ crowds.
   A. active   B. expressive   C. casual   D. orgiastic

8. Each of the following is a condition usually present in a situation of migration due to contracted labor EXCEPT
   A. laborers typically immigrate with their own cultural system intact
   B. people are moved under situations of duress
   C. when terms of servitude are completed, laborers have been able to expand their economic roles
   D. in America, contracted migrant workers have been denied basic services and protections

9. Which of the following statements about power as a stratification variable is FALSE?
   A. In its institutional expressions, it is distributed through political processes
   B. If used effectively, it will increase and be used again with greater ease
   C. It tends to emerge as an earlier, rather than later, object of explicit conflict in societies
   D. It determines whether a person has control over access to other stratification resources

10. In modern America, according to David Riesman, Americans in general have become more
    A. inner-directed
    B. other-directed
    C. traditional
    D. autonomous

11. Among young married American women, generally high separation rates occur among those with
    A. only one child
    B. high family incomes
    C. less than a high school education
    D. high job pressures

12. Rising taxes, along with the reduction of city services, has all of the following effects EXCEPT
    A. lowered city revenues
    B. appeals for federal assistance
    C. flight of businesses from cities
    D. creation of a multi-nucleic growth pattern

13. Which of the following would be a characteristic used to determine cognitive minorities in a society?
    A. Language
    B. Ethnicity
    C. Political beliefs
    D. Gender

14. The fourth phase of demographic transition is MOST closely illustrated by
    A. the Czech Republic
    B. Italy
    C. Sweden
    D. China

15. The term for the custom that requires individuals to choose marriage mates from outside certain groups is
    A. endogamy
    B. hyperlineality
    C. polygamy
    D. exogamy

16. Which of the following is NOT a common criticism of Robert Merton's theory of social deviance as a mode of adaptation?
    It
    A. oversimplifies the reasons for deviance
    B. fails to consider the role of deviate subcultures or groups in influencing and supporting certain activities
    C. overemphasizes the forms of deviance for which there are established, formal sanctions
    D. overemphasizes lower-class deviance

17. Indirect institutional discrimination
    A. is unenforceable
    B. is punished only by social condemnation
    C. refers to patterns of discrimination that have been incorporated into the formal norms of a society
    D. is a criminal offense in most societies

18. According to the concentric-zone model of urbanization, simple one- and two-family dwellings of semiskilled workers can be found in zone
    A. 2   B. 3   C. 4   D. 5

19. Where it is still in use, the term *race* is defined as a matter of difference in
    A. physical type
    B. mentality
    C. technological development
    D. culture

20. What type of argument favors the clustering together of people into urban arrangements?
    A. Psychological
    B. Sociological
    C. Criminologist
    D. Environmentalist

21. The absolutist perspective on social deviance includes each of the following assumptions EXCEPT:
    A. People who violate socially accepted standards of behavior are essentially different from conventional or conforming people
    B. There is a consensus in society on the importance of rules
    C. Deviance can be partially explained by determining why prevailing norms have developed
    D. Explanations for deviant behavior can be found through an analysis of the pathological environments in which deviants are raised

22. Converts to religious cults
    A. feel that previous religious experiences have been a success
    B. have many friends outside the cult
    C. tend to be politically conservative
    D. are oriented to religion as a solution to problems

23. Which of the following is an essential viewpoint of symbolic interactionism?
    A. Interaction can be correctly diagrammed as message-response.
    B. Society is possible only through a system of shared symbols.
    C. People interact only through the exchange of consensual symbols.
    D. Symbols are interpreted in the same way by all people.

24. Which of the following is NOT a type of hierarchy that figures in the multiple-hierarchies theory of social stratification?
    A. Social   B. Political   C. Religious   D. Economic

25. Making deals with upper class people, thereby making them more elite through the granting of special favors, is an example of
    A. cumulative causation   B. cause and effect
    C. conspicuous consumption   D. sufficient cause

KEY (CORRECT ANSWERS)

1.	D	11.	C
2.	A	12.	D
3.	A	13.	C
4.	B	14.	C
5.	C	15.	D
6.	D	16.	C
7.	A	17.	B
8.	B	18.	B
9.	C	19.	A
10.	B	20.	D

21. C
22. D
23. B
24. C
25. A

TEST 4

DIRECTIONS: Each question or incomplete statement is followed by several suggested answers or completions. Select the one that BEST answers the question or completes the statement. *PRINT THE LETTER OF THE CORRECT ANSWER IN THE SPACE AT THE RIGHT.*

1. Where multiple spouses are permitted by law, _____ considerations are MOST likely to limit the practice of polygamy.
   A. economic   B. religious   C. health   D. political

2. The MOST significant problem associated with the use of self-administered questionnaires in sociological research is
   A. potential for low response rates
   B. high costs
   C. slower administration
   D. results biased according to literacy of population

3. What is the term for an economically competitive situation in which a few major corporations control the vast majority of the means of production in a particular field?
   A. Trust-busting
   B. Monopoly
   C. Interlock
   D. Oligopoly

4. The Pacific coast from Los Angeles to San Diego is developing into an example of a(n)
   A. strip city
   B. SMSA
   C. multi-nucleic pattern
   D. blockbuster

5. In a country facing possible starvation, a(n) _____ would MOST likely be employed for the purpose of national survival.
   A. increase in personal freedoms
   B. decline in government control
   C. decrease in personal freedoms
   D. return to a free enterprise economic system

6. Which of the following is a latent function of the American economic system?
   A. Distribution of goods and services
   B. Creation of a desire for goods
   C. Generation of a gross national product
   D. Production of goods and services

7. According to George Mead's theory of self-development, a child acquires a sense of his/her self as an object in the _____ stage of development.
   A. preparatory   B. play   C. game   D. cognitive

8. The extent of social movement experienced by individuals within their own occupational careers is termed
   A. horizontal mobility
   B. voluntary mobility
   C. intragenerational mobility
   D. contracted labor

9. Gambling is MOST common in cultures that believe in
   A. industry
   B. astrology
   C. vengeful gods
   D. benevolent gods

10. In what way does old age tend to be more difficult for women than for men?
    A. Greater likelihood of heart attack or early death
    B. Forced sensitivity about appearance
    C. Reduced activity
    D. Role loss

11. The term for the point at which population would be just right for full development of natural resources and economic potential is _____ population.
    A. optimum   B. plateau   C. ultimate   D. peak

12. To structural-functional theorists, the MOST desirable form of intergroup relations is
    A. symbolic interactionism
    B. pluralism
    C. assimilation
    D. exchange

13. The purpose of an operational definition in sociological study is to
    A. represent entire categories of phenomena
    B. state the expected patterns and relationships among the variables
    C. describe relationships among relevant concepts
    D. specify exactly how a variable is to be measured in a particular study

14. The institutional sector MOST directly responsible for internal social control is
    A. polity   B. family   C. education   D. religion

15. According to Marx, each of the following is a superstructure of society EXCEPT
    A. law   B. economics   C. religion   D. politics

16. According to the work of Merton, a person who joins a religious commune would be seen as a
    A. ritualist   B. rebel   C. retreatist   D. conformist

17. The term *ethnicity* is defined as a matter of difference in
    A. biological features
    B. mentality
    C. industrialization
    D. culture

18. Each of the following is a pull factor in human migration EXCEPT
    A. better climate
    B. possibility of new and different activities
    C. racial persecution
    D. increased opportunity for income

19. Industrialized families tend to be
    A. neolocal   B. patrilocal   C. matrilocal   D. matrilineal

20. Which of the following types of norms is typically developed during primary socialization?
    A. Gender identity   B. Achievement
    C. Independence   D. Universalism

21. According to most research, the upper lower class is differentiated from the lower lower class on the basis of
    A. ability to speak English   B. dependency
    C. the type of work performed D. ethnic origin

22. Most sociologists agree that the urban personality is one based on
    A. a strong identification with place
    B. fragmented social relationships
    C. strong feelings of familial responsibility
    D. enduring friendships

23. Religion's MOST important sociological function is to
    A. weaken the forces of stratification
    B. help divert their attention from political to economic concerns
    C. create meaning for people
    D. integrate people into their society

24. Crime and poverty are MOST likely to be associated together
    A. where relative deprivation is obvious
    B. in poor countries
    C. where absolute deprivation is present
    D. in poor rural areas

25. Changes in behaviors, beliefs, values, and attitudes among minority members to approximate more closely the patterns of the dominant societal group are known collectively as
    A. acculturation   B. structural assimilation
    C. dissolution   D. conformity

KEY (CORRECT ANSWERS)

1.	A	11.	A
2.	D	12.	C
3.	D	13.	D
4.	A	14.	A
5.	C	15.	B
6.	B	16.	C
7.	B	17.	D
8.	C	18.	C
9.	D	19.	A
10.	B	20.	A

21.	B
22.	B
23.	D
24.	A
25.	A

EXAMINATION SECTION
TEST 1

DIRECTIONS: Each question or incomplete statement is followed by several suggested answers or completions. Select the one that BEST answers the question or completes the statement. *PRINT THE LETTER OF THE CORRECT ANSWER IN THE SPACE AT THE RIGHT.*

1. According to the socialization theory of social deviance,

    A. deviance is primarily a product of conflicting prevailing norms within a society
    B. deviance is a product of the weakening of a societal consensus about fundamental values
    C. deviance is sometimes taught and learned in primary group settings
    D. societal definitions and the treatment of deviance are a consequence of social inequalities

    1.____

2. Systems of stratification in which groups and individuals are ranked relative to the ownership of land are known as _____ systems.

    A. realty   B. estate
    C. plantation   D. caste

    2.____

3. Generally, people who work in bureaucratic organizations tend to value

    A. unchanging routines   B. self-direction
    C. political futures   D. conformity

    3.____

4. Which of the following is NOT a function of a modern society's political institution?

    A. Defending from outside encroachment
    B. Allocating power
    C. Occupational allocation
    D. Establishing and maintaining a civic ideology

    4.____

5. What type of people are most likely to adopt foreign ideas and ideologies in the process of cultural diffusion?

    A. The discontented   B. Military members
    C. The affluent   D. The poor

    5.____

6. The idea that stratification is simply the social structural by-product of people's attempts to maximize their shares of the social resource system is a basic assumption of the _____ theory of social stratification.

    A. social conflict   B. structural
    C. natural superiority   D. self-esteem

    6.____

7. According to the concentric-zone theory of urban growth, the zone in transition is undesirable for residences because

    A. rents are typically too high
    B. it is an area of urban blight
    C. it is devoted mainly to parks and recreation areas
    D. it is the financial center of the city

    7.____

8. According to most studies, _____ is most important in determining the academic success of American students.

    A. school financing
    B. home background
    C. quality of schools
    D. teaching methods

9. It is NOT true that the use of field work in sociological study

    A. usually generates more in-depth information than other methods
    B. provides flexibility for the researcher to alter strategies and follow up new leads that arise
    C. allows the influence of specific variables to be controlled by the investigator
    D. is more difficult to accurately generalize than other methods

10. In the classification system established by Robert Merton, discrimination in the absence of prejudice is a behavior that typifies a(n)

    A. bigot
    B. timid bigot
    C. fair-weather liberal
    D. all-weather liberal

11. Which of the following is NOT one of the primary functions of a modern society's family institution?

    A. Primary socialization
    B. Biological reproduction
    C. Material support of members
    D. Establishment of authority relations

12. In the attempt to reduce birthrates, developing countries have to contend with

    A. traditional attitudes
    B. industry
    C. opposition from international groups
    D. agricultural development

13. In human societies, cooperative interactions include each of the following EXCEPT

    A. cultural pluralism
    B. amalgamation
    C. enclaves
    D. assimilation

14. Which of the following statements about languages is true? They

    A. are similar in the way they conceptualize reality
    B. are present among many nonhuman species
    C. interpret nature and reality differently
    D. are of rather recent origin

15. With respect to the six-class schema of the American class structure, trends that appeared in the 1980s suggest that

    A. the size of the upper upper class will shrink considerably in a post-industrial society
    B. more upward mobility will become available to members of the working poor
    C. the underclass will become even more dependent
    D. the size of the middle strata will become reduced

16. Primary groups can be characterized in each of the following ways EXCEPT

    A. valued for extrinsic rewards
    B. direct contact
    C. spontaneity
    D. emotional warmth

17. The highest outlays in U.S. government spending are devoted to

    A. income security
    B. education
    C. health
    D. defense

18. The deconcentration explanation for the recent decline in American urban areas views this trend as a

    A. product of a change in cultural attitudes
    B. temporary setback to urban expansion
    C. fundamental break with the past
    D. response to health concerns

19. Which of the following stratification systems is/was LEAST ascriptive in nature?

    A. Western European estate systems
    B. India's Hindu caste system
    C. American migrant farm labor
    D. South Africa's apartheid policies

20. The main criticism of the multiple-nuclei model of urban spatial organization is that it

    A. ignores ethnic differences
    B. names mere subcenters as hubs in order to fit the model
    C. tends to ignore *pull* factors in urban migration
    D. ignores the topography of an urban center

21. Status-ranking systems generally appeared in human societies with the emergence of

    A. political systems
    B. division-of-labor practices
    C. the concept of wealth
    D. agriculture

22. The differential association theory attributes crime to

    A. learning
    B. social-class deprivation
    C. evil intent
    D. abnormal genetics

23. A cooperative state of dominant-subordinate relations in which cultural differences are maintained is known as

    A. secularism
    B. cultural pluralism
    C. ethnocentrism
    D. the melting pot

24. The generalized migration from rural areas to urban areas
    A. is unique to modern times
    B. advanced rapidly as a result of the age of discovery
    C. has been a rapid development since ancient times
    D. was given its greatest push by the industrial revolution

25. People whose opinions are most important to one's self-image are referred to as
    A. significant others   B. peers
    C. other-directed   D. secondary groups

KEY (CORRECT ANSWERS)

1. C
2. B
3. B
4. C
5. A

6. A
7. B
8. B
9. C
10. C

11. D
12. A
13. C
14. C
15. D

16. A
17. A
18. C
19. C
20. B

21. B
22. A
23. B
24. D
25. A

TEST 2

DIRECTIONS: Each question or incomplete statement is followed by several suggested answers or completions. Select the one that BEST answers the question or completes the statement. *PRINT THE LETTER OF THE CORRECT ANSWER IN THE SPACE AT THE RIGHT.*

Questions 1-2.

DIRECTIONS: Questions 1 and 2 refer to the figure below, a chart showing the relative rates of education completion in the United States according to race.

Years of School Completed, by Race, 1940-1980 (percent distribution)									
Race and Year	Percent High School Graduate					Percent College Graduate			
	Total	North-east	North Central	South	West	Total	North-east	North Central	South	West
All races										
1980	66.5	67.1	68.0	60.2	74.5	16.2	17.2	14.7	15.0	19.3
1970	52.3	52.9	53.7	45.1	62.3	10.7	11.2	9.6	9.8	13.2
1900	41.1	41.0	41.7	35.3	50.8	7.7	8.1	6.9	7.1	9.6
1950	34.3	35.7	35.4	26.7	45.6	6.0	6.6	5.5	5.3	7.7
1940	24.5	24.0	25.0	20.3	34.8	4.6	4.9	4.2	4.0	6.1
White										
1980	68.8	68.7	69.3	63.5	77.2	17.1	18.0	15.2	16.3	20.2
1970	54.5	54.2	55.0	49.1	63.3	11.3	11.7	10.0	10.8	13.5
l960	43.2	41.9	42.8	39.8	51.9	8.1	8.4	7.1	7.9	9.9
1950	36.4	36.7	36.4	31.6	46.7	6.4	6.8	5.6	6.2	7.9
1940	26.1	24.4	25.4	24.6	35.4	4.9	5.1	4.3	4.8	6.2
Black										
1980	51.2	56.4	54.9	44.9	68.7	8.4	8.4	7.9	8.0	11.4
1970	31.4	37.8	36.5	24.4	48.9	4.4	4.1	4.0	4.4	5.9
1960	20.1	26.9	25.3	14.7	34.3	3.1	2.9	2.9	3.1	4.1
1950	13.0	20.4	19.7	8.8	26.2	2.1	2.2	2.3	1.9	2.9
1940	7.7	11.7	12.6	5.4	18.4	1.3	1.7	1.8	1.1	2.2

1. In general, it appears that proportionally fewer black students complete their high school education in

    A. more recent years
    B. the South
    C. the West
    D. the Northeast

1.____

2. In 1970, what percentage of all students in the U.S., regardless of race, graduated from college?

    A. 7.7   B. 10.7   C. 11.3   D. 41.1

2.____

3. When middle- and upper-class people return to deteriorating central city neighborhoods, _____ occurs.

    A. devaluation
    B. gentrification
    C. inflation
    D. flight

3.____

41

4. The term that classifies a marriage in terms of *form* is

   A. neolocal
   B. monogamous
   C. blended
   D. egalitarian.

5. Which of the following is NOT a common criticism of the structural-functional theory of gender roles in a society? It(s)

   A. fails to explain stratification of gender roles
   B. ignores difference between instrumental and expressive roles
   C. focuses too much on oppression
   D. dysfunctional consequences of gender roles are ignored

6. Dramaturgical analysis

   A. focuses on the entire arc of an individual's socialization process
   B. relies primarily on the influence of reference groups during the socialization process
   C. is concerned with *why*, rather than *how*, people do the things they do
   D. examines the moment-to-moment social performance of individuals as stage or theater

7. Another term for voluntary associations is

   A. normative organizations
   B. reference groups
   C. membership groups
   D. microsocieties

8. Which of the following sociologists is not of the *Chicago School* that emerged during the first quarter of the 20th century?

   A. Louis Wirth
   B. William Ogburn
   C. Peter Berger
   D. Robert Park

9. Which of the following statements about competition and conflict among societal members is generally FALSE?

   A. The transition from competition to conflict is marked by a decline in effective norms.
   B. Conflict is not always negative in its effect.
   C. Conflict is a highly rule-bound form of social interaction.
   D. The needs of competitors generally promote a greater division of labor in the social structure.

10. Which of the following types of families is considered to be most out of step with traditional American values?

    A. Dual-income
    B. Voluntarily childless
    C. Reconstituted
    D. Dual-career

11. According to the classifications established by Joseph Gusfield, a political activist who openly challenges the legitimacy of a normative order would be classified as a(n) _____ deviant.

    A. sick
    B. enemy
    C. repentant
    D. cynical

12. The idea that human life is shaped by both individual traits and social forces is called   12.____

    A. objectivism   B. multidimensional model
    C. interactionism   D. stratification

13. The claim that certain social practices or institutions are common to all societies is   13.____
    known as

    A. secularism   B. relativism
    C. conceptualism   D. universalism

14. Which of the following is NOT included in a mixed economy?   14.____

    A. Social security and welfare measures
    B. Laissez-faire policies
    C. Giant corporations and small businesses
    D. Governmental regulation

15. In average income, developing countries could be compared with the _____ class.   15.____

    A. lower   B. lower middle
    C. middle   D. upper middle

16. Other than those involving married couples, what type of household is currently most   16.____
    prevalent in the United States?

    A. Female-headed   B. Male-headed
    C. Nonfamily   D. Sibling arrangement

17. In sociological study, a _____ sample is the term for a selection of homogeneous sub-   17.____
    populations in a manner that insures certain desired proportions of subpopulations in the
    sample.

    A. stratified   B. random
    C. mixed   D. purposive

18. General rules stating what people in a society should or should not think, say, or do   18.____
    under given circumstances are known sociologically as

    A. mores   B. norms   C. codes   D. laws

19. Social life is viewed as interdependent entities yielding social order and continuity by the   19.____
    _____ theory of sociology.

    A. social conflict   B. symbolic interactionism
    C. clinical   D. structural-functional

20. A category of persons whose stratification position is determined by unchangeable sta-   20.____
    tus norms, and who are powerless to alter either those defining norms are the resulting
    resource positions they create, is known as a(n)

    A. underclass   B. caste
    C. status community   D. behavioral minority

21. Each of the following is considered a barrier to sociological thinking EXCEPT

    A. the tendency to view social life in individualistic terms
    B. widespread familiarity with subject matter
    C. cultural relativism
    D. the belief that human behavior cannot be predicted

22. The _____ method of stratification analysis has most clearly led to a portrayal of U.S. social class as primarily a matter of status or prestige.

    A. objective
    B. scaled
    C. subjective reputational
    D. subjective self-placement

23. The most important DISADVANTAGE to using unstructured interviews during sociological research is

    A. costly time consumption
    B. *closed* questioning
    C. requirement that questions be asked in the same words and order
    D. no mechanism for pursuing interesting leads

24. Which of the following is NOT typically considered to be a latent function of religion?

    A. Alienation
    B. Conversion
    C. Imperialism
    D. Prejudice

25. If crowd types are shown along a continuum, the complete opposite of the active crowd is the _____ crowd.

    A. casual
    B. conventional
    C. expressive
    D. orgiastic

KEY (CORRECT ANSWERS)

1.	B	11.	B	21.	C
2.	B	12.	C	22.	C
3.	B	13.	D	23.	A
4.	B	14.	B	24.	B
5.	C	15.	A	25.	A
6.	D	16.	C		
7.	A	17.	A		
8.	C	18.	B		
9.	C	19.	D		
10.	B	20.	B		

TEST 3

DIRECTIONS: Each question or incomplete statement is followed by several suggested answers or completions. Select the one that BEST answers the question or completes the statement. *PRINT THE LETTER OF THE CORRECT ANSWER IN THE SPACE AT THE RIGHT.*

1. The contention that women are *too emotional* to hold high-level positions in corporate America, and therefore demonstrate their inability to perform executive-level work, is an example of

    A. direct institutional discrimination
    B. patriarchy
    C. blaming the victim
    D. alienation

2. The *sociological imagination* is a concept first introduced by

    A. Margaret Mead
    B. C. Wright Mills
    C. Peter Berger
    D. David Riesman

3. Stratification arrangements in a society are most clearly extensions of the society's

    A. legislative practices
    B. basic economic norms and values
    C. ethnic composition
    D. attitudes toward race and gender

4. The identification or a specific range, type, or category of real life events or activities that fall within a general sociological concept is a(n)

    A. proposition
    B. nominal definition
    C. variable
    D. operational definition

5. Which of the following is NOT a component of Marx's class system?

    A. In the long run, a capitalist society will be divided into only two classes.
    B. The capitalist system will sustain itself indefinitely through terror and oppression.
    C. Social structures are becoming organized according to people's relationships to productive capital.
    D. All capitalist systems are built upon the exploitation and oppression of the working class.

6. The relativist approach to social deviance defines deviance in terms of

    A. societal perceptions and reactions
    B. objective norms
    C. the inherent deviance of certain behaviors
    D. pathologies

7. Conflict theorists would explain a society's gender roles in terms of

    A. self-perpetuating stereotypes
    B. their existence as instruments of oppression in society
    C. subgroup differences
    D. their contributions to societal survival

8. The concentric-zone theory of human ecology assumes that

   A. the populations of a city work together to generate revenues
   B. cities have more than one center
   C. a city has eight distinct zones
   D. cities have heterogeneous populations

9. Religious sects are characterized by each of the following EXCEPT they

   A. accept all who wish to join
   B. are of recent origin
   C. emphasize purity of belief
   D. are led by self-ordained leaders

10. An example of internal colonialism is

    A. the Dutch East Indies
    B. the U.S. Virgin Islands
    C. Mexican farm laborers in the United States
    D. the Portuguese Azores

11. Which of the following sociologists believed that social evolution depends upon a competitive struggle for survival?

    A. Robert Merton
    B. Auguste Comte
    C. Margaret Mead
    D. William Graham Sumner

12. Which of the following statements about child abuse is FALSE?

    A. The younger the child, the more likely the child will experience some form of physical violence within the family setting.
    B. Both boys and girls are equally likely to be victims of sexual abuse.
    C. Both boys and girls are equally likely to be victims of physical abuse.
    D. At least half of all sexual abuse is perpetrated by family members.

13. Direct observation would be the most appropriate approach for gathering information during sociological study when the research questions focus on

    A. past events
    B. behavioral patterns
    C. theoretical circumstances
    D. cognitive or emotional patterns

14. Which of the following is NOT typically an element of a caste system?

    A. Support of religious attitudes or myths
    B. Marriage confined to within the caste
    C. Virtually no mobility
    D. Clear physical differences between castes

15. What is the term for a social collectivity whose members possess a feeling of common identity and interact in a regular, patterned way?

    A. Group   B. Strata   C. Aggregate   D. Category

16. Today, the MOST widely accepted explanation for social stratification is the _____ theory.

    A. social conflict
    B. structural
    C. multiple hierarchies
    D. self-esteem

17. Rivers or seacoasts give rise to the urbanization pattern known as

    A. concentric-zone
    B. sprawl
    C. redlining
    D. strip cities

18. What is the term for the legal power delegated to an elected or appointed official?

    A. Absolute power
    B. Contingent power
    C. Authority
    D. Influence

19. An example of a utilitarian organization is a

    A. military boot camp
    B. nuclear family
    C. parent-teacher association
    D. large business corporation

20. In the _____ phase of demographic transition, birthrates begin to decline

    A. first   B. second   C. third   D. fourth

21. The largest and oldest churches in a society's religious sector are called

    A. congregations
    B. denominations
    C. sects
    D. diocese

22. Which of the following is a normative group?

    A. University
    B. Prison
    C. Business corporation
    D. Girl Scouts

23. Each of the following determines where cities will grow EXCEPT

    A. iron and coal deposits
    B. population growth rate
    C. railroads
    D. rivers and seaports

24. Which of the following is NOT a reason why laboratory experiments are not often used in sociological research?

    A. Prevalent view of social life as multicausal
    B. Inability to effectively control subjects
    C. Prevailing interest in collective rather than individual phenomena
    D. High financial costs

25. Preindustrial families tended to be

    A. neolocal
    B. patrilocal
    C. matrilocal
    D. polygynous

KEY (CORRECT ANSWERS)

1. C
2. B
3. B
4. B
5. B

6. A
7. B
8. D
9. A
10. C

11. D
12. B
13. B
14. D
15. A

16. A
17. D
18. C
19. D
20. C

21. B
22. D
23. B
24. B
25. B

TEST 4

DIRECTIONS: Each question or incomplete statement is followed by several suggested answers or completions. Select the one that BEST answers the question or completes the statement. *PRINT THE LETTER OF THE CORRECT ANSWER IN THE SPACE AT THE RIGHT.*

1. The term for a sample of public opinion planned to demonstrate all groups in the right proportion is a _____ sample.

    A. legitimate
    B. random
    C. representative
    D. total

2. When communities and groups cooperate not out of shared values and goals, but from a recognition of mutual benefit, _____ exist(s).

    A. parasitism
    B. exchange
    C. amalgamation
    D. enclaves

3. What is the term for the application of sociological principles and research findings to the solution of human problems?

    A. Clinical sociology
    B. Normative sociology
    C. Social psychology
    D. Sociological prescription

4. Socioeconomic status is a composite measure that includes all of the following factors EXCEPT

    A. income
    B. prevalence of religious beliefs
    C. occupational prestige
    D. educational attainment

5. What is the term for the cooperative process in which subordinate status populations become more and more like the dominant community, and eventually become absorbed into it?

    A. Dissolution
    B. Assimilation
    C. Conformity
    D. Amalgamation

6. In comparing a society's status resources to other stratification variables, which of the following statements about status resources is false?
   They

    A. neither increase nor decrease with use
    B. show a high degree of institutional specificity
    C. are derived mainly from money received for the performance of occupational roles
    D. tend to be the most resistant to change

7. Agriculture became necessary as a way of life in human history because of

    A. discoveries in husbandry
    B. inadequate hunting skills
    C. population growth
    D. sudden climatic changes

8. Community control of American schools is considered democratic, but federal regulations have been more helpful in promoting all of the following EXCEPT

   A. uniform standards
   B. equal opportunities for minorities
   C. help for poor districts
   D. untracked course structures

9. The American housing preference seems to be

   A. individual homes   B. townhouses
   C. urban apartments   D. joint dwellings

10. According to the work of Milton Gordon, the MOST important measure of any group's assimilation process is

    A. the occupation of upper-middle and upper class strata
    B. participation in the legislative process
    C. the emergence of intermarriage patterns
    D. the degree to which group members complete higher-education degrees

11. In conducting a sociological study, a researcher conducts surveys, interviews, and field studies, and then used the information to form a sociological theory. This is an example of

    A. nominal definition
    B. the deductive method
    C. research without a hypothesis
    D. the inductive method

12. In the simplest societies, religion and polity are combined to create the governmental form of

    A. oligarchy   B. theocracy
    C. dogma   D. aristocracy

13. In dramaturgical analysis, a person's attempts to control social interaction are described as

    A. labeling   B. gesellschaft
    C. impression management   D. deviance

14. What is the term for the cooperative process by which different status communities, through intermarriage, mix biologically and culturally?

    A. Pluralism   B. Assimilation
    C. Reconstitution   D. Amalgamation

15. Which of the following is NOT a contradiction to the structuralist-functionalist theory of social stratification in American society?

    A. High physicians' salaries
    B. Family violence
    C. Divorce rates
    D. High school dropout rates

16. Which of the following characteristics is more typical of anthropology than of sociology?

    A. Interest in society
    B. A conflict model of society
    C. Great attention to primitive or preliterate societies
    D. Concern with all kinds of social groups

17. What is the term for a negative set of characteristics attributed to an entire category of people in a generalized manner?

    A. Stereotype   B. Brands
    C. Stigma   D. Prejudice

18. According to the work of Etzioni, the typical corporation engaged in trade, manufacturing, or finance is a(n) _____ organization.

    A. coercive   B. utilitarian
    C. normative   D. exploitative

19. Which of the following would be a characteristic used to determine behavioral minorities in a society?

    A. Body type   B. Religion
    C. Political beliefs   D. Ethnicity

20. According to most research, especially that of Kiesler, people who _____ will strive most to be accepted by a group with whom they have worked with for a period of several days.

    A. fear they are not rated well by the group
    B. are liked most by the group
    C. are least competent
    D. are highly extroverted

21. Of the four conditions governing the population movement, _____ is the most disadvantageous.

    A. voluntary migration   B. displaced persons
    C. force labor   D. contracted labor

22. The symbolic interactionism theory of sociology was introduced by

    A. G.H. Mead   B. Marx
    C. Parsons   D. Durkheim

23. According to the six-class schema of the American class structure, each of the following patterns has emerged in the 20th century EXCEPT

    A. within the middle strata, there are relatively few barriers to movement across substrata boundaries
    B. the class structure is internally diverse
    C. for the greater part of the century, most Americans were situated neither among the extremely rich nor the extremely poor
    D. the proportion of Americans situated in the upper upper class has tended to increase over time

24. In the United States, each of the following is a significant degenerative condition that leads to mortality EXCEP   24._____

    A. heart disease   B. HIV
    C. stroke   D. cancer

25. In the United States, the MOST powerful countervailing force is typically   25._____

    A. the media   B. special-interest groups
    C. social movements   D. business corporations

KEY (CORRECT ANSWERS)

1.	C	11.	D
2.	B	12.	B
3.	A	13.	C
4.	B	14.	D
5.	B	15.	A
6.	C	16.	C
7.	C	17.	A
8.	D	18.	B
9.	A	19.	D
10.	C	20.	A

21. C
22. A
23. D
24. B
25. D

EXAMINATION SECTION
TEST 1

DIRECTIONS: Each question or incomplete statement is followed by several suggested answers or completions. Select the one that BEST answers the question or completes the statement. *PRINT THE LETTER OF THE CORRECT ANSWER IN THE SPACE AT THE RIGHT.*

1. Technical sociological terms cannot be justly criticized when they serve   1._____

    A. to prevent dangerous findings from becoming assessible to irresponsible laymen
    B. to distinguish sociological writing from popular literature
    C. to express ideas in a precise, unambiguous way
    D. as a test of the dedication and familiarity with the field of aspiring sociologists

2. Which of the following statements is TRUE?   2._____

    A. From generation to generation, human behavior is consistent.
    B. From generation to generation, societies change radically.
    C. Human behavior displays no consistency.
    D. Human behavior in modern society displays a high degree of consistency even though many aspects of that society are changing.

3. In American society, a group that is trying to move up in the class structure: 3._____

    A. Eventually finds that it is an impossible task to achieve a higher status
    B. Often finds that some people will accept their claims to that status while others will deny it to them
    C. Have a relatively easy time if they concentrate all their efforts to achieve this
    D. Tend to reject the values of the established elite and impose new values

4. Material culture is a form of culture because it is   4._____

    A. artificial
    B. not biologically determined
    C. created and used according to knowledge and skills
    D. objective and not affected by individual variations in usage

5. The term *hypergamy* is used to refer to marriage between a   5._____

    A. man and woman of the same caste
    B. man of high caste and a woman of low caste
    C. man of low caste and a woman of high caste
    D. Moslem and Hindu

6. The parents' association of a rather large high school would be considered a(n)   6._____

    A. association   B. quasi group
    C. social category   D. primary group

7. Which of the following is an ascribed status?   7._____

    A. Chief Justice of the Supreme Court
    B. Olympic decathlon gold-medal winner

53

C. Mayor of Chicago
D. Prince of Wales

8. With which approach would you MOST associate the phrase *social change*? 8.____

   A. Functional   B. Historical
   C. Dysfunctional   D. Scientific

9. *Common sense* may be an obstacle to sociological inquiry because it 9.____

   A. is often wrong
   B. rests upon ordinary experience
   C. leads people to decry the desirability or necessity of the scientific study of man
   D. is a widespread characteristic of Americans

10. In spite of the informality of the Norton Street Gang, 10.____

    A. it involved a set of mutual rights and obligations for all members
    B. it was capable of concerted action for neighborhood improvement
    C. the leader had absolute control and was entitled to unquestioning support
    D. status of members was determined solely by performance in objective tests, such as sports contests

11. The term *polygyny* means 11.____

    A. marriage between one man and several wives
    B. marriage between one woman and several husbands
    C. a compound family
    D. marriage between one person (of either sex) and his or her spouses

12. Early students of the formation of individual personality, such as Cooley, Meade, Freud, and Piaget, established the important fact that 12.____

    A. it depends on the character of interactions early in life
    B. it explains the universal occurrence of childhood games
    C. the human infant is completely indeterminate until shaped by society
    D. personality must be well-developed before language learning can occur

13. The requirement that one must marry outside of his clan or group is called 13.____

    A. endogamy   B. exogamy
    C. incest taboo   D. extended family system

14. People who mow their lawns each Sunday may be classified as a 14.____

    A. social group   B. social category
    C. statistical aggregate   D. social class

15. In an associational society, 15.____

    A. roles are segmental
    B. relationships are transitory
    C. family life is not as important as in a communal society
    D. all of the above

16. Two *ideal* types of societies which sociologists do NOT use today are known as   16.____
    I. militant and industrial
    II. sacred and secular
    III. communal and associational
    IV. mythic and rationalistic
    The CORRECT answer is:

    A. I, II   B. I, IV
    C. II, III   D. I, III

17. The relation between the phenomena to which *society* and *culture* refer is   17.____
    I. society is a precondition for the emergence of culture
    II. culture is a precondition for the emergence of society
    III. society and culture are both the result of a common factor, evolution
    IV. society and culture are analytically distinct but always associated
    The CORRECT answer is:

    A. I, III   B. II, IV
    C. I, II, III   D. III, IV

18. Sociological concepts are characteristically   18.____
    I. applied to statistical aggregates rather than individual instances
    II. derived from situations in which people interact
    III. more general than those in fields which deal with the individual, such as psychology
    IV. applied to idiosyncrasies rather than general patterns
    The CORRECT answer is:

    A. I, III   B. II, IV
    C. II, III   D. I, II

19. Which of the following has the LEAST relevance for social organization? That   19.____

    A. women rather than men bear children
    B. human beings require a minimum number of calories periodically
    C. human beings have a limited lifespan
    D. adult human beings vary in weight

20. Beliefs and values   20.____
    I. differ in that beliefs are ideas whereas values are desirable objects
    II. differ in that beliefs concern questions of truth whereas values concern questions of decision-making
    III. are both crescive institutions
    IV. are types of shared normative commitments
    The CORRECT answer is:

    A. I *only*   B. II, III
    C. II, IV   D. I, II

21. The three MAIN senses in which *society* is used to refer to are: 21.____

A. The fact of social relationship, a level of group organization, and a complex of institutions
B. A type of interaction, a level of organization, and a set of philosophical ideals
C. an institution, an idea, and a set of techniques
D. man's relation to his environment, to himself, and to his goals

22. *Diffusion* refers to

    A. the process by which cultures will adopt certain traits and reject others
    B. the process through which certain traits upset the equilibrium of one society but not another
    C. the transfer of certain traits to highly nationalistic countries
    D. the transfer of technical skills to underdeveloped areas

23. Baseball fans may be classified as a(n)

    A. social group
    B. social class
    C. social category
    D. statistical aggregate

24. The effect of geography on social organization varies depending on the

    A. technology of the society
    B. individualism of the members
    C. cultural emphasis on aggression
    D. biological capacities of the races

25. Sociologists are GENERALLY convinced that differences among societies

    A. are to be explained by characteristics of cultural and social organization
    B. are related to geography rather than biology
    C. are superficially striking but theoretically trivial
    D. signify different stages of development of culture

KEY (CORRECT ANSWERS)

1.	C	11.	A
2.	D	12.	A
3.	B	13.	B
4.	C	14.	C
5.	B	15.	D
6.	D	16.	D
7.	D	17.	D
8.	B	18.	D
9.	C	19.	D
10.	A	20.	D

21. A
22. A
23. D
24. A
25. A

———

TEST 2

DIRECTIONS: Each question or incomplete statement is followed by several suggested answers or completions. Select the one that BEST answers the question or completes the statement. *PRINT THE LETTER OF THE CORRECT ANSWER IN THE SPACE AT THE RIGHT.*

1. Mary, Sue, and Jane have known each other for many years. They all attend the same church and participate actively in church functions. Each week, they get together at Jane's house in order to study French.
   These three girls may be called a(n)

   A. ethnic group
   B. communal society
   C. social group
   D. secondary group

2. Primary groups

   A. can be functional within formal organizations because they satisfy the members
   B. can be dysfunctional within formal organizations because they contradict the formal values and encourage dissatisfaction
   C. can be neutral within formal organizations because they involve emotional rather than rational association
   D. all of the above

3. The family as we know it in the United States is(,)

   A. not found elsewhere in the world
   B. comparatively speaking, the most stable and best-developed type in the world
   C. an example of the dysfunctions of highly industrialized society
   D. one of many types of family systems to be found throughout the world

4. The analysis by Whyte of the Norton Street Gang showed the importance of

   A. leadership
   B. organization
   C. affective relationships
   D. all of the above

5. The money economy

   A. creates the bureaucratic organization
   B. is unrelated to the growth of bureaucracy
   C. facilitates the development of bureaucracy
   D. hinders the operation of an efficient bureaucracy

6. Four black men shoot pool every Thursday night.
   They may be called by a sociologist a

   A. social group
   B. communal society
   C. social category
   D. minority group

7. Sociological evidence shows that
   I. cities are more disorganized than rural areas because of the lack of primary associations
   II. industrialism results in a decrease of interaction among individuals

III. primary groups arise even in slums, cities, and mass societies
IV. society is merely an association of primary groups

The CORRECT answer is:

A. I, II
B. III *only*
C. I, IV
D. I, III

8. Differences in behavior, attributed by *racist* theories to differences in race, are MORE often attributable to differences in

A. intelligence
B. language
C. cultural expectations
D. population size

9. The American middle-class family

A. takes great pride in its ancestry
B. maintains ties with close relatives
C. is usually isolated from close relatives and maintains little contact with them
D. all of the above

10. The American stress on the link between love and marriage is

A. unique
B. universal
C. relatively infrequent in other societies
D. a result of democracy

11. Scientific sociology is thought to be possible because

A. the universe is assumed to be orderly
B. refinements of logic and the scientific method are applicable to more social phenomena
C. the effects of physical and biological conditions on human activity are found to be increasingly important
D. more information about social affairs is becoming available to scholars

12. The N.A.A.C.P. is an example of a(n)

A. ethnic group
B. association
C. communal group
D. all of the above

13. Two important features of culture are that it is

A. innate and universal
B. learned and shared
C. moral and uncommunicable
D. popular and explicit

14. A theory is a(n)

A. untested hypothesis which explains a unique and unexpected occurrence
B. general statement of relations among types of events
C. set of definitions of basic concepts and their logical relations
D. specific prediction logically derived from an abstract generalization

15. Statements about the similar actions of members of the same group are ALWAYS in probability terms because
    I. sociology is not sufficiently developed to use precise mathematical analysis
    II. science is necessarily probabilistic since any experiment can theoretically result in disconfirmation of a law
    III. social contacts of individuals are so complex that no single group affiliation represents all the social influences on its members' actions
    IV. some individuals are not completely socialized due to errors in child-rearing or genetic anomalies
    The CORRECT answer is:

    A. I, III   B. II, IV
    C. I, II   D. III, IV

16. A popular aphorism such as *a man is known by the company he keeps* is NOT an adequate substitute for sociological knowledge because

    A. such common sense opinions are always wrong
    B. it has no basis in fact
    C. a systematic study would probably show that under some conditions it was not true
    D. men should be judged for what they are and not for their associates

17. Social relationships are important phenomena not only because men live together, but also because they
    I. seek to advance themselves at one another's expense
    II. require control to prevent continual strife
    III. must cooperate if their offspring are to survive to maturity
    IV. respond to one another on the basis of what is expected of them
    The CORRECT answer is:

    A. II *only*   B. I, III
    C. II, IV   D. II, III

18. One of the weaknesses in defining society as a set of institutions is that

    A. social life includes activities outside the scope of institutions
    B. institutions are not sufficiently coherent to form a system
    C. society is reduced to a sub-category of culture
    D. deviant behavior is not accounted for

19. Institutions are

    A. shared definitions of appropriate conduct
    B. formally organized permanent groups
    C. major requirements that must be fulfilled by any society if it is to survive
    D. customs which develop among people contrary to enacted laws

20. Which of the following questions about television would a sociologist – as a social scientist – be MOST likely to ask?

    A. Is it leading people to waste too much time?
    B. What kinds of people watch news programs?
    C. Is television bad for children?
    D. Should the *Great Debate* of 1960 be repeated?

21. The variations in the incest taboo reflect

    A. racial differences
    B. differences in family structure
    C. religious differences
    D. class differences

22. The increasing use being made of sociological findings and viewpoints suggests that

    A. the rate of discovery is higher in sociology than in other fields
    B. more information is waiting to be discovered in sociology than in other fields
    C. the subject matter of sociology is becoming more interesting to intelligent students in all fields
    D. the problems of contemporary life require more systematic understanding in social terms

23. *Personality* refers to the phenomenon in the individual's make-up of

    A. organization of habits, ideas, goals, etc. into a coherent system
    B. individual variations in temperament and magnetism
    C. outstanding and idiosyncratic patterns which deviate from cultural norms
    D. cultural creativity and voluntary behavior found only in social primates

24. Two basic facts underlying sociological inquiry are human

    A. behavior is patterned and human beings are social creatures
    B. respones are imitative and human beings are peaceful
    C. activity is based on prestige rankings and human beings are acquisitive
    D. history is progressively more complex and human beings are rational

25. Primary groups help to satisfy the human need for

    A. praise   B. sex
    C. emotional response D. interaction

KEY (CORRECT ANSWERS)

1.	C	11.	A
2.	D	12.	B
3.	D	13.	B
4.	D	14.	B
5.	C	15.	D
6.	A	16.	C
7.	D	17.	D
8.	C	18.	C
9.	B	19.	A
10.	C	20.	B

21. B
22. D
23. A
24. A
25. C

TEST 3

DIRECTIONS: Each question or incomplete statement is followed by several suggested answers or completions. Select the one that BEST answers the question or completes the statement. *PRINT THE LETTER OF THE CORRECT ANSWER IN THE SPACE AT THE RIGHT.*

1. The concept of *society* as distinct from the *state*　　　　　　　　　　　　1._____

    A. begins in Plato's REPUBLIC and LAWS
    B. is associated with the flowering of scholastic philosophy
    C. derives from political philosophy of the sixteenth and seventeenth century
    D. is due to the pioneer researches of Herbert Spencer

2. Because members desire the support and approval of their primary groups, the groups　　2._____

    A. exercise great social control
    B. foster conformity and discourage individuality
    C. cannot persist if there is any internal conflict
    D. are more necessary than the political state

3. Disagreements among sociologists about sociological concepts reflect　　　　3._____

    A. differences in knowledge
    \B. different ways of looking at social phenomena
    C. biased versus non-biased approaches
    D. all of the above

4. An important characteristic of culture is that it is　　　　　　　　　　　　4._____

    A. enacted
    B. objective
    C. transmitted by ideas
    D. inherited through the family

5. The fundamental observation underlying the role and status concept is that　　5._____

    A. people act in accordance with commonly held norms
    B. people are expected to act in different ways, depending on who or what they are
    C. people's actions are based on the power of others to reward or punish them
    D. the influence of an institution over an individual depends on approval of the other people who support the institution

6. The Hawthorne studies pointed out the importance in industry of　　　　　　6._____

    A. patterned activity　　　　　　B. conflict
    C. informal organization　　　　D. authority

7. The difference between status and role is that status is　　　　　　　　　　7._____

    A. social and role is cultural
    B. a position and role is a norm governing behavior
    C. an enacted institution and role is a crescive institution
    D. an idea and role is an institution

8. Both functional and historical analyses must deal with the problems of change. They differ, however, in that functional analysis

   A. deals with evolution whereas historical analysis deals with revolution
   B. tries to minimize change whereas historical analysis encourages it
   C. is limited to contemporary societies whereas historical analysis is limited to pre-modern times
   D. deals with changes within a stable unit whereas historical analysis deals with changes of the unit itself

9. Race is important in sociology because

   A. many differences in social organization and cultural patterns are caused by differences in race
   B. each race imposes a particular set of norms on its members
   C. races differ in the extent to which they are organized into groups
   D. race is a characteristic of great concern to the members of many societies

10. The *tabula rasa* theory of culture and personality is refuted by the fact that
    I. persons in different social milieus have different values
    II. most sociological statements are about probabilities, not certainties
    III. the same socialization achieves different results in persons of different temperament
    IV. persons often hold the same norm, but with differing emotions
    The CORRECT answer is:

    A. I, II   B. II, IV   C. II, III   D. III, IV

11. Which of the following is cited by Murdock as a universal feature of human societies?

    A. The legal profession   B. Organized armies
    C. Families   D. Psychoanalytic therapy

12. Relations among the workers in the Bank Wiring Room were

    A. found to be uniformly intimate and based on opposition to management
    B. formal and impersonal by comparison with each worker's relations with his family and friends
    C. encouraged by management as an outlet for tensions experienced on the job
    D. patterned and in part hierarchical, but independent of the official authority structure

13. Whether or not a primary group is functional within a formal organization depends on the

    A. degree of harmony between group goals and formal goals
    B. degree of formality of group operation
    C. personalities of the members
    D. relative size of the organization and the group

14. Sociology can study patterns without reference to individuals because

    A. culture and society operate independently of any particular individual
    B. individuals raised exclusively in one society almost always conform to its cultural expectations
    C. individual patterns are the province of psychology
    D. individual actions cannot affect the general patterns of culture

15. Individual variations are important to sociological consideration of

    A. statistical categories
    B. conformity and deviance
    C. morality and free will
    D. conflict

16. Racial categories in science are based on

    A. temperamental factors revealed in the history of the people and the behavior of individuals
    B. physical capacities, such as tolerance for heat or cold
    C. distribution of talents, skills, and specialized intelligence
    D. distribution of inherited external characteristics

17. Negative results of institutional patterns are known as

    A. eufunctions
    B. latent functions
    C. dysfunctions
    D. functional deviance

18. In all probability,

    A. there will, unfortunately, always be a distinction between the functional and the historical approaches
    B. the functional and historical approaches may come closer together, even though at this phase of sociology they have little in common
    C. the functional and historical approaches will be brought together since they already share a good deal in common
    D. sociologists will discover a new way to analyze society and will forego the functional and historical approaches, since neither will be satisfactory in the atomic age

19. One of the ambiguities in Cooley's account of primary groups is that

    A. all social groups have a sense of belonging together
    B. the *common spirit* is a non-scientific concept and does not apply to any concrete group
    C. all groups can be considered primary groups
    D. no groups have face-to-face contacts that are not formalized

20. The family of orientation is important to the individual because

    A. it provides him with complete sexual gratification
    B. it is the one and only true primary group
    C. it gives him the most meaningful experience in which an individual participates
    D. sociological investigations have proved that orphaned individuals can find little fulfillment in life

21. Evolutionary theories in sociology were often weak because they

    A. did not use the language of functionalism which is widespread in sociological work
    B. placed too much emphasis on relationships and not enough on total societies
    C. were deterministic rather than probabilistic
    D. attempted to coerce data about societies into preconceived categories

22. Women with red hair would be classified as a

    A. social category
    B. statistical aggregate
    C. social group
    D. social class

23. In a primary group, hostile relationships

    A. cannot be tolerated
    B. arise only with non-group members
    C. are not subject to group patterns of control
    D. are often generated and regulated by group norms

24. Sociological and anthropological studies of the origin of the family show that

    A. families were originally patrilineal
    B. families were originally matrilineal
    C. very little can be concluded about the origin of the family
    D. nothing can be known about primitive families

25. In a communal society, a sociologist would say that social roles are

    A. inclusive   B. segmental   C. acquired   D. achieved

KEY (CORRECT ANSWERS)

1. C	11. C
2. A	12. D
3. B	13. A
4. C	14. A
5. B	15. B
6. C	16. D
7. B	17. C
8. D	18. C
9. D	19. A
10. D	20. C

21. D
22. B
23. D
24. C
25. A

TEST 4

DIRECTIONS: Each question or incomplete statement is followed by several suggested answers or completions. Select the one that BEST answers the question or completes the statement. *PRINT THE LETTER OF THE CORRECT ANSWER IN THE SPACE AT THE RIGHT.*

1. In Warner's Yankee City study,

    A. classes tended to rate each other similarly
    B. the lower-lower class thought of themselves as the *no count lot*
    C. the lower-upper class found no distinction between themselves and the upper-upper class
    D. none of the above

2. In the United States,

    A. the life expectancy is different for different classes
    B. the age of marriage is higher in the lower classes
    C. divorce rate increases as class and status level rise
    D. many upper class men would rather remain bachelors than marry beneath their class

3. From a sociological standpoint, the statement which BEST describes the function of the rituals of rebellion of the Zulu women is to

    A. secure a good crop
    B. commit public obscenities and act like men
    C. serve as a reward and a release to the women and to maintain the normal social structure
    D. allow the women to let off steam

4. Which of the following refers to a status?

    A. Competent worker   B. Professor
    C. Successful man   D. Liar

5. Historical analysis focuses its attention on

    A. social change
    B. behavior of people at a specific time or place
    C. both of the above
    D. neither of the above

6. In 1950, Alex Inkeles

    A. revealed that the Soviet Union is a true classless society
    B. revealed that the Soviet Union consists of two major groups, the elite and the mass
    C. was able to divide the people of the Soviet Union into four distinct classes
    D. was able to divide the Soviet population into approximately ten distinct classes

7. A student government organization is an example of a

    A. social category   B. primary group
    C. secondary group   D. community

8. For bureaucracy to function effectively, the authority of the officeholder should be commensurate with his

   A. power
   B. talent
   C. training
   D. responsibility

9. Observation of the Bank Wiring Group revealed that rate of output

   A. was controlled by the plant administrator
   B. was controlled by informal social norms among the workers
   C. was the product of individual rates of work among the employees
   D. varied unpredictably, causing disruption of management expectations

10. Three girls work in the same office. They are all the same age, all married, of the same religion, and extremely friendly.
    They constitute a(n)

    A. primary group
    B. ethnic group
    C. association
    D. minority group

11. Initial membership in a social class is

    A. inclusive   B. ascribed   C. organized   D. segmental

12. The inherited patterns with which the individual is born include

    A. grasping, sucking, capacity for emotions
    B. knee jerk, maternal instinct, self-preservation
    C. self-preservation only
    D. intelligence, incest avoidance, belligerence

13. The introduction of bureaucratic methods

    A. always occurs for the same reason
    B. produces havoc within the society or organization
    C. is related to religious values
    D. is usually tied to specific situations within the society or organization

14. With which approach would you MOST associate the phrase *maintenance of social order*?

    A. Functional
    B. Historical
    C. Institutional
    D. Scientific

15. George Herbert Mead developed an account of the origins of the social personality based on

    A. the looking-glass self
    B. taking the role of the other
    C. the introjection of parental values
    D. role-expectations being incorporated into the actor's need-disposition system

16. Bureaucratic organization

A. makes no demands on the personalities of its members
B. requires that its members have no personal values
C. has no relationship to societal values
D. none of the above

17. Geographical determinism is contradicted by the

    A. fact that similar cultures are found in different environments
    B. fact that man is able to change his environment to suit his needs
    C. fact that man is culturally adaptable to all forms of climate, but remains biologically the same
    D. theory that geographical conditions themselves are constantly changing

18. Sociologists would rather discover

    A. uniformities among all groups than the same uniformities among all voluntary groups
    B. uniformities among all college fraternities than the same uniformities among all voluntary groups
    C. uniformities among all American voluntary groups than the same uniformities among all voluntary groups in the world
    D. differences between types of groups than uniformities among all groups

19. The intensive study made at Hawthorne, which was provoked by the recognition of the importance of workers' social organization, was conducted in

    A. Relay Assembly Test Room
    B. Bank Wiring Room
    C. small groups laboratories
    D. an Italian working-class neighborhood

20. Which of the following groups would a sociologist call a *family?*

    A. A woman of 72 years, her husband of 75 years, and their 55-year-old daughter
    B. A man of 40 years, his daughter of 5 years, and his mistress of 35 years
    C. A man of 30 years, his divorced wife of 25 years, and their twin girls of 2 years
    D. None of the above

21. Jargon is less criticized in the physical sciences than in the social sciences because

    A. physical scientists employ mathematical expressions rather than complicated sentences
    B. physical scientists are more understandable to the average man
    C. the subject matter of physical scientists is more concrete and familiar to the practical layman
    D. the practical achievements of physical scientists cause laymen to think of them as more expert

22. The Hawthorne studies were important to the study of primary groups because

    A. the demonstration of the importance of primary groups in the studies provoked a wave of sociological interest
    B. the studies demonstrated that modern society is based on rational, bureaucratic organizations while primary groups have less and less relevance to modern life

C. they were the first studies to include explicitly the primary group concept in the research design
D. they proved that complex organizations are merely collections of primary groups

23. Which of the following is a role?

   A. Executive secretary
   B. Indulgent father
   C. Resident neurosurgeon
   D. All of the above

24. Crescive and enacted institutions differ with respect for

   A. the severity of penalties applied to violations
   B. their origin and method of development
   C. dependence on public opinion
   D. the intensity of commitment to them in all parts of the population

25. Biological characteristics cause diversity in the personalities of members of a society through variations in
   I. race
   II. temperament
   III. intelligence

   The CORRECT answer is:

   A. I only
   B. I, II
   C. I, III
   D. II, III

KEY (CORRECT ANSWERS)

1. D
2. A
3. C
4. B
5. C

6. D
7. C
8. D
9. B
10. A

11. B
12. A
13. D
14. A
15. B

16. D
17. A
18. A
19. B
20. A

21. D
22. A
23. D
24. B
25. D

EXAMINATION SECTION
TEST 1

DIRECTIONS: Each question or incomplete statement is followed by several suggested answers or completions. Select the one that BEST answers the question or completes the statement. *PRINT THE LETTER OF THE CORRECT ANSWER IN THE SPACE AT THE RIGHT.*

1. Class was considered an important feature of societies by

    A. Karl Marx
    B. Aristotle
    C. James Madison
    D. all of the above

2. Weber's *ideal type* is a(n)

    A. utopian plan
    B. imaginary system
    C. model of a structure
    D. type of organization

3. Freud discussed the development of the individual's achievement goals and standards of progress which he called

    A. super-ego
    B. ego ideal
    C. looking-glass self
    D. role-expectations

4. The similarity between bureaucracy and military organization rests especially upon the fact that

    A. there are salary gradations in both
    B. there is an established and clear-cut line of authority in both
    C. both involve coercion
    D. both involve consensus

5. Conflict occurs often in marriage because

    A. the husband tries to dominate the wife
    B. the wife tries to dominate the husband
    C. blurred definitions of masculine and feminine roles exist
    D. too many people rely on books for information about marriage

6. An extended family is made up of

    A. mother, father, and offspring
    B. parents, their married offspring, the children of the married offspring
    C. one man and his several wives
    D. one wife and her several husbands

7. The American lower-class Black family

    A. centers around the father and his brothers
    B. is highly disorganized and lacks a center
    C. centers around the mother and her kin
    D. exemplifies the rise of the conjugal family in industrial society

8. Piaget's classic work in the development of the child's personality was based on his

   A. treatment of neurotic and schizophrenic orphans
   B. speculative philosophy
   C. observations of children at play
   D. experiments with children kept in isolation

9. The *looking-glass self* is a concept developed by

   A. Mead   B. Cooley   C. Freud   D. Piaget

10. Which of the following statements is TRUE?

    A. *Eufunction* and *function* are exactly the same.
    B. *Functional alternative* and *functional requisite* are exactly the same.
    C. *Eufunction* and *dysfunction* are exactly the same
    D. None of the above

11. Individuals tend to act alike if they

    A. confront the same problems
    B. are biologically related or physically similar
    C. have similar backgrounds of social experience
    D. use the same type of language

12. The classification of races in biology and anthropology

    A. was carried out mostly by German scientists in the Nazi era
    B. is not regarded as respectable scientific work
    C. is important to the sociological study of differences in the rate of progress of different societies
    D. is less relevant to sociology than are *common sense* theories of race

13. The individual can be considered the product of his society and culture because

    A. genetic endowment determines few patterns of behavior
    B. human beings can survive only by constant association with others who share the same expectations
    C. other factors, such as biology, race, and climate, do not shape personality
    D. conformity with the norms is expected by others

14. We must include in the analysis of change

    A. organized efforts to effect change
    B. institutionalized sources of innovation
    C. contacts with other groups
    D. all of the above

15. People who have the potentiality to form into groups but have no formal organization are known as

    A. ethnic groups   B. quasi-groups
    C. communities   D. primary groups

16. In the United States, the

    A. number of white collar employees has decreased
    B. middle class has decreased slightly
    C. number of unskilled workers has decreased
    D. need for skilled labor has decreased

17. Some of the dysfunctional aspects of bureaucracy result from
    I. man's natural inclination to break rules
    II. inflexible adherence to the rules of the organization
    III. insufficient attention to the rules
    The CORRECT answer is:

    A. I only B. I, II C. III only D. II, III

18. Biological determinism can be claimed for the differentiated roles of men and women in

    A. no areas of social organization
    B. child-bearing
    C. professional life
    D. government

19. The popularity of *baby manuals* in the United States is related to

    A. the small size of the family unit
    B. the prestige of science
    C. the changing roles of women
    D. all of the above

20. Which of the following *common sense* notions was shown to be wrong by scientific research?

    A. Educated men are more prone to psychological breakdown in military service than the uneducated
    B. Men with rural backgrounds took the hardships of military life better than urbanites
    C. Black soldiers were less ambitious than white soldiers
    D. All of the above

21. Which of the following statements is TRUE?
    I. Functions may be manifest to some but not to others.
    II. Latent functions may at times become manifest.
    III. The rain dances of the Zuni Indians have no positive functions.
    The CORRECT answer is:

    A. I, III B. II, III C. II only D. I, II

22. Early students of the social development of the personality did NOT emphasize the effects of

    A. the nuclear family
    B. the child's play group
    C. language learning
    D. adolescent peer groups

23. The category *secondary group* includes

    A. social groups, social categories, statistical aggregates
    B. communities, communal societies, associational societies
    C. associations, ethnic groups, social classes
    D. social groups, communities, ethnic groups

24. Most adult Americans drink coffee, which is a tropical product first refined in Asia Minor, during and between meals.
    This is an example of

    A. diffusion   B. amalgamation
    C. assimilation   D. accommodation

25. The relation of society to the individual is an important sociological issue because
    I. individuals cannot survive without some contact with others
    II. individual decisions pose a theoretical threat to the order of society
    III. culture and society are conceptual approaches to understanding the collective actions of individuals and have no separate existence
    IV. society imposes rules of conformity on individuals, thus inhibiting their individuality and creativity

    The CORRECT answer is:

    A. I, III   B. II, IV   C. II, III   D. I, II

KEY (CORRECT ANSWERS)

1.	D	11.	C
2.	C	12.	D
3.	B	13.	A
4.	B	14.	D
5.	C	15.	B
6.	B	16.	C
7.	C	17.	D
8.	C	18.	B
9.	B	19.	D
10.	D	20.	D

21. D
22. D
23. C
24. A
25. D

TEST 2

DIRECTIONS: Each question or incomplete statement is followed by several suggested answers or completions. Select the one that BEST answers the question or completes the statement. *PRINT THE LETTER OF THE CORRECT ANSWER IN THE SPACE AT THE RIGHT.*

1. Racial classifications are rendered difficult by

    A. overlapping distributions of characteristics
    B. underlying similarity and brotherhood of all men
    C. members of one race *passing* as members of another
    D. reluctance of people to report their races accurately to investigators and interviewers

2. Scientific concepts in sociology are similar to the ordinary language in which society is discussed by the layman in that

    A. they are equally precise
    B. they are equally explicit
    C. both are highly abstract
    D. both are conventional among those who employ them

3. Students throughout the United States would be classified as

    A. a social group
    B. a social category
    C. a primary group
    D. both A and C

4. The study of the relations of society to the individual are of special significance now because of

    A. the rise of totalitarian mass societies
    B. increasing bureaucracy in modern society
    C. increased importance of mass media in maintaining social solidarity
    D. all of the above

5. Conflict in society is

    A. always disruptive
    B. sometimes institutionalized and functional
    C. always a reflection of a weakened or challenged consensus in society
    D. none of the above

6. Concepts have an important influence in social science because they

    A. direct the sociologist's attention into specific areas
    B. contain fundamental general laws which underlie later research
    C. are an explicit statement of the biases and prejudices of the investigator which would otherwise go unnoticed
    D. are the terms most often used in sociological reports and papers

7. The assumption that one's own culture is a normal characteristic of mankind is known as

    A. naturalism
    B. ethnocentrism
    C. egocentrism
    D. socialization

8. Cultural and social diversity is the basis of an ethical position known as

   A. value-neutrality
   B. cultural relativism
   C. ethnocentricism
   D. panethical tolerance

9. Although the family is based on biological facts, it is NOT explained by them since

   A. religious sanctions are necessary to create a true family
   B. forms of the family differ widely in different human societies
   C. the family also fulfills many non-biological functions
   D. sex and reproduction can also occur outside of the family

10. Families in America

    A. no longer function as economic units of production
    B. continue to function as a collective enterprise of production
    C. are still the main influences in training their children for occupational roles
    D. have transferred the task of socializing the young to the schools

11. Stratification can be conceptually divided into three types of ranking:

    A. caste, class, conformity
    B. power, class, status
    C. achievement, ascription, asymmetry
    D. elite, mass, outcast

12. In modern Western society,

    A. property continues to the main determinant of class structure
    B. the dominance of corporations in the economy renders class differences among individuals unimportant
    C. wealth and occupation have little to do with one another
    D. none of the above

13. The traditional gross diversions of the caste system in India are

    A. intellectuals, soldiers, workers
    B. aristocrats, commoners, intellectuals, politicians
    C. religious men, fighters, merchants, peasants
    D. intellectuals, politicians, warriors, workers

14. Which characteristic did Alexis de Tocqueville think was peculiar to the American people?

    A. Class-consciousness
    B. Idealism
    C. Scientific achievement
    D. Equality

15. American politics is noteworthy because

    A. the struggle between parties representing different class interests is especially bitter
    B. all social class interests are represented by each party
    C. it is not a scene of explicit class conflict
    D. leadership comes from a small elite class only

16. An important characteristic of bureaucratic organization is that it separates the *office* from the

    A. office-holder
    B. organization
    C. job
    D. salary

17. Size of organization and complexity of tasks

    A. hamper bureaucratic methods
    B. introduce problems for which bureaucratic methods are well-suited
    C. are not related to bureaucracy
    D. create red tape

18. In American society, a mother-in-law's permanent residence with the family is looked upon as

    A. *unfortunate* because she will be meddlesome
    B. *fortunate* because she will probably be a tax deduction
    C. *neither fortunate nor unfortunate* but a fact of life that one must cope with
    D. *fortunate* because she has acquired much wisdom and can add richness to family life

19. MOST systems of residence in the patrilineal societies which Murdock studied were

    A. patrilocal
    B. neolocal
    C. matrilocal
    D. matri-patrilocal

20. A convincing demonstration of the influence of social relationships on individual patterns is the

    A. different perceptual sensitivities of individuals from different social backgrounds
    B. differences in innate intelligence among individuals from different social classes
    C. greater tolerance of extremes of temperature among individuals from different societies
    D. greater political maturity of members of European societies

21. The change in residence patterns of the Bemba of Northern Rhodesia came about because
    I. the women began to find more work as industrialism spread to Rhodesia and thus were able to exert greater influence
    II. following the English style, it became more fashionable to associate with the father's kin
    III. men were able to find jobs in the copper mines

    The CORRECT answer is:

    A. I *only*
    B. I, III
    C. I, II
    D. II, III

22. The scientific study of society began in

    A. classical Greece and progressed with the other specialized sciences
    B. the nineteenth century in France and has made greatest progress in the twentieth century
    C. the 1920's at the University of Chicago
    D. classical Greece but was hampered in its growth until the recent past by the bias of ethnocentrism

23. Society can be thought of as that group which contains

    A. an effective government with authority over its operations
    B. a self-maintaining elite which exercises a monopoly over decision-making
    C. members whose total lives are lived in association with one another
    D. the largest number of face-to-face relationships

24. The basic characteristic of social relationships is

    A. reciprocal expectation
    B. mutual benefit
    C. identical goals
    D. cooperative sentiments

25. The informal structure, *bureaucracy's other face,*

    A. tends to weaken the organization
    B. lessens the organization's efficiency
    C. prevents fulfillment of the organization's official goals
    D. all of the above might or might not be true, depending on the bureaucracy

KEY (CORRECT ANSWERS)

1.	A	11.	B
2.	D	12.	D
3.	B	13.	C
4.	D	14.	D
5.	B	15.	C
6.	A	16.	A
7.	B	17.	B
8.	B	18.	A
9.	B	19.	A
10.	A	20.	A

21. D
22. B
23. C
24. A
25. D

TEST 3

DIRECTIONS: Each question or incomplete statement is followed by several suggested answers or completions. Select the one that BEST answers the question or completes the statement. *PRINT THE LETTER OF THE CORRECT ANSWER IN THE SPACE AT THE RIGHT.*

1. When criminals commit crimes such as murder, theft, and rape, 1.____

    A. these crimes and crime in general probably have some latent functions for society
    B. it is because crime is a functional requisite of society
    C. the crimes are totally dysfunctional
    D. none of the above

2. Feudalism as a recurrent institutional pattern 2.____

    A. is found in all societies
    B. develops at a certain stage in the history of every society
    C. is found in several societies at different periods of time
    D. was universal in all societies at a certain time

3. The Norton Street Gang was characterized by 3.____

    A. strict control of all members by Doc, the leader
    B. rejection of the conservative norms of the ethnic community, especially in sexual matters
    C. clearly expressed offices and duties for each member, in accordance with the club charter
    D. none of the above

4. Social categories and statistical aggregates both 4.____
    I. do not possess the attributes of a group
    II. have the potentialities for being groups
    III. contain people who possess similar social attributes
    IV. contain people of similar status
   The CORRECT answer is:

    A. I *only*   B. II, IV   C. II, III   D. I, II

5. The PRINCIPAL difference between sociological consideration of man and society and philosophical consideration of man and society is that sociology is 5.____

    A. concerned with objective discription and generalization rather than evaluation of forms of social life
    B. more closely related to physical, chemical, and biological theories and research
    C. concerned with concrete specific facts rather than abstract theorization
    D. concerned with the present rather than the future

6. Montesquieu's theories of climatic influences 6.____

    A. served as the justification for modern totalitarian dictatorships
    B. are the basis for modern sciences of government and international relations
    C. have been brought into question by recent findings, but are still suggestive
    D. are now rejected by sociologists on the basis of studies of Eskimo adaptation

7. Personal feelings of guilt

   A. arise as psychological responses in the individual irrespective of the society in which he lives
   B. do not arise unless the individual is socialized to expect them
   C. are responses to actual or potential violations of social norms and are sometimes encouraged by social situations
   D. operate as psychological, but not social, forces

8. American marriage patterns are distinguished by emphasis on

   A. having children
   B. legitimacy of sexual relations
   C. love
   D. compatibility of temperament

9. Marx's use of the word *class* was based on man's relationship to

   A. sources of power
   B. the accumulation of inherited wealth
   C. his family position
   D. means of production

10. Individual status in India's caste system was

    A. achieved
    B. ascribed
    C. both achieved and ascribed
    D. achieved on the basis of education

11. Sociologists

    A. find social mobility to have increased greatly over past decades
    B. find social mobility to have decreased greatly
    C. are not certain whether social mobility has increased or decreased
    D. have found social mobility to have increased slightly

12. Bureaucratic organization requires
    I. that its members possess creative talent
    II. the absence of personal relationships
    III. cooperation between members

    The CORRECT answer is:

    A. II   B. I, II   C. II, III   D. I, III

13. The American middle-class family is considered

    A. matriarchal   B. patriarchal   C. matri-patrilocal   D. equalitarian

14. A MAJOR obstacle to objectivity in sociology is

    A. government pressure to prevent the discovery and publication of politically dangerous facts
    B. increasing contacts among dissimilar societies and rapid change within societies
    C. strong sentiments felt by sociologists about social issues
    D. bureaucratic inefficiency in communication of findings among sociologists in different areas

15. Borrowing of one society's patterns by another is dangerous because

   A. language barriers impede proper communication and transmission of ideas
   B. patterns may work within one society's particular institutional setting but may be disruptive in a different setting
   C. necessary techniques and tools are not always available in the borrowing society
   D. political control of the borrowed patterns may be weaker in the new than in the original society

16. The *tolkach* in the Soviet economy

   A. performs only activities which are functional for the economy
   B. performs only activities which are dysfunctional for the economy
   C. performs both functional and dysfunctional activities
   D. is gradually disappearing because of his many dysfunctions

17. By inculcating a proper respect for rules and procedures, the organization almost inevitably leaves the official with an exaggerated

   A. concern with routines and regulations
   B. concern for the goals of the organization
   C. sense of his own importance
   D. all of the above

18. James Smith has been in prison for five year. During this time, he and his wife have faithfully written to each other every day. In their letters, they have expressed intimate feelings and opinions.
   Their relationship

   A. cannot be considered a primary one since there is no face-to-face contact
   B. is a primary group relationship
   C. cannot be considered a primary relationship since there is no intrinsic value in the relationship
   D. cannot be considered a primary relationship since there is no commitment to an explicit goal

19. Biology and geography cannot be dismissed in the study of society because they

   A. are used in the ideologies of totalitarian movements
   B. set limits to the operation of society
   C. determine the operation of society
   D. are important branches of knowledge developed within a culture, especially Western culture

20. In modern Western society, the MOST important single determinant of status is

   A. family   B. occupation
   C. education   D. wealth

21. Early students of the social foundation of personality emphasized the operations of
    A. maternal care
    B. interaction in school situations
    C. experiences at feeding times
    D. role-taking in the primary group

22. Functional analysis can often be accused of neglecting the effects of
    A. social psychology
    B. social change
    C. religion and ethics
    D. geography

23. Social mobility is based to a great extent upon
    A. education
    B. connections
    C. age and sex
    D. race

24. Owners of Chinese laundries may be classified as a(n)
    A. associational group
    B. social category
    C. association
    D. social group

25. In modern societies, social units are USUALLY defined by
    A. life expectancy of the population
    B. political ideology
    C. political organization and geographic boundaries
    D. language or languages spoken

KEY (CORRECT ANSWERS)

1. A
2. C
3. D
4. D
5. A

6. C
7. C
8. C
9. D
10. B

11. C
12. D
13. D
14. C
15. B

16. C
17. A
18. B
19. B
20. B

21. D
22. B
23. A
24. B
25. C

TEST 4

DIRECTIONS: Each question or incomplete statement is followed by several suggested answers or completions. Select the one that BEST answers the question or completes the statement. *PRINT THE LETTER OF THE CORRECT ANSWER IN THE SPACE AT THE RIGHT.*

1. Alcoholics Anonymous is an example of a(n)

    A. social class
    B. primary group
    C. social category
    D. association

2. Women would be classified as a

    A. social category
    B. statistical aggregate
    C. social group
    D. social class

3. Castes in India

    A. are formalized and extend throughout India
    B. are informal and extend throughout India
    C. develop differently in each separate locality
    D. are controlled by the government

4. Throughout the United States, many new highways and turnpikes are being built. Their main purpose is for transportation.
The fact that many people are employed in building the roads is

    A. of little concern to the sociologist
    B. of the greatest concern to the sociologist
    C. to be considered by the sociologist along with other consequences of road-building
    D. known as a manifest function

5. The influence of biology on social organization

    A. explains all features common to every society
    B. is only general, since different societies handle biological facts quite differently
    C. is greater in non-industrial than in industrial societies
    D. operates by means of the sex drive, which gives rise to culture when it is frustrated and sublimated

6. Whyte's study of the Nortons exemplifies the method of

    A. controlled comparison
    B. experimental task groups
    C. participant observation
    D. permissive leadership

7. Uniform behavior can be expected of members of a social group despite individual differences since
    I. the members have been socialized to follow common norms
    II. group organization results in rewards for conformist behavior and penalties for deviant behavior
    III. admittance to the group is dependent on conformity to group norms
    IV. groups with nonconforming members tend to disintegrate

    The CORRECT answer is:

    A. I, III   B. II, IV   C. III, IV   D. I, II

8. Bureaucracy's advantage over other forms of organization lies in its

   A. impersonal procedures
   B. technical superiority
   C. use of democratic methods
   D. filing system

9. The conservatism of many U.S. small businessmen today can be seen as a(n)
   I. response to social change
   II. response to a threat to their status
   III. attempt at innovation

   The CORRECT answer is:

   A. I, III   B. III only   C. II, III   D. I, II

10. The social importance of punishment was noted by

    A. Simmel   B. Durkheim   C. Riesman   D. Marx

11. Which of the following associations is CORRECT?

    A. Transitional growth and industrializing societies
    B. High growth potential and poor agricultural societies
    C. Incipient decline and industrialized societies
    D. All of the above

12. Studies of attitudes of youth toward scientists show that scientists in general are regarded as

    A. making an important contribution
    B. being unsociable
    C. displaying selfless dedication
    D. all of the above

13. Durkheim saw religion as a *social fact* because it

    A. cannot be practiced individually
    B. is part of the real world
    C. acquires its sacred quality through collective rituals
    D. all of the above

14. The distinction between the Marxist and liberal views of the state can be summarized as

    A. the state as representative of a particular class vs. the state as representative of all classes
    B. the state as representative of a particular class vs. the state as arbiter between classes
    C. the state as an ideological weapon vs. the state as a maker of laws
    D. all of the above

15. Social scientists will be able to attain more insight into the effects of technology on culture as

    A. industrialization takes place in different cultural and structural contexts
    B. long as some areas of the world remain non-industrial

C. the study of economics progresses
D. cultural changes become more visible

16. One factor working against the characteristic urban pattern of *spatial proximity and social distance* is the

   A. development of distinctive neighborhoods
   B. educational system
   C. religious system
   D. all of the above

17. Organic solidarity is based upon

   A. the similarity of the members of the society
   B. the mutual dependence of the members of the society
   C. an underdeveloped technology
   D. technological determinism

18. The Norton Street Gang was significantly affected by

   A. patterns of formal authority within the group
   B. the changes introduced by the experimenter into their work situation
   C. conditions prevailing in the institutions of the whole society at that moment in history
   D. the high rate of turnover of the members

19. Bureaucratic roles

   A. are open to those who have the competence to fill them
   B. can be filled by any member of the society
   C. are closed to non-college graduates
   D. can be carried out only by those who are able to withhold information

20. Bureaucracy is a form of organization which

   A. originated during the Industrial Revolution
   B. is exclusively a twentieth century phenomenon
   C. can be traced back to ancient Egypt
   D. exists in all societies

21. The distinctive feature of government is the

   A. exercise of power
   B. monopoly of the legitimate use of force
   C. development of bureaucracy
   D. resolution of conflict

22. Religious rituals are often found to occur in connection with

   A. anxiety-provoking experiences
   B. rites de passage
   C. situations involving an unpredictable outcome
   D. all of the above

23. Science is a component of Western culture which is 23.____

   A. unrecognized by the layman
   B. less important now than it was in the seventeenth century
   C. just as important now as it was in antiquity
   D. a central focus of present and future social life

24. From 1900 to 1940, the birth rate of the United States and MOST of Western Europe showed 24.____

   A. no consistent trend
   B. a steady increase
   C. a sharp increase
   D. a steady decrease

25. Internal conflict may serve to maintain social order because it 25.____

   A. allows for the existence of opposing interests within the bounds of the society
   B. decreases social solidarity
   C. increases social solidarity
   D. restricts external conflict

KEY (CORRECT ANSWERS)

1. D
2. A
3. C
4. C
5. B

6. C
7. D
8. B
9. D
10. B

11. D
12. D
13. C
14. B
15. A

16. A
17. B
18. C
19. A
20. C

21. B
22. D
23. D
24. D
25. A

EXAMINATION SECTION
TEST 1

DIRECTIONS: Each question or incomplete statement is followed by several suggested answers or completions. Select the one that BEST answers the question or completes the statement. *PRINT THE LETTER OF THE CORRECT ANSWER IN THE SPACE AT THE RIGHT.*

1. The culture-of-poverty theories of the late 1960s implied that cultural values concerning the control of sexual
activity and the value of marriage were the _____ rather than the _____ of poverty.

   A. best aspects of; worst aspects of
   B. results; causes
   C. causes; results
   D. causes; unintended consequences

2. Two kinds of conflicts that underlie much of the controversy and discussion of major public issues concerning the family are

   A. child care and the family wage
   B. women's autonomy and beliefs about *natural* roles
   C. women's autonomy and income assistance to the poor
   D. women's dominance and child care

3. Too much emphasis on the *structural causation of* changes in family structures among the poor ignores evidence regarding

   A. proliferation of low wage jobs
   B. increasing male joblessness in the inner city
   C. the benefits of postponing childbearing
   D. racial prejudice

4. The proponents of welfare reform argue that work requirements for mothers will have positive consequences. Which of the following is NOT one of positive consequences they predict?

   A. Increased self-esteem will make them better mothers.
   B. Holding a job will help families establish set routines.
   C. Children will benefit from enriched daycare facilities.
   D. Employed mothers will be better role models.

5. If current rates of immigration and births were to continue, by the year 2050 the percent of the U.S. population comprised of white Europeans would be approximately _____ percent.

   A. 60   B. 50   C. 35   D. 25

6. _____ networks are superior in allowing people to be upwardly mobile.

   A. Marriage-based   B. Female-centered kin
   C. Male-centered kin   D. Cohabitation-based

7. Most government involvement in family support is based on a concern about

   A. votes
   B. keeping employees happy and working
   C. dependents, especially children and the elderly
   D. distributing excess monies fairly to all groups

8. Which of the following was NOT one of the changes that contributed to the end of traditional courtship patterns in the United States?

   A. Migration from rural areas to cities
   B. Higher standards of living
   C. Growth in passionate love as a basis for marriage
   D. Extended period of adolescence as a stage of development

9. The longer a woman remains on welfare, the _____ she is to give birth.

   A. more likely
   B. less likely
   C. there is no correlation
   D. none of the above

10. In samples of welfare households, most current household heads grew up in the _____ class.

    A. welfare   B. middle
    C. working   D. poor relief

11. The *family duty* blueprint was undermined by

    A. changes in the sexual division of labor
    B. the sexual revolution
    C. the automobile
    D. the emergence of dating among youth

12. Most laboratory studies of married couples as they discussed problems revealed that _____ was a better predictor
of a distressed or nondistressed marriage than _____.

    A. verbal behavior; nonverbal behavior
    B. open conflict; nonverbal behavior
    C. nonverbal behavior; verbal behavior
    D. expressed anger; body language

13. Since the 1960s, there has been a shift away from relative care of preschoolers to center care of preschoolers. This is due to

    A. women on welfare relying on state subsidized center care
    B. the increasing proportion of single parents
    C. decreasing labor force participation among women with infants
    D. increased father involvement in childcare

14. According to research on images of romance, romances set in the American West are increasingly about 14.____

    A. resolution of gender disputes through violence
    B. how to resolve male-female conflict over the increasing commitment of women to work
    C. preference for cohabitation over marriage
    D. the declining influence of feminism on American women and their attitudes

15. According to belief on changing images of romance since the 1970s, the overall bestselling genre of popular fiction in the U.S. today is 15.____

    A. science fiction for women
    B. time-travel
    C. mystery fiction for women
    D. romance

16. An article on the blueprints of love and research on contemporary images of romance both use which of the following research methods? 16.____

    A. Content analysis of popular writings
    B. Surveys of readers
    C. Demographic analysis
    D. All of the above

17. During the Victorian Era, married women's supposed lack of erotic interest in all probability actually gave these women 17.____

    A. some measure of control over pregnancy
    B. control over their husbands
    C. the opportunity to have extramarital affairs
    D. freedom from sexually-transmitted diseases

18. The companionship blueprint for the family is an example of the belief that 18.____

    A. trust, commitment, and permanence are devalued in contemporary society
    B. the 20th century family has increasingly emphasized private over public functions
    C. middle class families are taking on the sexual values of working class families
    D. American attitudes and behavior about divorce are increasingly tolerant

19. An egalitarian division of labor between married partners often collapses with the 19.____

    A. birth of a child
    B. wife quitting her job
    C. husband losing his job
    D. death of parents

20. The tendency of adults to marry those very similar to themselves in race, education, religion, and other characteristics is referred to as 20.____

    A. the New Home Economics
    B. heterogamy
    C. the dating-rating complex
    D. none of the above

21. American politicians began to talk specifically about family policy in the 21.____

    A. 1950s   B. mid-1970s   C. mid-1980s   D. 1990s

22. Which of the following has NOT contributed to the increase in single-parent families?

    A. A cultural shift away from marriage
    B. Scarcity of semi-skilled manufacturing jobs
    C. Income assistance programs
    D. True love as a basis for marriage

23. The independent marriage emphasizes

    A. rigid gender role typing
    B. affection, friendship, and sexual gratification
    C. authority, duty, and conformity to social norms
    D. self-development and flexible roles

24. American family households most likely to be headed by a married couple are from the _____ racial-ethnic groups.

    A. African-American
    B. Asian-American
    C. non-Hispanic white
    D. Hispanic

25. The total fertility rate is defined by demographers as the

    A. proportion of women in a given population able to bear children
    B. proportion of men who father children over a period of 20 years
    C. proportion of men in a given population who are not infertile
    D. average number of children that women would bear over their lifetimes

KEY (CORRECT ANSWERS)

1. C
2. C
3. C
4. C
5. B

6. A
7. C
8. C
9. B
10. C

11. A
12. C
13. B
14. B
15. D

16. A
17. A
18. B
19. A
20. D

21. B
22. D
23. D
24. B
25. D

TEST 2

DIRECTIONS: Each question or incomplete statement is followed by several suggested answers or completions. Select the one that BEST answers the question or completes the statement. *PRINT THE LETTER OF THE CORRECT ANSWER IN THE SPACE AT THE RIGHT.*

1. Middle-class Americans in the 1930s and 1940s, despite increased acceptance of pre-marital sex, considered love to be _____ sexual intimacy.   1._____

    A. a barrier to
    B. the result of
    C. the best deterrent of
    D. a necessary condition for

2. _____ percent of young adults in the U.S. eventually marry.   2._____

    A. 45   B. 60   C. 75   D. 90

3. Which of the following responses to partner pregnancy is widely shared among unmarried fathers?   3._____

    A. The fathers strongly condemned abortion.
    B. There was a fairly high probability of marriage before the birth of the child.
    C. Nonmarrying, absent fathers tended to be involved in drugs or crime.
    D. Parents strongly encouraged marriage or co-residence.

4. When cohabitating relationships end, most result in marriage.   4._____

    A. True   B. False

5. The *family cap* is defined as   5._____

    A. limitations on state-supported day care subsidies under the new act
    B. the new work requirement for mothers on welfare
    C. the suggested lifetime limit on welfare benefits
    D. no additional benefits for mothers who give birth while on welfare

6. In the 1970s, the sexual double standard   6._____

    A. disappeared
    B. lingered on
    C. became politically incorrect
    D. increased

7. Contemporary romance novels for women idealize   7._____

    A. family
    B. motherhood
    C. fertility
    D. commitment, trust, and permanence

8. The transitions in marriage forms in the U.S. are consistent with   8._____

    A. a greater emphasis on service to others
    B. a greater emphasis on individualism
    C. a greater threat of economic problems
    D. none of the above

9. Parents have _____ choices for arrangements for their infants than for their older pre-schoolers.

   A. fewer
   B. more
   C. better
   D. about the same number of

10. The *earned income credit* is

    A. a program of cash assistance to poor, single-parent families in New York State
    B. the same as the family wage
    C. a new modification of the Aid to Families with Dependent Children program
    D. a refundable tax credit to low-income families with children (where a parent is employed)

11. The income gap between more educated and less educated women in the U.S. is

    A. stabilizing
    B. narrowing
    C. increasing
    D. causing more divorces

12. American states _____ in how they regulate family child care homes.

    A. vary very little
    B. collaborate
    C. vary widely
    D. compete with one another

13. Which of the following is NOT a component of the market model of marriage?

    A. Supply of men and women in a marriage market
    B. Rational choice
    C. Resources of men
    D. Preference

14. When there are alternative job opportunities available to young men other than those related to parents' resources (such as farms, for example), the marriage age of young men tends to

    A. increase
    B. decline
    C. remain unchanged
    D. increase initially then decline

15. Women and men experience romantic love

    A. similarly
    B. differently
    C. at different points in the life span
    D. in inverse life order

16. The typical college woman in the 1940s and 1950s

    A. was having premarital sexual intercourse more frequently than the typical girl in the 1930s
    B. had premarital sexual intercourse at the same rate as the typical college man
    C. tended to have sexual intercourse only when going steady or while engaged
    D. went out only on group dates

17. The _____, as well as subsequent U.S. Supreme Court decisions, banned discrimination against women in hiring and wages.

    A. 1964 Civil Rights Act
    B. 1970 Title XX Amendment
    C. Equal Rights Amendment
    D. 1969 Women's Work Amendment

18.

HOUSEHOLD AND FAMILY CHARACTERISTIC PERCENTAGES BY HOUSEHOLD TYPE

Household characteristics	Female heads	Married heads	Single heads	Elderly heads
Household size				
1	2.6	0.2	79.8	93.8
2	34.9	9.0	7.9	4.8
3	29.8	22.1	3.6	0.7
4	16.3	26.1	2.8	0.5
5	8.1	19.2	2.4	0.0
6 or more	8.4	23.4	3.6	0.2
Average	3.2	4.5	1.5	1.1
Living arrangement				
Home	99.6	99.4	78.1	18.8
Nursing home	0.0	0.2	20.0	81.2
Other	0.4	0.4	2.0	0.0
Marital status				
Never married	39.7	-	73.8	13.8
Married	-	100.0	-	3.9
Separated	27.2	-	8.2	16.6
Divorced	31.4	-	12.1	4.2
Widowed	1.7	-	5.8	61.5
Number of generations in household				
1	3.8	9.6	97.2	98.0
2	94.7	88.8	2.8	1.8
3	1.6	1.6	-	0.2
Number of Children				
0	3.9	11.6	100.0	98.7
1	41.8	23.2	-	1.2
2	29.5	26.9	-	0.0
3	14.2	19.0	-	0.0
4 or more	10.7	19.2	-	0.2
Average	1.9	2.3	-	-
Ages of Children				
Less than 6	40.2	36.3	-	-
6-17	56.3	59.1	-	-
18 or more	3.3	4.6	-	-

The above table presents household and family characteristics of one research sample of welfare households. This table _____ the theory that large, extended families live together on welfare.

   A. does not support
   B. supports
   C. does not speak to
   D. all of the above

Questions 19-20.

DIRECTIONS: Questions 19 and 20 are to be answered on the basis of the following table.

ESTIMATES OF COHABITATION AND MARRIAGE
BEFORE THE AGE OF 25, BY BIRTH COHORT (%)

Birth Cohort	MALES		FEMALES	
	Cohabit	Marry	Cohabit	Marry
2000 - 2004	33	38	37	76
1995 - 1999	29	51	26	67
1990 - 1994	24	55	16	72
1985 - 1989	11	66	7	79
1980 - 1984	8	68	3	82

19. What is the MOST likely reason why more women are married by age 25 than men?

    A. Men avoid marriage.
    B. Men are more likely to cohabit.
    C. Men tend to be older than the women they marry.
    D. Women are more likely to have been married more than once by age 25.

20. Which statement is the BEST description of how marriage and cohabitation experiences have changed over time for men?

    A. Fewer men by age 25 either marry or cohabit.
    B. Cohabitation seems to be *substituting* for early marriage.
    C. More men now postpone sexual relationships.
    D. None of the above

21. Marriages preceded by cohabitation have _____ rate of disruption than marriages not preceded by cohabitation.

    A. a higher
    B. a lower
    C. the same
    D. none of the above (the data are ambiguous)

Questions 22-25.

DIRECTIONS: Questions 22 through 25 are to be answered on the basis of the following table.

INFORMATION ABOUT WOMEN'S MARITAL STATUS, BY BIRTH COHORT AND AGE

Generation	15-19	20-24	Ages 25-29	30-34	35-39
Percent Ever Married*					
Generation X	6	37			
Late baby boomers	10	46	71	84	
Early baby boomers	12	62	83	89	91
World War II	15	69	90	93	95
Parents of baby boomers	16	69	89	94	95
Percent Married and Living With Husband					
Generation X	5	31			
Late baby boomers	9	38	58	67	
Early baby boomers	10	54	69	70	71
World War II	15	62	81	81	78
Parents of baby boomers	15	62	80	84	82
Divorced or Separated Women per 1,000 Married-Spouse Present Women*					
Generation X	-	161			
Late baby boomers	-	158	207	224	
Early baby boomers	-	111	174	229	254
World War II	-	65	86	123	179
Parents of baby boomers	-	81	75	83	98

*These percentages exclude women who were separated because their husbands were in military service.

22. According to this table, which birth cohort had the lowest probability of ever marrying by age 24?

    A. Generation X
    B. Late baby boomers
    C. Early baby boomers
    D. World War II

23. Which of the following birth cohorts had the highest probability of EVER divorcing or separating by age 34?

    A. Late baby boomers
    B. Early baby boomers
    C. World War II
    D. Parents of baby boomers

24. Which of the following cohorts had the highest probability of ever divorcing or separating by age 24?

    A. Generation X
    B. Late baby boomers
    C. Early baby boomers
    D. World War II

25. Based on the table *alone*, which of the following birth cohorts would you predict will have the highest LIFETIME divorce rate?

    A. Generation X
    B. Late baby boomers
    C. Early baby boomers
    D. One cannot tell from the table

KEY (CORRECT ANSWERS)

1.	D	11.	C
2.	D	12.	C
3.	C	13.	B
4.	A	14.	B
5.	D	15.	B
6.	B	16.	C
7.	D	17.	A
8.	B	18.	A
9.	A	19.	B
10.	D	20.	B

21. A
22. D
23. B
24. A
25. A

EXAMINATION SECTION
TEST 1

DIRECTIONS: Each question or incomplete statement is followed by several suggested answers or completions. Select the one that BEST answers the question or completes the statement. *PRINT THE LETTER OF THE CORRECT ANSWER IN THE SPACE AT THE RIGHT.*

1. No-fault divorce is defined as

    A. the right to make important decisions about children
    B. a ruling that a marriage has never been properly formed
    C. coordination of divorced parents in raising children
    D. granting of divorce due to irreconcilable differences

    1._____

2. In the era of restricted divorce, countries with a predominantly _____ religion were more liberal about divorce.

    A. Catholic   B. Muslim   C. Protestant   D. Anglican

    2._____

3. In regard to the family economy and mental health, the fact that women are more exposed to environmental stressors than men has been used to argue that _____ explains the gender gap in psychological distress and depression.

    A. work-family conflict
    B. role participation
    C. psychological compensation
    D. biological predisposition

    3._____

4. Across all types of maltreatment, prevalence rates of child abuse are highest among

    A. middle-class families
    B. low-income families
    C. two-parent families
    D. families with older mothers

    4._____

5. Women are forced to choose between

    A. equality and work
    B. parenting success and equality
    C. parenting success and marriage
    D. equality and marriage

    5._____

6. The TYPICAL waiting period for a divorce in the United States is

    A. one year or less   B. two years
    C. five years   D. three years

    6._____

7. The major cause of elder abuse is

    A. dependency of the elder person
    B. deviance of the abuser
    C. lack of attention to the problem
    D. all of the above

    7._____

97

8. According to prevalent thought on family roles and psychological distress/depression, the WIDEST *gender gap* in psychological distress levels is between _____ men and women.

   A. never married   B. divorced   C. widowed   D. married

9. The poor's response to marital breakdown has been

   A. annulment through the church
   B. bigamy
   C. separation without legal divorce
   D. to divorce quickly

10. Regarding the long-term impact of divorce on children, the *sleeper effect* is

    A. children of divorce on average finish fewer years of schooling
    B. sons of divorce are less likely to marry
    C. daughters of divorce are less likely to form committed, happy relationships in adulthood
    D. children of divorce are more likely to suffer depression during adulthood

11. Who of the following is MOST likely to commit acts of domestic violence?

    A. Employed men   B. Unemployed men
    C. Men with college degrees D. Men with graduate degrees

12. Under English law until the late 19th century, at the time of their marriage, husband and wife became

    A. the equivalent of a legal corporation
    B. two legal partners
    C. one legal person
    D. none of the above

13. A MAJOR negative outcome of divorce on children is

    A. a quarter of mothers practice *diminished parenting*
    B. a number of children are *overburdened* by their parents not being able to function
    C. feelings of abandonment and rejection years later
    D. all of the above

14. _____ likely to take time away from career to invest in family relationships.

    A. Wives are more
    B. Husbands are more
    C. Both wives and husbands are equally
    D. There is no definitive data

15. Men tend toward the _____ ideal in resolving the *second shift,* and women tend toward the _____ ideal.

    A. egalitarian; traditional   B. traditional; egalitarian
    C. traditional; economic   D. economic; sociological

16. Research shows that the average number of hours of housework married women do weekly has _____ since the 1970s.

    A. increased
    B. stayed the same
    C. decreased
    D. varied

17. Many corporations view their workers' families as a

    A. plus
    B. desirable connection to encourage
    C. big problem
    D. source of happiness for their workers

18. The two opposing theoretical perspectives explaining why husbands and wives differ in the amount of money they earn (on average) from jobs are

    A. New Home Economics and demographic change
    B. New Home Economics and the theory of patriarchy
    C. the theory of patriarchy and Marxist feminism
    D. Marxist feminism and demographic change

19. Which is the MOST tolerated form of family violence?

    A. Hitting children
    B. Hitting wives
    C. Hitting husbands
    D. Sexual abuse

20. Which of the following is the BEST description of the *medical model* of domestic violence?
    Domestic violence is seen

    A. as an illness and a source of injuries
    B. in the sense of relations of power and authority between men and women
    C. as a traditional way to preserve the family
    D. as arising from evolutionary processes

21. Parental *buffering* is

    A. parents protecting children from daily stressors
    B. one parent mediating between the children and the other parent
    C. reciprocal give-and-take between parents and children
    D. comforting children who are upset

22. Child maltreatment is _____ among single-parent families.

    A. less prevalent
    B. no more prevalent
    C. more prevalent
    D. there is no conclusive data on this subject

23. The BEST definition of *spillover* is

    A. being involved in more roles increases your psychological distress
    B. being involved in fewer roles increases your psychological distress
    C. stressors from one role have an impact on other aspects of life
    D. rewards from one role in life compensate for stressors in another

24. Men whose wives work generally earn _____ men whose wives do not work. 24._____

    A. less than
    B. more than
    C. the same as
    D. sometimes more, sometimes less than

25. _____ was the first jurisdiction anywhere in the Western world to eliminate fault grounds for divorce. 25._____

    A. New York   B. England
    C. Calgary (Canada) D. California

KEY (CORRECT ANSWERS)

1.	D	11.	B
2.	C	12.	C
3.	A	13.	D
4.	B	14.	A
5.	D	15.	B
6.	A	16.	C
7.	B	17.	C
8.	D	18.	B
9.	C	19.	A
10.	C	20.	A

21. B
22. C
23. C
24. A
25. D

TEST 2

DIRECTIONS: Each question or incomplete statement is followed by several suggested answers or completions. Select the one that BEST answers the question or completes the statement. *PRINT THE LETTER OF THE CORRECT ANSWER IN THE SPACE AT THE RIGHT.*

1. While the affectional bonds are normally very strong between a child and both parents, typically there is more _____ between mothers and children than between fathers and children.

    A. disciplinary strictness
    B. reciprocal give-and-take
    C. play-making
    D. authority

2. In the early 1990's, _____ percent of married women with pre-school-aged children were in the labor force.

    A. 50   B. 30   C. 40   D. 60

3. Reported cases of child abuse/neglect are defined as the total number of

    A. children abused or neglected at least once in a given year
    B. children reported under formal procedures to child protective agencies
    C. reports determined, after investigation, to be child abuse/neglect
    D. all of the above

4. Violence is more prevalent in _____ relationships than _____ relationships.

    A. marital; cohabiting
    B. marital; common law
    C. cohabiting; marital
    D. friendly; close

5. Studies done in the 1950s and 1960s showed that those women who seemed to have the most decision-making power in marriage were

    A. not employed
    B. independently wealthy
    C. employed
    D. none of the above

6. Mandatory reporting laws are a good solution to the problem of elder abuse.

    A. True   B. False

7. On average, husbands who work full-time work _____ wives who work full-time.

    A. fewer hours than
    B. the same hours as
    C. more hours than
    D. none of the above

8. The parental *alliance* involves

    A. agreeing on rules for children
    B. joint decision-making when appropriate
    C. relieving of child care duties
    D. all of the above

9. The *stalled revolution* refers to

    A. too many roles with conflicting demands
    B. family production of food and goods they need to survive
    C. the social system based on the domination of men over women
    D. the lack of adjustment by husbands to their wives' employment

10. Increasing income among poor families would eradicate child maltreatment. 10._____

    A. True   B. False

11. Husbands' greater economic power and authority in the contemporary United States is due in large part to 11._____

    A. the husbands' earnings and employment
    B. the tradition of patriarchy in the United States
    C. women's expectations that their husbands should have power
    D. their use of or threat of use of force

12. Divorced fathers _____ tend to be more involved in decisions about their children than divorced fathers 12._____

    A. with joint legal custody; without joint legal custody
    B. without joint legal custody; with joint legal custody
    C. without jobs; with jobs
    D. that are remarried; that are unmarried

13. Most companies provide some form of childcare assistance. 13._____

    A. True   B. False

14. Most wives receive alimony as part of their divorce settlement, at least for a limited time. 14._____

    A. True   B. False

15. A substantial proportion of elder abuse is _____ abuse. 15._____

    A. spouse   B. brother to sister
    C. sister to brother D. cousin

Questions 16-17.

DIRECTIONS: Questions 16 and 17 are to be answered on the basis of the following table.

PROFILE OF TIME ALLOCATION BY LIFE DOMAIN
AND SEX (BASE; MARRIED OR COHABITING ADULTS,
AGE 25-74, IN MACARTHUR NATIONAL STUDY OF MIDLIFE)

	HOME	
	MEN	WOMEN
Domestic chores per week	8.8 hrs	18.9 hrs
(range)	(0-60)	(0-60)
Contact with family not in HH at least once per day	29.4%	40.5%
Give advice /support	58.1 hrs /mo	85.5 hrs/mo
Give hands-on care % NONE Avg. helping	23.5% 25.7 hrs/mo	24.3% 36.1 hrs/mo

16. The table above is consistent with the view that

    A. men are more exposed to stressors than women
    B. women are more exposed to stressors than men
    C. men receive more social support than women
    D. women receive more social support than men

17. The number of hours the average married woman spends on weekly housework has _____ since the 1980's.

    A. stayed the same
    B. increased
    C. decreased
    D. increased greatly

Questions 18-19.

DIRECTIONS: Questions 18 and 19 are to be answered on the basis of the following figure.

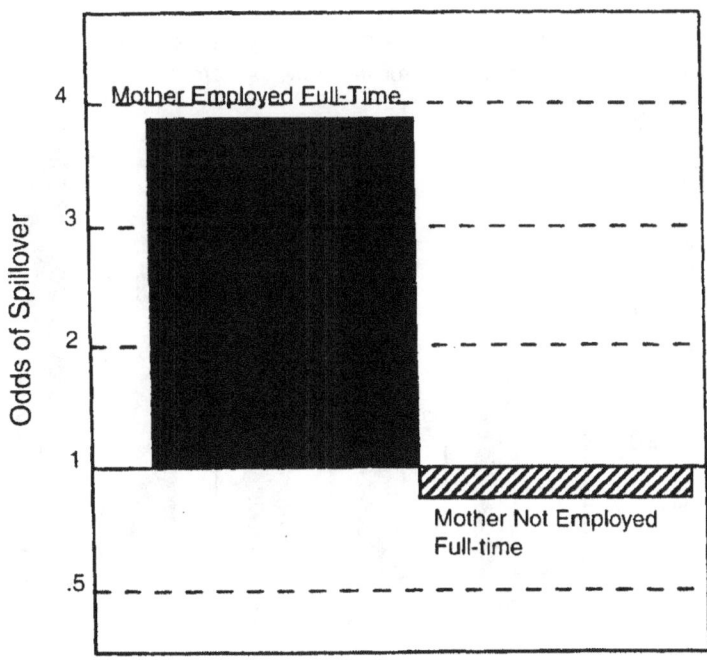

Odds Fathers' Tenson Spillover Given the Presence of other Daily Stresses

Father's Tension Spillover

18. The above figure shows the odds that a father's argument with someone will spillover (cause an argument later) into the home. The data shown in this figure imply that

    A. women may compensate for home stress by working longer hours
    B. men may compensate for home stress by working longer hours
    C. women experience more role overload than men
    D. men may benefit from being in more traditional marriages

19. The data in the above figure appear to be collected from

    A. the United States Census
    B. a daily stress study
    C. United Nations' studies
    D. school districts

Questions 20-21.

DIRECTIONS: Questions 20 and 21 are to be answered on the basis of the following figure.

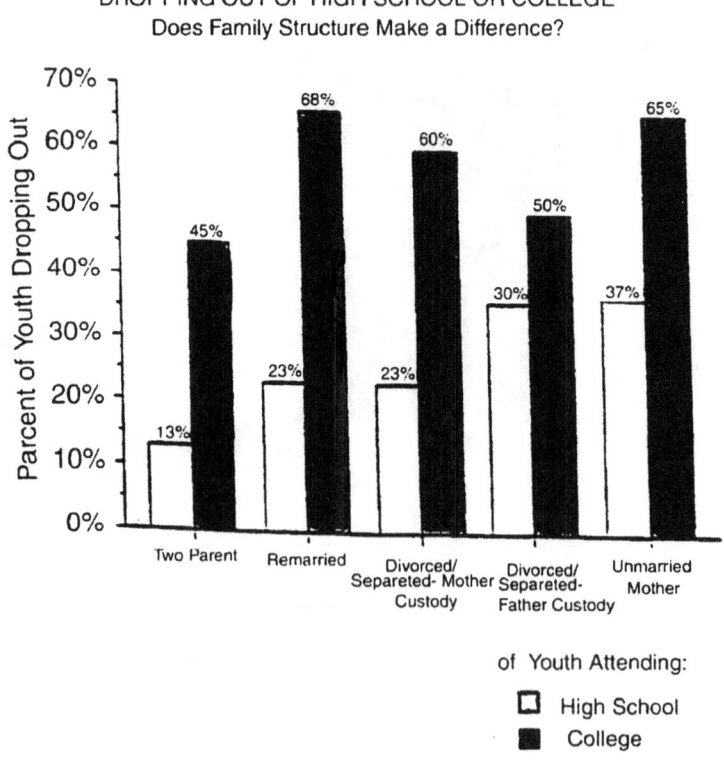

20. The data are from the National Longitudinal Survey of Youth, which oversamples low income families. In this study, the lowest high school dropout rate is for children of which of the following family types?

   A. Two parent
   B. Remarried parent
   C. Divorced parent, mother custody
   D. Unmarried (single) mother

20.____

21. What is the MOST likely reason why the college dropout rate is lower in two parent and divorced father custody families?

   A. Mothers have less control over children
   B. Fathers tend to have higher income than mothers
   C. Separated parents share equally
   D. Dropouts are unaffected by parental status

21.____

Questions 22-23.

DIRECTIONS: Questions 22 and 23 are to be answered on the basis of the following table.

MARRIED MOTHERS' LABOR FORCE ATTACHMENT

	1970	1980	1990
With children under age 18			
Percentage who worked last year	51	63	73
Percentage who worked full-time, year-round	16	23	34
With children under age 6			
Percentage who worked last year	44	58	68
Percentage who worked full-time, year-round	10	18	28
With children aged 6-17			
Percentage who worked last year	58	68	78
Percentage who worked full-time, year-round	23	29	40

22. Of the following groups, which *increased* its year round, full-time employment the MOST from 1970 to 1990?
Women with children

   A. under age 18
   B. under age 6
   C. age 6-17
   D. all of the above

22.____

23. Which increased its year-round, full-time employment the LEAST?
Women with children

   A. under age 18
   B. under age 6
   C. age 6-17
   D. all of the above

23.____

Questions 24-25.

DIRECTIONS: Questions 24 and 25 are to be answered on the basis of the following tables.

Mean responses to the question: Employed mothers can have just as good a relationship with their children as mothers who are not employed.

Class mean	MEN	WOMEN
	2.39	2.10
25-29	3.07	2.80 (NS)
30-39	3.10	2.47
40-49	3.05	2,20
50-59	3.35	2.60
60+	3.62	2.73

Mean responses to the question: To grow up emotionally healthy, children need to be raised in an intact family with <u>both</u> parents.

Class mean	MEN 2.94	WOMEN
		3.54
25-29	2.75	3.19 (NS)
30-39	2.59	3.32
40-49	2.79	3.67
50-59	2.31	3.18
60+	2.15	2.40

1. Response categories: Strongly Agree = 1; Strongly Disagree = 7
2. ALL differences are significant, unless noted otherwise.

The first row presents data from the class survey. Rows 2 through 6 present data from the national survey, grouped by age.

24. Taking both tables together, which statement is the MOST correct summary of the trends?

    A. Middle-aged respondents (early baby boomers) are more socially liberal than current college students.
    B. Women are more socially liberal than men (in general).
    C. Men are more socially liberal than women.
    D. None of the above

25. The pattern of gender and family-related attitudes in this table is most consistent with the issues presented in reading

    A. Mark Rank, FAMILY DYNAMICS
    B. Arlie Hochschild, JOEY'S PROBLEM: EVAN AND NANCY HOLT
    C. Betsy Morris, IS YOUR FAMILY WRECKING YOUR CAREER
    D. none of the above

KEY (CORRECT ANSWERS)

1.	B	11.	A
2.	D	12.	A
3.	B	13.	B
4.	C	14.	B
5.	C	15.	A
6.	B	16.	B
7.	C	17.	C
8.	D	18.	D
9.	D	19.	B
10.	B	20.	A

21. B
22. B
23. C
24. B
25. B

EXAMINATION SECTION
TEST 1

DIRECTIONS: Each question or incomplete statement is followed by several suggested answers or completions. Select the one that BEST answers the question or completes the statement. *PRINT THE LETTER OF THE CORRECT ANSWER IN THE SPACE AT THE RIGHT.*

1. In the United States, levels of lifetime childlessness were higher for women who reached their peak child-rearing years in the _____ than in any other generation of women in the 20th century.

    A. 1950s   B. 1930s   C. 1960s   D. 1990s

    1._____

2. According to sociological structural-functionalists, in the 1950s the two *natural* roles that provided the basis of a family were the _____ roles.

    A. breadwinner and homemaker
    B. husband and wife
    C. parental and childbearing
    D. conjugal and extended

    2._____

3. A census survey is distinguished from a social survey by

    A. collecting data in many different countries at once
    B. collecting data from two different samples
    C. collecting data from the entire population rather than a sample
    D. the use of experimental techniques

    3._____

4. The BEST term to describe the attitude of many Americans toward marriage and family in the 1990s is

    A. reluctance   B. ambivalence
    C. intolerance   D. confusion

    4._____

5. Marriage and personal welfare are related. Which of the following statements aptly describes the relationship?

    A. Negative marital relationships have little impact on overall mental health.
    B. Marriage has a positive emotional impact on both men and women.
    C. Friendship is a more important source of social support than marriage in our society.
    D. Single people, on average, report better well-being than married people.

    5._____

6. The central mechanism of the psychoanalytic approach to explaining male/female differences is _____, while that of the socialization approach is _____.

    A. unconscious; conscious
    B. internalization; learning
    C. learning; internalization
    D. activity; internalization

    6._____

7. The National Center for Health Statistics 7.____
   A. conducts the United States census
   B. collects and publishes death, birth, and other records
   C. is the largest survey organization in the world
   D. is a health intervention program run by the federal government

8. The United States had the highest _____ of any western country in 1990. 8.____
   A. age at marriage   B. women's employment rate
   C. divorce rate   D. illegitimacy ratio

9. Before the arrival of the Europeans, most Native Americans lived in 9.____
   A. small kinship groups
   B. extended families similar to the Europeans
   C. tribal societies based on lineages
   D. husband/wife conjugal units

10. In prior American eras, women attained their social class position through their husband's 10.____
    A. occupation   B. family name
    C. income   D. education, level

11. In the United States, a person's (or family's) power, prestige, and privilege are based for the most part on 11.____
    A. income, type of college degree, and family background
    B. family background, region of country, and income
    C. area of the country, education, and income
    D. income, occupation, and education

12. The *good-provider role* involves conflicts between norms of 12.____
    A. religion and work   B. family and religion
    C. family and work   D. all of the above

13. _____ support efforts are apt to be more common among family members than friends. 13.____
    A. Regulatory   B. Companionship
    C. Positive   D. Recreational

14. The emergence of a protected extended stage of childhood in the 1800s occurred as a result of 14.____
    A. legal restrictions on how children could be treated
    B. a growing population of elderly and therefore grandparents
    C. greater economic resources of parents
    D. the spread of schooling and a decline of child deaths

15. The median income of _____ families with children is higher than the median income of _____ families with children, which in turn is higher than _____ families with children. 15.____
    A. dual earner; single-mother; working husband-homemaker
    B. working husband-homemaker; dual earner; single mother

C. single-father; working husband-homemaker; single mother
D. dual earner; working husband-homemaker; single mother

16. Better psychological well-being may lead to better social support, rather than vice-versa. 16.____
Which of the following is the social scientific term describing this possibility?

    A. The social support hypothesis
    B. Social integration
    C. Social *selection*
    D. Individualism

17. Those MOST likely to view marriage as an economic necessity rather than a source of 17.____
self-fulfillment would be the

    A. poor   B. middle class
    C. upper class   D. women

18. The primary family unit in Western nations is the 18.____

    A. nuclear family living in the vicinity of extended kin
    B. small, household-based single parent living with his or her children
    C. small, household-based family of parents and children
    D. small, household-based family of two adults

19. The *New Theory of Home Economics* was developed by 19.____

    A. Gary Becker   B. David Popenoe
    C. William Julius Wilson   D. Robert Bellah

20. The age group of women with the highest rate of unmarried births is aged 20.____

    A. 15-19   B. 20-24   C. 25-29   D. 30-34

21. Which types of research methods are typically used in historical research on the demo- 21.____
graphic characteristics of families in the past?

    A. *Family reconstitution* techniques
    B. Experiments
    C. Social surveys
    D. Inductive logic combined with guesswork

22. Two new demands being made on *good providers* are 22.____

    A. intimacy and support
    B. household responsibility and intimacy
    C. career commitment and household responsibility
    D. support and career commitment

23. The primary importance of the poverty line in the United States is its 23.____

    A. estimate of the truly poor in the United States
    B. ability to be used in an analysis of changes over time in poverty rates in the United States
    C. use as a political issue by the different political parties
    D. use in determining benefits for Social Security and other government programs

24. An example of the *helping* function of social bonds is

    A. empathic listening
    B. shared recreation
    C. reminder of role obligations
    D. feedback about inappropriate behavior

25. If, as a researcher, you were studying the way families discipline their children, handle their disagreements, or share their affection, you would be focusing on

    A. public family
    B. extended family
    C. sexual abuse
    D. private family

KEY (CORRECT ANSWERS)

1.	B	11.	D
2.	C	12.	C
3.	B	13.	A
4.	B	14.	D
5.	B	15.	D
6.	B	16.	C
7.	B	17.	A
8.	C	18.	C
9.	C	19.	A
10.	A	20.	B

21. A
22. B
23. B
24. A
25. D

TEST 2

DIRECTIONS: Each question or incomplete statement is followed by several suggested answers or completions. Select the one that BEST answers the question or completes the statement. *PRINT THE LETTER OF THE CORRECT ANSWER IN THE SPACE AT THE RIGHT.*

1. As a result of changing functions and responsibilities, American families today have a(n) _____ public role and a(n) _____ private role than families in colonial America prior to 1776.

    A. broader; narrower
    B. less extensive; less extensive
    C. enlarging; enlarging
    D. narrower; broader

    1._____

2. An adult daughter taking care of her elderly parents shopping for them, taking them to doctors, cooking for them, and so on is an example of the daughter's producing a

    A. private good
    B. negative externality
    C. functionalism
    D. public good

    2._____

3. In inflation-corrected dollars, the value of welfare and food stamp benefits have _____ over the last two decades.

    A. increased
    B. stayed the same
    C. decreased
    D. decreased, then increased

    3._____

4. Our political order based on individualism, personal choice, and egalitarianism has shaped our current view that family relationships are

    A. permanent and binding
    B. voluntary and easily terminated
    C. biologically-determined
    D. socially deviant

    4._____

5. In the first half of the 20th century in the United States, it was a common practice for the husbands to be paid enough money (in theory) so that their wives did not need to work for pay. This division of labor was known as the _____ system.

    A. working wage
    B. provider wage
    C. nuclear family
    D. family wage

    5._____

6. _____ has/have increased the number of single mother families in the United States.

    A. The *marriage squeeze*
    B. Generous welfare benefits
    C. Community support
    D. Changing values

    6._____

7. Since the 1970s, American families whose income lies in the middle of the income distribution of all United States families kept up with the cost of living primarily by

    A. husbands taking second jobs
    B. reliance on parental *gifts* for purchases such as down-payments on houses
    C. changes in the tax structure favoring married couples
    D. wives taking jobs outside the home

    7._____

113

8. The pattern of behaviors associated with a position in society is 8.____

   A. the sex-gender system   B. socialization
   C. the social role   D. biosocial evolution

9. Poor people often actively construct extended kin networks by 9.____

   A. living with their extended kin
   B. moving away from their places of birth and birth homes
   C. exchanging goods/services with others in need
   D. none of the above

10. According to the traditional research definition of the family, which of the following would NOT be labeled a *family*? 10.____

    A. Two cohabiting adults of the same sex
    B. A widow and her minor children
    C. Married couple raising children
    D. A married couple in the *empty nest* stage

11. Those families who increased their share of the total income of all families in recent years are those in the _____ fifth of all United States families. 11.____

    A. bottom   B. top
    C. second lowest   D. third lowest

12. *Affective individualism* has produced in families over time 12.____

    A. less individual privacy
    B. more emphasis on collective goals in society
    C. increasing status for women
    D. increasing abuse of children

13. Social scientists cannot always use *experimental* techniques to study an important issue because 13.____

    A. experiments do not adequately control for biological differences
    B. experiments are more expensive than surveys
    C. sociologists prefer using census and vital statistics
    D. in some cases, experiments do not reproduce *real-life* conditions

14. According to studies of people's sense of obligation to kin, researchers have found that most people feel _____ kin. 14.____

    A. little obligation to most
    B. no obligation to most
    C. moderate to high levels of obligation to most
    D. some obligation, but only to the very closest

15. Contrary to what they were considered to be in colonial America, children today are considered to be 15.____

    A. economic assets   B. emotional burdens
    C. companions   D. household workers

16. The decline of marriage in the 1970s and 1980s was due to the abandonment of intimate male-female co-residential relationships.

    A. True
    B. False

17. _____ has/have increased the number of single mother families in the United States.

    A. The shortage of employed, marriageable men
    B. The culture of poverty
    C. Changing values regarding childrearing
    D. Very generous welfare benefits

18. To understand why the *illegitimacy ratio* has gone up so fast in recent years, you need to take into account the following trends:

    A. Declining age at marriage; nonmarital birth rates
    B. Changing values of men; declining age at marriage
    C. Marital birth rates; delays in marriage
    D. Changing values of men; welfare benefits

19. Cherlin, in his book PUBLIC AND PRIVATE FAMILIES, holds to the _____ perspective when discussing group differences.

    A. functionalist
    B. cultural variance
    C. Marxist conflict
    D. cultural deviance

20. If you were concerned with the way families discipline their children, handle their disagreements, or share their affection, you would be focusing on

    A. the public family
    B. sexually-based primary relationships
    C. the external family
    D. the private family

KEY (CORRECT ANSWERS)

1.	A	11.	B
2.	D	12.	C
3.	C	13.	D
4.	B	14.	C
5.	D	15.	C
6.	D	16.	B
7.	D	17.	A
8.	C	18.	C
9.	C	19.	B
10.	A	20.	D

EXAMINATION SECTION
TEST 1

DIRECTIONS: Each question or incomplete statement is followed by several suggested answers or completions. Select the one that BEST answers the question or completes the statement. *PRINT THE LETTER OF THE CORRECT ANSWER IN THE SPACE AT THE RIGHT.*

1. Which of the following is NOT a factor contributing to the current generation of Americans' later marriage rates? 1.____

    A. Increasing work skills and experience of young women
    B. Increasing cohabitation among American unmarried couples
    C. Earlier childbearing
    D. Decreasing earning power of young men

2. The foremost practitioner of functionalism in sociology was 2.____

    A. Robert Kingsley   B. Talcott Parsons
    C. David Popenoe   D. Andrew Cherlin

3. Historians such as Phillipe Aries and John Demos argue that the concept of childhood as a distinct stage of life was not recognized prior to the 1700s primarily because 3.____

    A. families were trying to survive
    B. families had so few children
    C. people did not understand the needs of children
    D. so many infants and toddlers died

4. One reason that extended families (as opposed to nuclear families) were never predominant in the United States is because 4.____

    A. life expectancy was short and made it improbable that grandparents lived with their children
    B. United States citizens have always had a tendency to reject the social norms of their ancestors
    C. affectionate and emotional ties to family were emphasized only recently in United States history
    D. all of the above

5. Which of the following was NOT a characteristic of the type of family that began to emerge in the United States between 1776 and 1830 – and continued well into the 20th century? 5.____

    A. Increase in the number of children per family
    B. Increasingly child-centered families
    C. Increasing autonomy for women within the family
    D. Increased role segregation whereby women took care of home and family

6. A study of the history of the family reveals that the _____ family is as old as human civilization, but that the _____ family emerged much more recently. 6.____

    A. extended; nuclear   B. public; private
    C. private; public   D. nuclear; extended

117

7. The foremost proponent in sociology of the psychoanalytic approach to gender differences is   7._____

   A. Lillian Rubin   B. Theda Skocpol
   C. Andrew Cherlin   D. Nancy Chodorow

8. In the earlier half of the 20th century in the United States, it was a common practice for the husbands to be paid enough money (in theory) so that their wives did not need to work for pay. This division of labor was known as the   8._____

   A. breadwinner-homemaker model
   B. working wage system
   C. family wage system
   D. provider wage system

9. The central mechanism of the socialization approach to explain male/female differences is _____, while that of the psychoanalytic approach is _____.   9._____

   A. internalization; learning
   B. unconscious; conscious
   C. activity; memorization
   D. learning; internalization

10. A number of professional sociologists seem puzzled more by the _____ of stereotyped gender roles than by their _____.   10._____

    A. vast variety; existence   B. persistence; existence
    C. existence; variability   D. existence; persistence

11. Increasingly in the United States, prosperity is a characteristic of _____ families.   11._____

    A. dual-earner, two-parent
    B. highly-educated, single-earner
    C. one or two earners in highly technical fields
    D. white, highly-educated, single-parent

12. The primary importance of the poverty line in the United States is its   12._____

    A. estimate of the truly poor in the United States
    B. ability to be used as an analysis of changes over time in poverty rates in the United States
    C. use as a political issue by the different political parties
    D. use in determining benefits for Social Security and other government programs

13. The most important difference among the lower-class, working-class, and middle-class families is   13._____

    A. the discipline of their children
    B. their educational differences
    C. the emotional support they receive from extended family
    D. the relative autonomy of the parent-child unit from other kin

14. There is _____ in modern American family relationships.   14._____

    A. inequality   B. dominance
    C. anomie   D. reciprocity

15. Better psychological well-being may lead to better social support, rather than vice-versa. Which of the following is the best example of this opinion?   15._____

    A. People who are physically attractive have few friends.
    B. Happy people have more stable social relationships.
    C. Distressed people rely on friends for support.
    D. Well-adjusted mothers raise more children.

16. Which of the following is the best definition of social integration?   16._____

    A. Cohesion between members of a social group
    B. Psychological well-being
    C. Emotional support from others
    D. Social control

17. Marriage and personal welfare are related. Which of the following statements is not correct?   17._____

    A. Marriage has a positive impact on men, but a negative impact on women.
    B. Married people report better well-being than non-married people.
    C. Marriage is a major source of social support in our society.
    D. The quality of the marital relationship is important to mental health.

18. In what respect is the modern American family an economic unit?   18._____

    A. Parents influencing your choice of college
    B. Provision of critical emotional support
    C. Nurturance of infants
    D. Members providing goods and services for each other

19. Which of the following was an important change in family relationships after 1500 in Western society?   19._____

    A. Growing preference for personal and family privacy
    B. Increasing sense of obligation to the community, rather than one's nuclear family
    C. Increasing rates of homosexuality
    D. Marital choice based on practical reasons

20. According to the lecture on social support and family relationships, _____ people report lower psychological distress than _____ people, on average.   20._____

    A. single; married   B. married; single
    C. female; male   D. cohabiting; married

21. The median income of _____ families with children is higher than the median income of _____ families with children, which in turn is higher than _____ families with children.   21._____

    A. dual earner; single-mother; working husband-homemaker
    B. working husband-homemaker; dual earner; single mother
    C. single father; working-husband homemaker; single mother
    D. dual earner; working husband-homemaker; single mother

22. _____ has/have increased the number of single mother families in the United States, according to Charles Murray.

   A. The shortage of marriageable men
   B. Women's increasing economic independence
   C. The women's movement
   D. Welfare benefits

23. _____ has/have increased the number of single mother families in the United States, according to William J. Wilson.

   A. The shortage of marriageable men
   B. Women's increasing economic independence
   C. The culture of poverty
   D. Welfare benefits

24. The Yale-Harvard study called attention to which of the following demographic/social phenomena?

   A. The culture of poverty
   B. The women's movement
   C. The marriage squeeze
   D. Welfare dependency

25. Since 1500, there has been an increase in _____ in the average Western family.

   A. physical punishment and discipline
   B. religious practice and involvement
   C. violations of privacy
   D. affect expressed

KEY (CORRECT ANSWERS)

1. C
2. B
3. D
4. A
5. A

6. B
7. D
8. C
9. D
10. B

11. A
12. B
13. D
14. D
15. B

16. A
17. A
18. D
19. A
20. B

21. D
22. D
23. A
24. C
25. D

TEST 2

DIRECTIONS: Each question or incomplete statement is followed by several suggested answers or completions. Select the one that BEST answers the question or completes the statement. *PRINT THE LETTER OF THE CORRECT ANSWER IN THE SPACE AT THE RIGHT.*

1. The differences by race and class in reported sexual activity have narrowed in recent years, primarily due to the fact that

    A. middle-class sexual patterns have become very similar to sexual patterns among the working class and the poor
    B. sexual patterns among the working class and the poor have become very similar to middle-class sexual patterns
    C. there are more ethnic minorities in the middle class now than in the past
    D. none of the above

    1._____

2. In studies about cohabiting couples, on a day-to-day basis, they behave more like _____ than _____.

    A. married persons; single persons
    B. single persons; married persons
    C. engaged couples; single persons
    D. none of the above

    2._____

3. The major reason reported by American adults for cohabiting rather than marrying their partners is

    A. cohabiting requires less of a personal commitment
    B. cohabiting requires less sexual faithfulness
    C. to make sure the partners are compatible before marriage
    D. cohabiting allows more independence

    3._____

4. In surveys conducted with young adults in the 1980s, women with greater economic resources including better educated employed were _____ likely to marry than women with fewer economic resources.

    A. less   B. equally   C. nearly as   D. more

    4._____

5. Until the 20th century, sexual relations in marriage were seen mostly as a means of

    A. personal fulfillment
    B. satisfying the partner's desires
    C. pleasure for self
    D. producing children

    5._____

6. Most of the sociological research findings on 1950s couples find that they _____ so that their marriages would stay together.

    A. stifled anger and avoided conflict
    B. sought professional help
    C. used parents and siblings as a sounding board for problems rather than each other
    D. all of the above

    6._____

7. The new love myths of the 1990s tend to devalue qualities such as

   A. commitment, trust, and permanence
   B. sexual fidelity
   C. fertility and childbearing
   D. family

8. Since the number of births and deaths among Native Americans did not change dramatically between 1970 and 1980, how would the 72% rise in their population during this time period be explained?

   A. There was finally a category of Native American to check on United States census forms
   B. There was a high immigration rate from South and Central America
   C. More people began to think of themselves as Native Americans and reported themselves to the United States census as that
   D. None of the above

9. Sociologists study racial-ethnic variations in family patterns because

   A. different kinds of families can have different effects on individuals
   B. the variations have always been studies
   C. we as a society know very little about families other than our own
   D. none of the above

10. African-American women and men seem to weigh economic considerations more heavily than white men and women in deciding when to marry. This is most likely due to the fact that

    A. they are more materialistic
    B. they hold to the more traditional breadwinner-home-maker model of family life
    C. their economic situation in our society is more precarious
    D. they are less educated, on average

11. The program of financial assistance to low-income single-parent families that had become commonly known as *welfare* was

    A. the Job Training Program (JTP)
    B. Aid to Families With Dependent Children (AFDC)
    C. the Work Incentive Program (WIN)
    D. Social Security Supplemental Income (SSSI)

12. The most dramatic change in the assistance available to United States citizens through federally-funded and assisted welfare programs has centered upon changing AFDC recipients from _____ into _____.

    A. wage earners; homemakers
    B. young teenagers; mature mothers
    C. widowed mothers; divorcees
    D. homemakers; wage earners

13. The _____ is NOT a *mediating* structure.

    A. church
    B. neighborhood
    C. family
    D. government

14. Those considered to be the most nondeserving poor in our country are

    A. unwed mothers
    B. children
    C. unemployed able-bodied men
    D. widows

15. The current view among many Americans, shared by both liberals and conservatives, laypeople and politicians, is that persistent poverty is not just a problem of income but also of

    A. laziness
    B. ignorance
    C. prolonged dependence on cash assistance
    D. discrimination against women and racism

16. An example of an *explicit* family policy is

    A. the United States federal mortgage tax credit
    B. Sweden's pro-birth policies
    C. the G.I. Bill (1945)
    D. Medicare

17. An example of a *universal* family-related policy is

    A. Medicaid
    B. Aid to Families With Dependent Children
    C. low-income housing
    D. none of the above

18. The nonmarital birth ratio, i.e., the proportion of all births that occur to unmarried women, has _____ for teenagers in the United States in the 1990s.

    A. decreased
    B. stabilized
    C. remained unchanged
    D. increased

19. People with college educations lead the trend toward increased cohabitation.

    A. True
    B. False

20. On average, cohabitation relationships in the United States last _____ than marriages.

    A. a shorter time
    B. about the same time
    C. a longer time
    D. there is no comparative data collected on this

KEY (CORRECT ANSWERS)

1.	A	11.	B
2.	B	12.	D
3.	C	13.	D
4.	D	14.	C
5.	D	15.	C
6.	A	16.	B
7.	A	17.	D
8.	C	18.	D
9.	A	19.	B
10.	C	20.	A

EXAMINATION SECTION
TEST 1

DIRECTIONS: Each question or incomplete statement is followed by several suggested answers or completions. Select the one that BEST answers the question or completes the statement. *PRINT THE LETTER OF THE CORRECT ANSWER IN THE SPACE AT THE RIGHT.*

1. A shift in the social position of large numbers of people due to changes in the society is termed _____ mobility. 1._____

    A. social change
    B. structural social
    C. aggregate
    D. intergenerational

2. The normative elements of a social relationship are organized into 2._____

    A. groups   B. culture   C. folkways   D. statuses

3. A temporary cluster of individuals who may or may not interact is referred to as a 3._____

    A. crowd   B. group   C. category   D. population

4. A person who engages in social learning about universities because he wants to become a professor someday is engaging in 4._____

    A. directed learning
    B. socialization
    C. status learning
    D. anticipatory socialization

5. The basic pattern of social organization that arose during the industrial revolution was 5._____

    A. rational coordination
    B. contract
    C. status
    D. fealty

6. _____ is the path to understanding the world based on science. 6._____

    A. Theologism
    B. Determinism
    C. Positivism
    D. Phenomenology

7. Weapons are an example of 7._____

    A. a cultural anachronism
    B. material culture
    C. a latent culture
    D. nonmaterial culture

8. Colleges bring young people together and thus serve as a form of *marriage market*. This is an example of 8._____

    A. dysfunction
    B. functional prerequisite
    C. manifest function
    D. latent function

9. Suppose a Yanomamo moved to the United States and immediately moved into a college dormitory. As an initial reaction, he would experience

   A. culture shock
   B. anomie
   C. acculturation
   D. primary socialization

10. Movement from one to another equivalent status is called _____ mobility.

    A. horizontal
    B. static
    C. vertical
    D. equivalent

11. To initiate the most effective resocialization of a whole country, the socialization agent upon which attention should be focused is

    A. the family
    B. the schools
    C. peer groups
    D. the mass media

12. What would a *structural-functionalist* say about the role of education in social placement?

    A. Schooling evens out differences in students' aptitudes and abilities.
    B. Schools use social background instead of achievement to evaluate performance.
    C. Schooling enhances meritocracy.
    D. Formal education has had little impact on social mobility.

13. Which of the following statements is TRUE about social stratification?

    A. Social stratification is a characteristic of society.
    B. Social stratification is universal and invariant.
    C. There is little persistence of social positions across generations.
    D. Social stratification is supported by economics, not by patterns of belief.

14. What is the term for a social position that is received at birth or involuntarily assumed later in the life course?

    A. Role
    B. Master status
    C. Achieved status
    D. Ascribed status

15. What does social-conflict analysis say about educational tracking? It

    A. is the only strategy in a culturally diverse society
    B. is a necessary evil that enhances individual achievement
    C. affects a student's performance, but not his or her self-concept
    D. perpetuates privilege

16. The process of change that results from a society's gaining new information, particularly technology, is called

    A. sociocultural evolution
    B. cultural diffusion
    C. cultural transfer
    D. cultural innovation

17. The theoretical paradigm in sociology that assumes society is a complex system whose parts work together to promote stability is the _____ paradigm.

    A. structural-functional
    B. social-conflict
    C. symbolic-interaction
    D. social organization

18. What is the lifelong process of social experience by which individuals develop human potential and learn the patterns of their culture?

    A. Socialization
    B. Personality
    C. Human nature
    D. Behaviorism

19. Members of all societies rely on _____ to make sense out of everyday situations.

    A. social structure
    B. their status set
    C. their role set
    D. social substructure

20. The term for recognized social position that an individual occupies is

    A. prestige
    B. status
    C. social power
    D. occupation

21. The Global Society vignette on gestures shows that

    A. symbols carry universal meanings
    B. symbols carry that same meaning across cultures
    C. the meaning of symbols is culturally dependent
    D. symbolizing in other's cultures is always dangerous

22. Regarding research on rhesus monkeys, a reasonable conclusion would be that

    A. there is no comparison between monkeys and humans
    B. monkeys and humans *bounce back* from long-term isolation
    C. long-term social isolation will lead to permanent developmental damage in both species
    D. social isolation affects monkeys more than humans

23. Intragenerational mobility can be

    A. horizontal mobility
    B. vertical mobility
    C. both of the above
    D. neither of the above

24. _____ societies are characterized by technology that supports an information-based economy.

    A. Horticultural
    B. Agrarian
    C. Industrial
    D. Postindustrial

25. Systems of social stratification based on individual achievement are referred to as

    A. social differentiation
    B. caste systems
    C. class systems
    D. mobility systems

4 (#1)

KEY (CORRECT ANSWERS)

1. B
2. D
3. A
4. D
5. B

6. C
7. B
8. D
9. A
10. A

11. A/D
12. C
13. A
14. D
15. D

16. A
17. A
18. A
19. A
20. B

21. C
22. C
23. C
24. D
25. C

———

TEST 2

DIRECTIONS: Each question or incomplete statement is followed by several suggested answers or completions. Select the one that BEST answers the question or completes the statement. *PRINT THE LETTER OF THE CORRECT ANSWER IN THE SPACE AT THE RIGHT.*

1. The factor that accounts for the aging of our society is

    A. greater personal mobility
    B. the Baby Boom and greater personal mobility
    C. lower birth rates and greater longevity
    D. higher mortality and the Baby Boom

    1.____

2. The term for the traits that males and females, guided by their culture, incorporate into their personalities is

    A. gender
    B. gender identity
    C. gender orientation
    D. gender role

    2.____

3. The majority of immigrants to the United States comes from

    A. Asia
    B. Latin America
    C. Europe
    D. A and B

    3.____

4. *Pink-collar* work refers to what type of work?

    A. Clerical
    B. Service
    C. Interior decorators
    D. Professional

    4.____

5. Which of the following types of marriage is seen as *conventional*?

    A. Only the husband is employed, and the wife does the housework and child rearing.
    B. Both spouses work, and the wife does the housework and child rearing.
    C. Both spouses work and share household and child rearing responsibilities.
    D. Both spouses work, and the husband does the housework and child rearing.

    5.____

6. How many births per woman is the replacement level of fertility?

    A. 2.1   B. 1.0   C. 3.0   D. 1.9

    6.____

7. The unequal distribution of wealth, power, and privilege between the two sexes is called

    A. gender division of labor
    B. gender stratification
    C. gender discrimination
    D. sexist stratification

    7.____

8. What is TRUE about industrialization?

    A. Children become a greater asset.
    B. Family size increases.
    C. Children cost less.
    D. Children become financial liabilities.

    8.____

9. The _____ is the sociological term for the sharp drop in the United States birthrate after 1965.

   A. Baby Boom
   B. Baby Bust
   C. Baby Reversal
   D. Echo of the Baby Boom

10. The fastest growing age group in the United States population today is

    A. oldest-old (85+)
    B. infants (0-1)
    C. young-old (65-84)
    D. reproductive ages (15-44)

11. What is the term for a graphic representation of the age and sex of a population?

    A. Sex pyramid
    B. Age-sex pyramid
    C. Sex ratio
    D. Age-gender triangle

12. If you mine gold for a living, you are in the _____ production sector.

    A. primary   B. secondary   C. tertiary   D. septiary

13. What is the term for a category composed of people who share biologically transmitted traits that are deemed socially significant?

    A. Minority   B. Ethnicity   C. Race   D. Stereotype

14. Union leaders are concerned about the waning power of unions over the last decade. What strategy might be used to expand union membership?

    A. Reduce industrial sector jobs
    B. Re-focus recruitment efforts on newly created industrial jobs
    C. Create new international unions
    D. Reduce worker anxiety over job security

15. Which of the following was NOT a change brought about by the industrial revolution?

    A. The spread of factories
    B. Manufacturing and mass production
    C. Cottage industry
    D. Wage labor

16. The future size of the United States population is determined by

    A. natural increase (births-deaths)
    B. immigration
    C. both A and B
    D. none of the above

17. The two major characteristics of minorities are

    A. genetic background and lifestyle
    B. racial background and lifestyle
    C. vulnerability and subordination
    D. distinctive identity and subordination

18. What is the term for the significance a society attaches to biological categories of female and male?

    A. Primary sex characteristics
    B. Secondary sex characteristics
    C. Sexual orientation
    D. Gender

19. The myth of _____ is NOT one of the myths of old age identified by authorities in the field.

    A. unproductivity
    B. disengagement
    C. wealth
    D. serenity

20. A legally sanctioned relationship involving economic cooperation as well as normative sexual activity and childbearing is termed

    A. marriage
    B. a family unit
    C. kinship
    D. cohabitation

21. Multiculturalists find fault with the assimilation model because they believe it

    A. tends to paint minorities as the problem by defining them as the ones who must change
    B. tends to paint the majority as the group in need of change
    C. would lead to a true *melting pot*
    D. would lead to even more segregation

22. What is NOT a likely future trend for the United States family?

    A. Economic changes will cease to affect marriage and the family.
    B. Family life will become even more variable.
    C. More children will be growing up with weaker ties to fathers.
    D. The importance of new reproductive technology will increase.

23. The logic of endogamy

    A. helps to forge useful alliances and promotes cultural diffusion
    B. helps to keep inherited kinship traits consistent within the kinship group
    C. is economically beneficial
    D. allows those of similar social position to pass along their standing to offspring, thereby maintaining traditional social patterns

24. Which labor market includes occupations that provide extensive benefits to workers?

    A. Primary
    B. Secondary
    C. Unionized
    D. Professions

25. What is the term for the number of live births in a given year for every thousand people in a population?

    A. Fertility
    B. Birth rate
    C. Crude birth rate
    D. Fecundity

KEY (CORRECT ANSWERS)

1.	C	11.	B
2.	B	12.	A
3.	D	13.	C
4.	A	14.	C
5.	A	15.	C
6.	A	16.	C
7.	B	17.	D
8.	D	18.	D
9.	B	19.	C
10.	A	20.	A

21. A
22. A
23. D
24. A
25. C

EXAMINATION SECTION
TEST 1

DIRECTIONS: Each question or incomplete statement is followed by several suggested answers or completions. Select the one that BEST answers the question or completes the statement. *PRINT THE LETTER OF THE CORRECT ANSWER IN THE SPACE AT THE RIGHT.*

1. Perhaps the chief reason for the survival of many practices, customs, beliefs, and technological methods is

   A. stubbornness on the part of most people who say, *"It was good enough for grandpappy, and it's good enough for me"*
   B. pride
   C. selfishness
   D. that people are used to them
   E. the fear of *retribution from change*

   1.____

2. Euthenics is the study of the methods of improving the quality of the population through

   A. improving the understanding of basic social needs
   B. applying knowledge of hereditary differences in reproduction
   C. elaborating the Aryan design and transferring its components to give a wider view of the benefits of endogamy
   D. the revival of euthanasia
   E. testing the effects of crossbreeding

   2.____

3. A human individual who has been reared apart from human society and, hence, has not been socialized would be called a_____ man.

   A. maturational   B. marginal   C. feral
   D. symbiosistic   E. Transylvanian

   3.____

4. The idea of social planning has challenged man for centuries. Recently, under the influence of the social evolutionists, the idea was

   A. given support in all areas except in regard to proposals involving the aged
   B. denounced as representing a harmful and foolish tampering with the basic natural laws of society
   C. given unanimous approval
   D. denounced as anarchistic
   E. vituperated as communist inspired

   4.____

5. In addition to habit, the fear of_____ often lies behind resistance to innovation.

   A. the unknown   B. retribution   C. retaliation
   D. God   E. disruption

   5.____

6. Many frequency distributions, when plotted, form a bell-shaped curve. The result is a

   A. curved adano   B. median curve   C. circular arc
   D. normal curve   E. parti-circle

   6.____

7. Among the basic factors conducive to social change, _____ is of primary importance.   7.____

   A. the education of the masses
   B. religious training
   C. the demise of all secondary groups
   D. social accumulation
   E. a heterogeneous population

8. Social disorganization, which is a result of rapid and uncoordinated change, usually   8.____

   A. can be discerned only by an expert sociologist
   B. inhibits further change
   C. leads to further change
   D. can be suppressed by military force
   E. produces the kind of resentments which lead to complete social stagnation

9. Many, perhaps most, sociologists agree that values, when they become organized into generalized ideologies,   9.____

   A. are the blocks over which new thoughts, new ideas, and inspired reasoning stumble
   B. completely inhibit social change
   C. like other factors in social change, are the result of still other changes, and they alone are the only pillars on which the advancement of the social process may stand
   D. usually degenerate into unquestioned dogma
   E. have an important influence on individual and collective behavior, hence, on social processes

10. Invention and diffusion are basic social processes since they   10.____

    A. both meddle in things that should be left alone
    B. are the only ways by which new elements may be introduced into a society's culture
    C. exist only in the minds of opportunists
    D. both stem from the basic need in humanity to change things and to leave humanity's mark on nature
    E. are largely a matter of chance

11. It has long been recognized that the age-old distinction between static and dynamic societies is   11.____

    A. more apparent than real
    B. non-existent since there is no such thing as a *dynamic* society
    C. one of degree rather than of kind
    D. ridiculous to one who possesses a grain of sense
    E. non-existent since there is no such thing as a *static* society

12. A teacher who is constantly warning students about possible punishments or who frequently sends them to the *office* is

    A. a victim of suggestive social control
    B. using internal social control methods
    C. obviously sexually maladjusted
    D. probably a sado-masochist
    E. relying mainly on regulative control

13. Informal social control is exemplified in the functions of the mores in controlling behavior, especially

    A. in complex societies with greater division of labor
    B. in primitive or atavistic societies
    C. among societies which place greater importance on sub-groups with different sets of mores
    D. in connection with the state
    E. in militaristic or totalitarian societies

14. *Big-business* organizations of houses of ill repute, under the control of single persons or small groups of persons, have

    A. declined as a result of their failure to improve their recruitment techniques
    B. apparently declined as a result of local governmental suppression
    C. declined as a result of the advancing age of the prostitutes in such houses
    D. been taken over by more responsible business firms
    E. disappeared as a result of the decline in public's need for their services

15. Much of the problem of gambling is attributable to

    A. anti-gambling legislation
    B. the fact that anti-gambling legislation is not supported by the mores of large groups of people
    C. the greed of the average person
    D. the American pioneer spirit
    E. the difficulty of prosecuting known gamblers as a result of recent anti-wiretap legislation

16. Drug addiction and alcoholism have been accounted for in many different ways. They have in common:

    A. The ability to produce an euphoric state of mind, which is beneficial to those suffering from mental stress and mental disorders
    B. The tendency for the addiction to become cumulative
    C. A great clarity of vision and thinking
    D. Pleasant dreams from which one never awakes
    E. The fact that they both produce the same kind of behavior pattern

17. Where drug addiction and alcoholism are concerned, stern repressive measures

    A. have never been attempted
    B. have proved to be the only effective way in which to deal with these problems
    C. have alleviated the problems in most states
    D. have largely been abandoned
    E. seem to be ineffective

18. In recent decades, alcoholics and drug addicts have come to be regarded as _____ people.

    A. depraved   B. deprived   C. ill
    D. sinful   E. welfare

19. One of the persistent problems of modern society

    A. is centered around the apathetic attitude demonstrated by most people toward the plight of the underprivileged and the so-called *common man* in society
    B. is its inability to cope as yet with the numerous difficulties involved in the forming of any new sociological group
    C. is that of providing facilities which will meet the need for wholesome and adequate recreational activities
    D. is the question of adequate prison accommodations
    E. will be overcome without doubt during this decade as a result of technological advances

20. Transference of many recreational activities to commercial auspices often

    A. affects individuals rather than groups
    B. places the ego-oriented motive first
    C. results in a most degrading situation for the social worker
    D. leads to the complete destruction of the honest man's efforts towards rehabilitation
    E. puts the profit motive first

21. In general, rural areas, with regard to educational facilities,

    A. are making energetic attempts to approach urban standards
    B. have always been superior to urban areas
    C. are, every day, in every way, getting better and better as compared to the crowded cities
    D. lag behind urban areas
    E. have not improved since 1900

22. The premise that a person should be able to advance as far as his ability and his achievement will take him

    A. is sound, provided that the world rids itself of all the sensitive and shy people who cannot find it within themselves to conform to the breakneck and often cut-throat process of *rising to the top*
    B. recalls the saying, *"If he can't go forward, then he must be backward"*
    C. is quickly losing ground as the liberals become more and more powerful
    D. is actually a communistic idea and has its source in many of the writings of Karl Marx
    E. is belied by gross inequalities in educational opportunity

23. _____ has been found to be more prevalent in urban than in rural areas.

    Friendship   Heterosexuality   Atrophy
    Suicide   Bestialism

24. The constant movement of people presents many problems. One of the problems of families who migrate as units is:

    A. acute homesickness, which is the main reason for marital breakups and separations of migrating families who return home
    B. invariably insufficient preparation for the long road ahead
    C. the high rate of illiteracy that often is found among migrating families
    D. cutting loose from old ties and adjusting to a new social environment
    E. finding socially-acceptable jobs for themselves and their children

25. The struggle between nations, both in war and in peace, essentially involves the

    A. inner struggle of man himself regarding *right* and *wrong*
    B. egotistic need in man to belong to a group that is superior
    C. *power-mania* which is, in most instances, less prevalent today than in past decades
    D. deep-rooted, and often unconscious, desire in man to join or relate spiritually with his fellow man
    E. attempt to improve or defend the economic position of the nations involved

26. The dominant ideologies in the first half of the twentieth century were democracy, fascism, and communism.
Sociologists contend that all ideologies

    A. are beliefs which describe the nature of man and his connections with God
    B. contain verifiable statements concerning human relationships
    C. *are* personified in the youth who plunges into the icy waters of life in search of sunken treasure, only to find "....*cockles and mussels alive, alive, O!*"
    D. contain inconsistencies and irrational elements, none of which is verifiable
    E. seem to attract the psychologically retarded person, e.g., the person who would send out an army of paper dolls to fight a forest fire

27. A phenomenon intimately associated with warfare in recent centuries is

    A. communism   B. atheism   C. nationalism
    D. barbarism   E. patriotism

28. War is a problem that differs from other social problems in that

    A. man cannot exist without the basic need for excitement and violence that war provides
    B. it is too closely connected to the laws of nature for society to control
    C. it will quite possibly outlive society itself
    D. it cannot be resolved within any one society
    E. it can be justified and tolerated by the individual and does not need the support of the masses

29. Where unemployment is high, members of the majority group will

   A. most often band together in search of a solution to this problem that will benefit mankind as a whole
   B. seek new recruits for their group, thus making themselves the strongest pressure group through sheer weight of numbers
   C. favor discrimination in order to hold the few scarce jobs
   D. no doubt be singled out for the blame
   E. panic and, if not subdued quickly, become a dangerous and uncontrollable *mob*

30. It has been pointed out that many persons are imprisoned unnecessarily, that they are fit to return to society upon conviction, and that the only justification for imprisoning them is

   A. to prevent them from doing harm to themselves
   B. revenge
   C. that an adequate period of parole supervision is required
   D. to see that mercy is tempered by justice
   E. to teach them a trade

31. When the reform school alumnus or the released prisoner drifts back into illegal activities, it is usually because

   A. rehabilitation has been rejected by him
   B. crime and the excitement often accompanying danger are in his blood
   C. he takes great pride in his chosen profession
   D. he is vocationally ill-prepared for some other profession than crime
   E. he is tempted more by the ability to *take* rather than *make* money

32. _____ crime involves a complex division of labor, varying with the type of illegal activity, but often interrelated under the hegemony of a small combination of leaders at the top.

   A. Specialized   B. Juvenile   C. Orthodox
   D. Systematic   E. Urban

33. Which of the following statements is an example of overgeneralization in use among those who attribute crime to a single cause?

   A. The family that prays together, stays together.
   B. I knew he wouldn't amount to anything.
   C. All work and no play makes Jack a dull boy.
   D. The parents are to blame.
   E. Give 'em one inch and they'll want six.

34. The *things* which are done in response to an earthquake or flood

   A. are not social problems but, rather, problems of the individual
   B. are usually done by those who have been deprived of religious counseling
   C. may become a social problem
   D. are not of importance to society itself
   E. will only serve to bring about more earthquakes and floods

35. One of the CHIEF religious problems in the U.S. is 35.____

    A. the importation of too many different religions from other countries
    B. inadequate facilities
    C. that there are more churches built than are needed or can be financially supported
    D. the guilt feeling which is imposed upon those who do not attend church by those who do
    E. inadequate membership in approved religious groups

36. Of the following fields, which one is considered MOST closely related to religious feeling? 36.____

    A. Science   B. Politics   C. Art
    D. History   E. Anthropology

37. The multiplicity of religious bodies is, to a great extent, a product of 37.____

    A. rebellion in what is now the Protestant Church, against all imposed doctrines
    B. chaotic disagreement among religious groups
    C. lack of foresight
    D. successive splits within Christianity resulting from the Protestant Reformation
    E. the trend toward Unitarianism

38. In many communities,_____ function as symbols of social class. 38.____

    A. banks   B. recreation halls   C. churches
    D. museums   E. parks

39. Among the economic trends in the United States, perhaps the MOST striking long-term trend is that toward 39.____

    A. organized labor   B. equal economic opportunities
    C. long-term speculation   D. large-scale production
    E. special interest groups

40. Human ecology MOST frequently involves a relationship of mutual advantage. This is called 40.____

    A. symbolic logic   B. *simpatico* relations
    C. celibacy   D. symbiosis
    E. associationism

KEY (CORRECT ANSWERS)

1.	D	11.	C	21.	D	31.	D
2.	B	12.	E	22.	E	32.	D
3.	C	13.	B	23.	D	33.	D
4.	B	14.	B	24.	D	34.	C
5.	E	15.	B	25.	E	35.	C
6.	D	16.	B	26.	D	36.	C
7.	D	17.	E	27.	C	37.	D
8.	C	18.	C	28.	D	38.	C
9.	E	19.	C	29.	C	39.	D
10.	B	20.	E	30.	B	40.	D

TEST 2

DIRECTIONS: Each question or incomplete statement is followed by several suggested answers or completions. Select the one that BEST answers the question or completes the statement. *PRINT THE LETTER OF THE CORRECT ANSWER IN THE SPACE AT THE RIGHT.*

1. In the United States, the decrease in the death rate during the last 300 years   1.____

    A. is, to sociologists, a great cause for alarm
    B. will eventually result in catastrophe due to overpopulation
    C. was matched by a long-range decrease in the birth rate
    D. affected many more females than males
    E. proves that Americans are healthier than any other group

2. Recent, long-range population forecasts for the United States have predicted that the population   2.____

    A. will continue to increase at an alarming rate
    B. is dangerously in need of replenishment
    C. will be stable or declining
    D. will exceed that of Asia within the next century
    E. will start to decrease at an alarming rate

3. Social epidemics involve social contagion throughout a huge mass of people. They are MAINLY supported by   3.____

    A. prejudice   B. intellectual arguments
    C. public opinion polls   D. emotional responses
    E. market research

4. If John Smith lived in the family home or locality of his wife, he would be   4.____

    A. involved in role conflict
    B. under the influence of maternal rule
    C. subject to psychological emasculation
    D. living in a matrilocal residence
    E. a member of a polyandric society

5. When marriage takes place in one's own social group, it is termed   5.____

    A. culture diffusion   B. dispersion of caste
    C. exogamy   D. endogamy
    E. incest

6. Anthropology resembles, particularly, sociology in that   6.____

    A. both are historical studies
    B. they are both inextricably linked with the study of political theory
    C. both depend for their validity upon the study of religious thought
    D. it is more concerned with the generally applicable rather than the unique
    E. it is more concerned with the unique than with the generally applicable

7. Of mutual interest to anthropologists and sociologists is the

   A. relationship between cultural tradition and religion
   B. study of ancient cultural patterns
   C. relationship between unemployment and social discontent
   D. relationship between culture and personality
   E. study of prehistoric animals and man

8. A pattern of behavior related to a social position is a

   A. habit   B. sociogram   C. status
   D. more   E. role

9. Rational coordination is

   A. the ability to move about within the limits of rational society
   B. the ability to coordinate and bring together two opposing units
   C. specialized, impersonal management of an organization
   D. mind over matter
   E. intellectual control over simple motor activity

10. According to one noted sociologist, _____ are *nurseries of human* nature.

    A. colleges   B. military schools   C. fraternities
    D. social groups   E. primary groups

11. Marriage of several males to several females is called Group Marriage. An approximation of this is found in the Marquesas, a Pacific Island tribe. Group Marriage, in its pure form,

    A. is found only among the most primitive peoples
    B. exists in certain areas of Brazil and Paraguay
    C. is regarded as a necessary evil in the Marquesas
    D. is unknown
    E. was found to exist only in a small area of New Guinea

12. Human kinship to the great apes is close, and today scientists are learning that

    A. communication with apes may someday be possible
    B. apes have a rather complex language
    C. man and ape can probably mate successfully
    D. apes have a complex, though primitive, social system
    E. this man-ape parallel carries over to group behavior as well

13. In relation to the study of culture, anthropological research reveals this essential fact:

    A. Cultural evolution always proceeds from the simple to the complex
    B. Culture is hereditary in some societies
    C. Wherever common cultural features dominate a complex society, sub-cultures are not present
    D. Culture is diffused from society to society in a continual process
    E. Culture is not influenced by biological factors

14. Anthropology rejects the attitude known as ethnocentrism because it   14.____

    A. encourages disbelief in one's own culture
    B. inhibits cultural growth
    C. encourages war and aggression
    D. fosters unwarranted territorial expansion
    E. gives rise to psychoneuroses

15. If one believes in the superiority of his own culture, he   15.____

    A. is snob-cultural, according to Cooley
    B. is euthenics-oriented
    C. is an abysmal ignoramus who doesn't deserve a culture at all
    D. is simply subscribing to the norms and mores of his society
    E. cannot make an objective approach to the study of society

16. Another name for human geography is   16.____

    A. etiology   B. anthropogeography   C. ethnography
    D. geology   E. graphology

17. Although the subject matter of sociology and anthropology overlaps to a great extent,   17.____
    there are several valid differences.
    One of these is:

    A. Anthropology is the older of the two disciplines
    B. Sociology is more concerned with the study of simple societies
    C. Anthropology is more concerned with the literate peoples of the world
    D. Anthropology deals more with habitat than with inhabitants
    E. Sociology is more concerned with the study of complex societies

18. Social psychology is claimed by both psychology and sociology AND is   18.____

    A. often regarded as a mere upstart by serious scientists
    B. beyond dispute, no relation of either
    C. sometimes said to belong to neither
    D. often thought of as a pseudo-science
    E. an exact science

19. Aside from being important as a huge strategic area of land, China is also noteworthy   19.____
    because

    A. of what new civilizations can learn from its antiquity
    B. it is a case study in the effect of Western industrialization and culture traits upon a
       peasant society
    C. it houses the largest chest of cultural treasure in the world
    D. its preparation of food is superior to all other methods
    E. its government is Communist and efficient

20. One of the major changes already under way in China before World War II was the

    A. complete passing of *Traditional China*
    B. formation of a political party by the Chinese gentry
    C. rise of a small, but powerful, industrial group
    D. destruction of all treaty ports for the benefit of Western traders
    E. start of an anti-Buddhist movement, which almost succeeded in destroying this religious belief among the peasants

21. A true normal curve has certain precise mathematical characteristics. For instance,

    A. the measurements of human variation show the greatest number of cases toward the extreme center of distribution
    B. a perfect positive is expressed by +1.00, a perfect negative by +.0
    C. the mean, median, and mode coincide
    D. it must coincide with the significance range
    E. it is skewed to the right or to the left, but never toward the center

22. _____ is a technique which involves a deliberate attempt by the investigator to influence the behavior he is studying.

    A. Entrapment
    B. Participant-observer confrontation
    C. Field study
    D. Action research
    E. Relationship experimentation

23. The men who developed the atomic and hydrogen bombs were _____ scientists.

    A. social   B. pure   C. pseudo-
    D. political   E. applied

24. History has much in common with the other social sciences. It DIFFERS from them, particularly, in

    A. that it tends to be primarily concerned with uniformities
    B. that it tends to be less objective
    C. the way in which it verifies sources and generalizes its findings
    D. that it is primarily concerned with unique sequences of events
    E. its approach to the elements of human behavior and the way in which it deals with these

25. The verbally deep-seated resistances which help to block the road toward the application of scientific method to human problems is symbolized in the phrase,

    A. No man is an island
    B. Every individual is a rule unto himself
    C. If you can't fight them, join them
    D. You can't fight City Hall
    E. It's bigger than both of use

26. The source of MOST cultural change is 26.____

    A. dissatisfaction with the present cultural system
    B. social unrest
    C. diffusion
    D. social disorganization
    E. war and migration

27. Where there is no distinct functioning state, governmental functions 27.____

    A. may be turned over to the masses
    B. are often exercised by religious establishments
    C. collapse
    D. are non-existent
    E. are, especially in very primitive societies, turned over to the youngest member of the group

28. Religion functions as a 28.____

    A. shield, not a sword
    B. cultural crutch
    C. constant source of sanction for the mores
    D. filter to prevent the dangerous tars and nicotines of truth
    E. justification for the individual's behavior

29. Studies show that, today, the opportunity for a factory worker to rise to a top position in a large-scale company is 29.____

    A. as great as is his natural ability
    B. greater, if he is a member of a minority group
    C. small
    D. greater than it was a century ago
    E. unrelated to his intellectual capacity

30. A trend in contemporary American government which has been the subject of much controversy is 30.____

    A. isolationism
    B. the increase in governmental functions
    C. the support of state's rights
    D. the sharpening decline of foreign aid
    E. the decline in the powers of the federal court system

31. Among agricultural people, the_____ family predominates. 31.____

    A. emancipated   B. maternal   C. paternal
    D. equalitarian   E. matricentric

32. The_____ family maintains its continuity through many generations. 32.____

    A. incestuous   B. royal or hemophilic
    C. consanguine   D. conjugal
    E. systematic

33. Some very primitive tribes in Australia have extremely complex   33._____

   A. concepts of right and wrong
   B. sexual techniques
   C. industrial systems
   D. kinship systems
   E. eating and gustatory habits

34. Suburban areas are growing rapidly while the rural farm population is   34._____

   A. turning to pursuits other than agriculture
   B. expanding at a more rapid rate than ever before
   C. declining
   D. facing a long period of technological unemployment
   E. increasing

35. *Natural areas* are   35._____

   A. any parks or public grounds within a city
   B. those areas where buildings or living quarters are not permitted
   C. small areas in cities which are not the products of a definite plan
   D. game farms which are landscaped according to the natural habitat from which the game came
   E. similar to some reservations where the terrain is kept in its natural state and the people live in much the same way as in primitive times

36. Strictly speaking, the *neighborhood* is   36._____

   A. a product of the sociologist's imagination
   B. completely non-existent within a large city
   C. a primary group
   D. stronger in an urban community
   E. seldom neighborly in a large city

37. Urban communities tend toward_____ more strongly than rural communities do.   37._____

   A. secondary groups   B. social mobility
   C. primary controls   D. a *Peyton Place* society
   E. anonymity of the individual

38. Of the many types of villages, one of the MOST predominating is the   38._____

   A. resort village   B. company town
   C. rural village   D. coal town
   E. industrial village

39. People from_____ areas tend to be more xenophobic than people from_____ areas.   39._____

   A. urban; rural   B. rural; urban
   C. industrial; pastoral   D. riparian; lacustrine
   E. Eastern; Western

40. Social control is weakened by	40._____

	A. sporadic behavior patterns of the troublesome individual
	B. inferior religious training
	C. group isolation
	D. the power given to primary control methods
	E. the isolation of individuals from society

41. Sociological research in the United States has suggested that children of non-manual	41._____
workers are much more likely to

	A. learn rapidly than any other children
	B. take pride in the possession of a college degree
	C. be well-adjusted to the strains of living in a demanding society than are children whose intelligence level is lower
	D. attend college than are the children of manual workers
	E. engage in illegal activities than are their playmates

42. Sociological research studies reveal that there has been a great increase in the United	42._____
States in

	A. communistic activities among the people of this country
	B. the use of harmful drugs to overcome the ever-increasing tensions of this modern age
	C. upper class snobbery
	D. the size of the middle class
	E. anodynamic activities during the past ten years

43. The cable cars of San Francisco have lasted far beyond the need for them because	43._____

	A. the citizens of this area were wary of the extremely costly bill proposed by the Mayor for the new city improvement program
	B. it was much too enervating to walk up the hills of that city
	C. the people of the city identified their way of life with them
	D. that peculiar malady, car-sickness, was prevalent among the people of San Francisco
	E. the cable cars were an historical tradition in that city

44. If an intoxicated operator of a vehicle swerved wildly into the midst of a crowd of people	44._____
waiting for a bus, instantaneously, the crowd

	A. in their panic, would feel a close bond with one another which, as in most moments of crisis, prevents violence which might, and usually does, occur in similar types of situations
	B. would file suit against the driver
	C. would become caught up in their own individual shock and, thus, the crowd would become a gathering of individuals
	D. would become a mob
	E. would become as one, each individual reaching out for mass salvation

45. Riots are   45.____

    A. always due to governmental ineffectiveness
    B. according to Martinez, *seeds of revenge growing in the hearts of the deprived*
    C. more prevalent in Europe than in the United States
    D. not only foolish and childish pranks, but totally useless as well
    E. typified by random destructiveness

46. Leaders of the *crowd or mob* use catch phrases and epithets   46.____

    A. because they are usually frustrated writers who are full of hate
    B. which symbolize the object against which the crowd is to move as a mob
    C. because they are lacking in basic ideological philosophy and devices
    D. in order to make an easily recalled historical record of the event
    E. to bolster their own egos and those of the *mob*

47. CORE members of a public are   47.____

    A. those who fight for segregation
    B. those who back all civil rights movements
    C. *interstitial members*
    D. those who strive to show the benefits or disadvantages of segregation or integration by going to the center or core of the problem
    E. those having the greatest interest in the issue over which the *public* was created

48. Propaganda is   48.____

    A. a dishonest means to an equally dishonest end
    B. extremely harmful in any form
    C. a clever and insidious institution dedicated to turning the nation's mentality into a public putty factory
    D. the transmission of ideas and attitudes in order to influence the opinions of others
    E. derived from the legend of the intoxicated goose who, being perennially in this condition, needed to be propped up to be fed

49. An example of a model propaganda campaign would be   49.____

    A. the reconstruction of the South
    B. prohibition
    C. the promotion of the Edsel automobile
    D. the *love thy neighbor campaign* of 1940
    E. motherhood

50. Social movements, in order to survive, MUST   50.____

    A. proceed cautiously
    B. have the support of the entire nation
    C. have full governmental support
    D. learn to accept defeat
    E. be oriented towards action

KEY (CORRECT ANSWERS)

1. C	11. D	21. C	31. C	41. D
2. C	12. E	22. D	32. C	42. D
3. D	13. D	23. E	33. D	43. C
4. D	14. B	24. D	34. C	44. D
5. D	15. E	25. B	35. C	45. E
6. D	16. B	26. C	36. C	46. B
7. D	17. E	27. B	37. E	47. E
8. E	18. C	28. C	38. E	48. D
9. C	19. B	29. C	39. B	49. A
10. E	20. C	30. B	40. C	50. E

EXAMINATION SECTION
TEST 1

DIRECTIONS: Each question or incomplete statement is followed by several suggested answers or completions. Select the one that BEST answers the question or completes the statement. *PRINT THE LETTER OF THE CORRECT ANSWER IN THE SPACE AT THE RIGHT.*

1. Change of position on the same status level is called

    A. horizontal mobility
    B. the status quo
    C. immobility
    D. upward mobility
    E. victory and defeat

2. The two MOST important determinants of an individual's social class are his income and

    A. his profession
    B. the social class position of the family into which he was born
    C. his popularity
    D. his reputation
    E. his degree of independence

3. In the United States, social climbing is

    A. unnecessary
    B. a leading cause of mental disease
    C. a criminal offense in some states
    D. improbable but not impossible
    E. a widely accepted activity

4. A BASIC characteristic of a rigid social caste system is

    A. the revolt of the masses
    B. the dictatorship of the proletariat
    C. marriage only within one's own caste
    D. oppression of minority groups
    E. upward mobility

5. When social class affiliation coincides with similar interests and affiliations all along the line, class consciousness is likely to be greater.
   The Communists, realizing this, have

    A. romanticized agricultural workers as *sons of the soil*
    B. promoted world revolution
    C. championed the superiority and entitlement to rule of the skilled working class
    D. tried to build up class consciousness in the lower classes by emphasizing their mutuality of interests in all aspects of life
    E. engaged in a continuing ideological war with the Socialists and the Maoists

6. The population of the world was recently estimated at 5,500 million, representing a _____ percent increase in the world's population over the last three centuries.
    A. 50   B. 100   C. 500   D. 1000   E. 2500

7. In the ESSAY ON THE PRINCIPLE OF POPULATION, Malthus

    A. advanced the idea that disease and war are necessary as the best possible checks on the population
    B. supported birth control by contraceptive and other means
    C. indicated that people would have to exercise voluntary restraints on reproduction
    D. foresaw the day when the continuous succession of wars, famines, and plagues would end
    E. realized that the food supply, broadly conceived to include other necessities, is also capable of great expansion with the development of new technologies and the more efficient division of labor

8. Every farmer's gate opens onto a road and that road leads to a village or town. This statement dramatizes the fact that the American farmer

    A. has close functional relationship with surrounding farmers
    B. even though he may live apart from others in the midst of the land he cultivates, is part of a community
    C. needs socialization in the village or town, and will occasionally enter the town for this reason
    D. will welcome certain contacts because farmers are generally isolated
    E. believes that *good fences make good neighbors*

9. Urban people associate with each other CHIEFLY on the basis of _____, rather than that of _____.

    A. proximity; common interests
    B. interest; locality
    C. economy; sociability
    D. homogeneity; heterogeneity
    E. ethnology; religion

10. Systematic crime is BEST exemplified by

    A. constitutional structure, feeblemindedness, mental illness
    B. specific relationships with the police, the courts, the politicians
    C. different concepts of punishment for the juvenile delinquent as opposed to the adult criminal
    D. a bank teller who decides to abscond with funds
    E. the methods of dealing with the criminal in his apprehension, trial, and subsequent treatment

11. The study of _____ deals with the treatment of criminals by society.

    A. criminology   B. penology
    C. multiple causation   D. methodology
    E. ecology

12. Symbiosis is the process by which

    A. two or more individuals or groups live together in close physical proximity in some type of reciprocal, functional relationship
    B. people are not distributed evenly in a locality, but tend to cluster for economic reasons

C. social interaction is affected by geographic environment and spatial distribution
D. members of a particular group gradually come to occupy some of the territory formerly occupied by a different group
E. a few people spread out over a relatively large area

13. The plan by which reliable knowledge of social phenomena can be obtained is known as

    A. motivational sociology
    B. social organization
    C. sociometry
    D. methodology
    E. intergroup relations

14. _____ is based on the analogy between society and a biological organism.

    A. Amelioration
    B. Social pathology
    C. Social coordination
    D. Genetics
    E. Agronomy

15. Jeremy Bentham outlined PARIOPTICON for the purpose of

    A. better observation of what goes on within prison walls
    B. deterring crime
    C. rehabilitation
    D. defining the precise function of the jury system
    E. abolishing capital punishment

16. According to _____, sociology is built around the concepts of in-group and out-group, while folkways and mores are prescriptions for the treatment of members of one's own group as well as outsiders.

    A. Ruth Benedict
    B. William Sumner
    C. John Dewey
    D. Margaret Mead
    E. Emile Durkheim

17. The sociologist, in order to formulate his working hypotheses, needs what Weber calls,

    A. ideal types
    B. the norm
    C. mental constructs
    D. combinations of particular elements of reality
    E. one-way causation

18. _____ is the process of selecting a relatively small number of items from the total universe or population under investigation on the assumption that generalizations can be then formed and attributed to the whole population.

    A. The normal curve of distribution
    B. A measure of central tendency
    C. A frequency distribution
    D. Sampling
    E. The stratified statistic

19. Nazi and Fascist doctrine revived an old theory that war

    A. brings out the noblest virtues in mankind
    B. is part of the natural law
    C. is a cyclical phenomenon

D. would make the world safe for democracy
E. can be avoided if the *haves* will agree to share with the *have-nots*

20. Two fundamentally opposed views clash in the treatment of the criminal, once convicted. On one hand is the position, embodied in the structure of criminal law, that the criminal must be punished because of his crimes against society and as a deterrent from further crimes.
On the other hand is the standpoint that

   A. very few crimes justify the types of prison sentence, including capital punishment, meted out
   B. trial by jury has been considered unjust because it is impossible to be judged by a jury of one's peers
   C. the goal of treatment should be the protection of society and the rehabilitation of the criminal
   D. prison life and the types of punishment imposed breed revenge in the criminal mind and often result in homosexuality
   E. were paroles granted and good behavior rewarded more than it is at present, the criminal would react favorably towards society

21. Parole is

   A. a release under constant custody and supervision of an appointed officer
   B. a release from imprisonment under specific stipulations regarding one's conduct, with frequent reference and report to the parole officer
   C. a specified time period to give the criminal an opportunity to prove his ability to return to normal society; thereafter, having proved himself, he is granted complete freedom
   D. a system designed to facilitate rehabilitation of the criminal prior to release from prison
   E. equivalent to release on bail

22. The field of political sociology is divided into three sub-areas; one of these is

   A. primitive political systems
   B. political behavior in educational institutions
   C. political primaries and conventions
   D. social aspects of interaction between political groups
   E. prehistoric political behavior

23. It is generally agreed among criminologists that, considering the overcrowding in penal institutions, the inadequate opportunities for vocational training, the presence of guards who lack training in psychology or sociology, and the _____, the criminal becomes hardened and remains unprepared for a successful return to society.

   A. exchange of information and attitudes among prisoners
   B. fact that the rigorous duties and pressures of daily prison life leave no time for constructive thought
   C. coddling of juvenile delinquents
   D. oppressiveness of prison sentences
   E. failure to abolish capital punishment

24. The range of individual differences among criminals is 24.____

    A. after a long period in prison almost non-existent
    B. dependent upon their age
    C. as wide as that of the general population
    D. dependent upon the seriousness of the crimes they have committed
    E. usually very narrow

25. Criminals are almost invariably 25.____

    A. a separate type of people
    B. have no morals
    C. motivated by normal human desires
    D. *lone wolves* who do not seek or need the affection and approval of other people
    E. not found to subscribe to many of the mores to which law-abiding people adhere

26. Criminal behavior has been found to be PARTICULARLY high among 26.____

    A. immigrants
    B. the children of immigrants
    C. types of persons with a particular physical constitution
    D. children of broken homes
    E. members of certain religious groups

27. The kinship system of the United States is weak in contrast to that of the _____, for whom the kinship system of the United States is *backward* and even *primitive*. 27.____

    A. *Castro Cubans*   B. Australian aborigines
    C. Chinese communists   D. Russian communists
    E. French Canadians

28. Norms are supported by _____, which are forms of reward or punishment based on conformity or non-conformity. 28.____

    A. social attitudes
    B. sanctions
    C. logic and reason
    D. statutes and *unwritten laws*
    E. ethics

29. Since many norms are unconscious, _____ may arise when an individual is suddenly plunged into a different culture. 29.____

    A. chauvinism   B. hypertension
    C. hysteresis   D. xenophilia
    E. *cultural shock*

30. Sociologist David Riesman's depiction of modern man as *other-directed* in contrast to *tradition-directed* and *inner-directed* leads to the widely-held view that modern man 30.____

    A. espouses the principles of laissez-faire
    B. evaluates success in terms of the approval of his peers
    C. usually acts altruistically
    D. is, generally speaking, not creative
    E. conforms to the pattern of *checks and balances*

31. A doctor, a priest, and a career soldier all undergo forms of *resocialization*.
A modern and more extreme form of *resocialization* is

   A. education
   B. on-the-job or in-service training
   C. emulation
   D. *brainwashing*
   E. emigration or repatriation

32. The *ethos* of a culture may be embodied in well-established customs of dress, diet, conformity to rituals, etc.
Ethos is the sociological term for

   A. moral behavior   B. blind conformity
   C. dominant spirit   D. prejudices
   E. indoctrination

33. The essence of _____ groups is that they are personal, intimate, diffuse, spontaneous, and affective (permeated by emotion).

   A. tertiary   B. secondary   C. primary
   D. marital   E. centenary

34. Social stratification in the U.S.S.R. is characterized by slave laborers at one end and politicians and _____ at the other.

   A. the bourgeoisie   B. industrial managers
   C. the proletariat   D. the masses
   E. artists and writers

35. Marriage and parenthood are _____ statuses in that they are voluntary and not thrust upon the individual without his choice.

   A. achieved   B. ascribed   C. tributary
   D. assigned   E. sequential

36. The term *institution* refers to a(n)

   A. group
   B. organized way of doing something
   C. formalization
   D. government agency
   E. endowed foundation or educational institution

37. The crowd and the mob are dominated by

   A. reason   B. their members   C. communism
   D. emotion   E. forces of evil

38. People may succumb to _____ while in enforced isolation.
This is a disorganized response not dependent on, although related to, emotional contagion.

   A. anti-social behavior   B. panic
   C. false doctrine   D. cynicism
   E. resignation and despair

39. The practice of group psychotherapy BASICALLY utilizes the fact that
    A. people generally tend to prefer group discussion to individually working out a problem
    B. attitudes and other characteristics are often group-formed and group-influenced
    C. private treatment is beyond the income of the average man
    D. fears, hostilities, etc. can be acted out rather than spoken about
    E. it is based on practical life situations, i.e., employment, family problems, etc.

40. Cooperation is one of the most basic social processes.
    It might be exemplified by
    A. a child crying for its parent
    B. periodic mass unemployment
    C. the two-party system
    D. several men lifting a log
    E. a merchant selling his wares

41. Often conflicts result in a change in status of the hostile parties in such a way that a new level of adjustment is reached in which one party attains a status above the other.
    The higher status is then called
    A. status quo ante   B. superordinate status
    C. superior status   D. subordinate status
    E. status seeking

42. Lynchings, race riots, and group combat between opposing sets of rioters at athletic events are examples of
    A. the revolt of the masses   B. milling
    C. social unrest   D. mob behavior
    E. crisis

43. The effectiveness of propaganda is often observed to vary inversely with
    A. the use of catchwords or slogans
    B. an appeal to tradition
    C. the facilities of communication
    D. the educational status of the public
    E. constant repetition

44. The eugenic movement favors
    A. a wider use of birth control among the poorer classes and a greater reproduction rate among the more fortunate
    B. birth control and euthanasia
    C. the restoration of sexual ability by the use of monkey glands
    D. the construction and operation of homes for the aged
    E. the rhythm method of birth control and the concept of original sin

45. The large proportion of young people in the American farm population has led to
    A. improved methods of agriculture   B. migration from farms to cities
    C. a high crime rate in rural areas   D. crop rotation
    E. migration from cities to farms

46. Neighborhoods themselves _____, for, typically, their population is too small to support a full set of institutional services.

   A. are generally independent entities
   B. are examples of informal social groups
   C. must be racially integrated
   D. are not communities
   E. must be diversified

47. The family can be organized either on a _____ basis or on a _____ basis.

   A. consanguine; conjugal
   B. friendly; hostile
   C. political; social
   D. higher; lower
   E. homogeneous; heterogeneous

48. The majority of people seem to practice monogamy, if only for _____ reasons.

   A. religious   B. inconsequential
   C. sexual   D. economic
   E. personal

49. An abiding problem in the United States is posed by the _____ of the nation's resources.

   A. waste   B. conservation
   C. widespread use   D. abundance
   E. inadequacy

50. Laws against miscegenation forbid

   A. the breeding of cattle
   B. marriage to foreigners
   C. intermarriage between Caucasians and members of other races
   D. the integration of school facilities
   E. anti-semitic practices

9 (#1)

KEY (CORRECT ANSWERS)

1.	A	11.	B	21.	B	31.	D	41.	B
2.	B	12.	A	22.	D	32.	C	42.	D
3.	E	13.	D	23.	A	33.	C	43.	D
4.	C	14.	B	24.	C	34.	B	44.	A
5.	D	15.	A	25.	C	35.	A	45.	B
6.	D	16.	B	26.	B	36.	B	46.	D
7.	C	17.	A	27.	B	37.	D	47.	A
8.	B	18.	D	28.	B	38.	B	48.	D
9.	B	19.	A	29.	E	39.	B	49.	A
10.	B	20.	C	30.	B	40.	D	50.	C

———

TEST 2

DIRECTIONS: Each question or incomplete statement is followed by several suggested answers or completions. Select the one that BEST answers the question or completes the statement. *PRINT THE LETTER OF THE CORRECT ANSWER IN THE SPACE AT THE RIGHT.*

1. The system of apprehension and trial of persons who have broken the law is widely recognized as 1.____

    A. speedy and efficient
    B. criminal
    C. immoral
    D. inefficient
    E. unfair

2. It is now authoritatively recognized that delinquency and crime are products of 2.____

    A. inherited defects
    B. religious fanaticism
    C. sexual deviation
    D. the institutional configuration
    E. racial characteristics

3. Which one of the following statements concerning crime is TRUE? 3.____

    A. Many more males are arrested for criminal acts than females, and a large proportion of female arrests is for sex offenses.
    B. The percentage of delinquents from broken homes is low.
    C. Movies, comic books, radio, and television have proved to be the major causes of juvenile delinquency.
    D. Urban conditions are no more conducive to criminal activities than rural.
    E. Income level has been found to be inconsequential as a cause of crime.

4. _____ is the systematic effort to alleviate maladjustments between the individual and society. 4.____

    A. Social science
    B. Sociometry
    C. Sociology
    D. Social work
    E. Socialism

5. _____ is the study of the spatial arrangements of people in urban areas in relation to their environment. 5.____

    A. Systematic sociology
    B. Sympathetic contact
    C. Urban sociology
    D. Urban ecology
    E. Political economy

6. Social problems, almost by definition, are 6.____

    A. impossible to resolve
    B. the same as they have always been
    C. constantly becoming more aggravated
    D. fast disappearing
    E. problems which society makes for itself

7. A consanguine family, of which an older man is the functional head, is termed

   A. patrilineal   B. patriarchal   C. partilocal
   D. patrimonial   E. patrician

8. The process by which individuals or groups from one culture come to acquire the behavior and thought patterns of a different culture is termed

   A. osmosis   B. intervention   C. permeation
   D. correlation   E. acculturation

9. The process by which two or more groups who have had different attitudes and mores become alike (in these things) is termed

   A. conciliation   B. merger   C. monism
   D. assimilation   E. attrition

10. Durkheim's law states that the rate of suicide is INVERSELY proportional to

    A. the rate of birth
    B. periods of peace
    C. periods of war
    D. the degree of social cohesion
    E. the absence of economic stress

11. Cooley developed the conception of the interdependence and inseparability of the individual and society.
    This idea is crystallized in the following statement attributed to him:

    A. No man is an island
    B. Even the hermit will, at some time, seek out the group
    C. Man cannot exist in solitude
    D. Life is an organic whole
    E. Self and society are twin-born

12. An IMPORTANT sociological concept, introduced by Durkheim is the three-fold classification of suicide as (1) egotistic, (2) altruistic, and (3)

    A. depressive   B. introverted   C. manic
    D. anomic   E. psychic

13. On entering industrial life, the worker must adjust to conditions to which he has not previously been exposed. Which of the following is NOT such a condition?
    He

    A. is faced with long hours of work
    B. is frequently separated for many hours from his family
    C. is exposed to new social control systems
    D. is dealt with as an individual
    E. acquires status on the basis of production

14. According to Marx, the affairs of industry are NOT of great concern to the worker because

    A. most workers are basically lazy
    B. the affairs of industry are basically a capitalistic concern

C. there is no real relationship between the workers
D. he does not truly share in the profits
E. he has far more important concerns in his daily life

15. As the structure of society lost its homogeneity and specialization increased, some system was required for the orderly transmission of culture.
This requirement was fulfilled by the

A. church
B. school
C. state
D. military system
E. business world

16. The _____ population in the colleges is described as those students who tend to combine academic effort with a general lack of identification with the institution.

A. vocational
B. *beatnik*
C. athletic
D. nonconformist
E. collegiate

17. The modern college has been compelled by circumstance to assume _____ its students.

A. the financial support of
B. a policy of complete integration of
C. an *in loco parentis* attitude toward
D. total academic responsibility for
E. the additional role of the community with respect to

18. _____ has practically vanished as a function of the American family.

A. Economic interdependence
B. Economic production
C. Procreation
D. Recreation
E. Acculturation

19. The _____ family is the nearly universal one.

A. matriarchal
B. neo-local
C. polygamous
D. polyandrous
E. polygynous

20. Nearly all prejudice is based on _____ thinking.

A. deductive
B. analytical
C. inductive
D. stereotyped
E. intuitive

21. Which one of the following statements does NOT describe a function of group prejudice? It

A. provides a source of egotistic satisfaction
B. justifies various types of discrimination which are considered to be advantageous to the dominant group
C. provides an outlet for aggressive feelings
D. provides convenient scapegoats
E. excludes most of those who are patently *undesirables* from participation in community activities

22. In the absence of a unifying doctrine, the social scientist needs to experiment permanently with multiple perspectives.
    To acquire such experimental skills, he needs specific training in the history of _____, as well as knowledge of accepted methodologies.

    A. morals
    B. abandoned doctrines
    C. revealed truth
    D. logic
    E. holy writ

23. The PRIMARY function of the labor union is

    A. the racial integration of the working class
    B. group-bargaining
    C. retirement planning
    D. to conduct strikes
    E. acculturation

24. Class animosity does NOT increase in proportion to the _____ of social classes.

    A. competition
    B. differences in mores
    C. dominance and subjugation
    D. justifiable resentments
    E. separation

25. Sociology tends to cure pessimism, not in the old messianic way of promising a bright future, but in the pan-social way of

    A. preaching the doctrine of original sin
    B. pointing out the inevitability of death
    C. showing each one's life as a member of a great process
    D. adhering to the doctrine of fatalism
    E. encouraging people to think for themselves

26. Where there are inherited classes, there are also class standards of

    A. art
    B. economy
    C. industry
    D. science
    E. family structure

27. The wish for security is actually

    A. dominant in all individuals
    B. an inborn instinct
    C. the reason a man buys real property
    D. the desire to avoid danger
    E. the quest for admiration and power

28. Role behavior

    A. presupposes formative experiences
    B. connotes behavior with respect to other people
    C. focuses attention on the presentation of one's own image, regardless of the responses provoked
    D. is never changing despite the nature of the situation
    E. is best reflected in the actions of the dictators Hitler, Mussolini, and Stalin

29. Vice, drug addiction, and similar *segmental* behavior patterns are examples of

   A. inborn criminal instincts
   B. group behavior
   C. social class distinctions
   D. ambivalent behavior
   E. deviant behavior

30. The two MOST frequent types of psychosis in American society, as measured by the admission data of mental hospitals, are

   A. paranoia and schizophrenia
   B. schizophrenia and manic-depression
   C. hysteria and megalomania
   D. homosexuality and alcoholism
   E. drug addiction and nymphomania

31. Social psychology is the organization of biological, psychological, and sociological factors which

   A. constitute a group
   B. underlie the individual's behavior
   C. comprise a culture
   D. lead to rational thinking
   E. account for psychoses

32. As the child learns the meaning of words, the scope of his _____ others is broadened.

   A. suspicion of
   B. alienation from
   C. interaction with
   D. hostility towards
   E. superiority over

33. Sociologists use the term *social roles* in three different senses: (1) cultural roles, (2) personal roles, and (3)

   A. group roles
   B. interpersonal roles
   C. motivational roles
   D. situational roles
   E. status roles

34. The medieval family was dominated by comparatively settled traditions which reflected the needs of the general system of society.
   Marriage was ESSENTIALLY regarded as a(n)

   A. result of love
   B. alliance of interests
   C. coming-of-age
   D. auction of the wife to the highest bidder
   E. means of ending inter-family feuds

35. Economic independence declines with the advance of

   A. the employer-employee relationship
   B. agricultural techniques
   C. civil liberties
   D. the arms race
   E. specialization

36. Veblen traced the sharp division between worker and entrepreneur back to primitive times and the _____, who scorned routine labor in favor of exploits which testified to personal prowess.

    A. philosopher-kings
    B. emergence of the hunter and warrior
    C. shaman
    D. pharoahs
    E. Java man

37. As illustrated by the potlatch of the Kwakiutl Indians, the theory of _____ implies that, one shows, through extravagant waste, how much he has to throw away.

    A. diminishing returns   B. superabundance
    C. *waste not, want not*   D. capitalism
    E. conspicuous consumption

38. Durkheim showed the importance of _____, which impress on men their social nature and make them aware of something beyond themselves.

    A. natural disasters   B. native deities
    C. *unifying ceremonies*   D. patriotic songs
    E. religious rites

39. Lewis Mumford has described the evolution of society as a development from the old *wood and water economy,* which he calls _____, to the new advanced levels of electricity and atomic energy.

    A. eotechnical   B. biotechnical   C. ethnocentric
    D. naturopathic   E. organismic

40. It was the era of _____ which first brought the landless, traditionless serfs of Europe into the new factories, and the poverty-stricken peasants of India into the new textile mills.

    A. neolithic culture
    B. monolithic culture
    C. hypertechnic civilization
    D. primotechnic civilization
    E. paleotechnic civilization

41. In the famous study, MIDDLETOWN, the investigators found that the acquisition of money rather than _____ was the basic economic motive.

    A. greed   B. status   C. the job itself
    D. pleasure   E. education

42. A culture with primitive agriculture or domesticated herds, but possessing no metal working or writing, is termed

    A. barbaric   B. pastoral   C. littoral
    D. static   E. prehistoric

43. The use of human flesh as either a symbolic or regular food is often linked with ceremonials reflecting religious significance and is termed 43._____

    A. Catholicism   B. vampirism   C. cannibalism
    D. hara-kiri   E. necrophilia

44. A_____ is a hierarchical system of social control, its status depending on its origin and religious orthodoxy. 44._____

    A. cabal   B. culture   C. caste
    D. clan   E. class

45. A society in which women are the rulers is called 45._____

    A. misogymy   B. gynocracy   C. oligarchy
    D. triumvirate   E. Amazonian

46. The condition of one person's legally owning and controlling another and denying him freedom of action or movement is called 46._____

    A. imperialism   B. nationalization
    C. feudalism   D. slavery
    E. serfdom

47. A social group, usually with a definite locale, dialect, cultural unit, or unifying social organization, is a 47._____

    A. pueblo   B. caste   C. tribe
    D. nation   E. shaman

48. Myth, in the form of poetry and song, when sung in unison, is used ordinarily to express 48._____

    A. grievances   B. collective emotion
    C. class distinctions   D. happiness
    E. resentment

49. In primitive societies, the arts, such as music, dancing, poetry, and the plastic arts, are all considered together in a single complex.
In modern society, the arts 49._____

    A. perform a similar function
    B. are treated separately
    C. are practically unknown
    D. reveal class distinctions
    E. have wholly succumbed to industrialization

50. Vocal music probably FIRST consisted of 50._____

    A. Gregorian chants
    B. operatic arias
    C. the imitation of animals
    D. rhythmic work songs
    E. cries of pain

KEY (CORRECT ANSWERS)

1. D	11. E	21. E	31. B	41. C
2. D	12. D	22. B	32. C	42. A
3. A	13. D	23. B	33. D	43. C
4. D	14. D	24. E	34. B	44. C
5. D	15. B	25. C	35. E	45. B
6. E	16. A	26. B	36. B	46. D
7. B	17. C	27. D	37. E	47. C
8. E	18. B	28. B	38. C	48. B
9. D	19. B	29. E	39. A	49. B
10. D	20. D	30. B	40. E	50. D

EXAMINATION SECTION
TEST 1

DIRECTIONS: Each question or incomplete statement is followed by several suggested answers or completions. Select the one that BEST answers the question or completes the statement. *PRINT THE LETTER OF THE CORRECT ANSWER IN THE SPACE AT THE RIGHT.*

1. In sociology, a "social problem" is
    I. defined by academics
    II. a condition considered by many to be a deviation
    III. a condition violating a cherished norm
    IV. capable of precise definition
    V. capable of precise measurement
   The CORRECT answer is:

   A. I, V   B. II, III   C. I, IV, V
   D. I, III, IV   E. all of the above

2. The sociologist, in studying social problems, considers *values* as
    I. totally irrelevant
    II. important in the definition of a group-defined problem
    III. an integral element of social interaction
    IV. the subjective element of a social problem
    V. the objective element of a social problem
   The CORRECT answer is:

   A. I only   B. II, V   C. II, III
   D. II, III, IV   E. II, III, V

3. Contemporary sociologists *generally* consider facts to be
    I. the sum total of the scientific investigation
    II. always a matter of interpretation
    III. autonomous and free of their sources
    IV. a unit of information within a network of other facts
    V. almost entirely insignificant
   The CORRECT answer is:

   A. I only   B. V only   C. II, IV
   D. III only   E. II, III, IV

4. An *objective* social condition is one which
    I. can be measured statistically
    II. is open to public observation
    III. could conceivably be assessed by impartial observers
    IV. is free of dispute
    V. is agreed upon by consensus
   The CORRECT answer is:

   A. I, II   B. II, III   C. V only
   D. II, III, IV   E. none of the above

5. From the sociological point of view, society is
    I. an aggregation of individuals
    II. a collectivity
    III. a system of groups and institutions
    IV. an established order
    V. a fluctuating set of disparate elements
   The CORRECT answer is:

   A. V only
   B. I only
   C. I, II
   D. III, V
   E. III, IV

6. The FIRST major sociologist was

   A. George Herbert Mead
   B. Emile Durkheim
   C. Max Weber
   D. Margaret Mead
   E. Thomas Malthus

7. The forerunner of demographic sociology was
    I. Malthus
    II. concerned with population trends
    III. a student of economics
    IV. a philosopher
    V. British
   The CORRECT answer is:

   A. I, V
   B. II, III
   C. I, III, V
   D. II, IV, V
   E. all of the above

8. Social problems develop
    I. spontaneously from without
    II. gradually from within
    III. in phases from awareness to solution
    IV. when institutional arrangments come into conflict
    V. in all times and places
   The CORRECT answer is:

   A. I, V
   B. III, IV
   C. IV, V
   D. I, III, V
   E. II, III, IV

9. Social phenomena which have been considered social problems include
    I. witches
    II. the military-industrial complex
    III. automobiles
    IV. public water
    V. mercy killings
   The CORRECT answer is:

   A. I, V
   B. I, II
   C. II, III
   D. III, IV
   E. all of the above

10. The conceptual limits on what may be considered as a social problem
    I. are virtually nonexistent
    II. are the boundaries of objective reality
    III. include a necessary condition that the facts are correct
    IV. include a sufficient condition that someone considers it a problem
    V. are difficult to determine sociologically
    The CORRECT answer is:

    A. I, IV   B. I only   C. II, III
    D. III, IV   E. V only

11. The sociologist Etzioni distinguishes active from passive society by the criterion of
    I. whether a society has a collection of knowledge
    II. whether a society uses the information it has
    III. the decision-making abilities of leaders
    IV. the ability to convert power into action
    V. the consensus of preferences
    The CORRECT answer is:

    A. I, V   B. II only   C. III only
    D. IV, V   E. all of the above

12. Fatalism is antithetical to sociology because it
    I. breeds on ignorance
    II. leads to inaction
    III. makes people anti-intellectual
    IV. reduces alternatives
    V. is not scientifically based
    The CORRECT answer is:

    A. I, II   B. I, II, IV, V C. III, IV, V
    D. I, III, V   E. none of the above

13. To the sociologist, knowledge is
    I. almost impossible to attain
    II. theoretically impossible
    III. a source of power
    IV. a socially significant factor
    V. scientifically insignificant
    The CORRECT answer is:

    A. I only   B. II only   C. III, IV
    D. III, V   E. V only

14. According to Max Weber, *power* is
    I. someone implementing his/her will against resistance
    II. economic control
    III. political patronage
    IV. domination of circumstances
    V. comprised of social elements
    The CORRECT answer is:

    A. I, V   B. II, III   C. III, V
    D. IV only   E. all of the above

15. Sociologically speaking, norms
    I. are subjective and capricious
    II. supply order to the world
    III. help people gratify themselves
    IV. are philosophically useless
    V. are morally void

    The CORRECT answer is:

    A. I, V   B. II, III   C. III, IV
    D. I, III, V   E. V only

16. The standard conception of a "social norm" is
    I. a rule of conduct
    II. whatever people believe
    III. something that specifies what should or should not be done
    IV. applied only within a culture
    V. hot culture bound

    The CORRECT answer is:

    A. I, V   B. II only   C. I, III, IV
    D. I, III   E. V only

17. The term CULTURE denotes
    I. nothing in particular
    II. everything in general
    III. all the knowledge, values, beliefs, norms, and technology of a people
    IV. all the knowledge, norms, and technology in a people's history
    V. artistic achievements of a society

    The CORRECT answer is:

    A. I only   B. II only   C. V only
    D. II, III   E. III only

18. To the sociologist, *values* are
    I. criteria of desirability
    II. vague and subjective
    III. objective and quantifiable
    IV. used as justifications for behavior
    V. unavoidable

    The CORRECT answer is:

    A. I, V   B. II only   C. III only
    D. I, IV, V   E. I, III, V

19. American culture can be sociologically characterized by the values of
    I. sloth and hedonism
    II. achievement and work
    III. efficiency and freedom
    IV. progress and practical usefulness
    V. self-awareness and growth

    The CORRECT answer is:

    A. I only   B. V only   C. II, V
    D. II, III   E. II, III, IV

20. The sociological concept of SOCIALIZATION refers to
    I. institutional brainwashing
    II. private acculturation
    III. the process in which children learn social culture
    IV. processes within the school
    V. all early experience
    The CORRECT answer is:

    A. I, III
    B. II, V
    C. III, V
    D. I only
    E. IV only

21. A norm is considered *legitimate* when
    I. an individual considers himself bound by it
    II. society places punishments upon violations of that norm
    III. everyone believes it
    IV. sociologists determine its objective validity
    V. it becomes someone's duty
    The CORRECT answer is:

    A. I, V
    B. II, III
    C. III only
    D. IV only
    E. II, III, IV, V

22. A social institution is something that
    I. is based on patterns of norms
    II. can be observed directly
    III. cannot be observed directly
    IV. causes behavior which can be studied
    V. cause recurrent situations which can be studied
    The CORRECT answer is:

    A. I, II
    B. I, III
    C. I, IV
    D. I, III, V
    E. II, IV

23. Social institutions include
    I. family
    II. church
    III. business
    IV. government
    V. schools
    The CORRECT answer is:

    A. I, III
    B. I, II
    C. III, IV
    D. I, IV
    E. all of the above

24. Social institutions are
    I. always ahead of their time
    II. reflectors of current conditions
    III. essentially conservative
    IV. preserve the status quo
    V. always somewhat behind the times
    The CORRECT answer is:

    A. I only
    B. II, III
    C. III, IV
    D. III, IV, V
    E. I, IV, V

25. Social control is
    I. irremediable
    II. social forces designed to oppose deviation from norms
    III. state-controlled legal mechanisms
    IV. usually effected in the home
    V. both formal and informal
    The CORRECT answer is:

    A. I, III
    B. II, IV
    C. II, V
    D. II only
    E. II, III, IV

26. Informal social controls differ from formal ones in that
    I. the former are deliberately formulated
    II. the latter are deliberately formulated
    III. the former rely on public sentiment, the latter on agencies
    IV. police belong to the former and not the latter
    V. gossip belongs to the former and not the latter
    The CORRECT answer is:

    A. I, III, V
    B. II, III, IV
    C. II, III, V
    D. II, IV
    E. I, IV, V

27. Sociologists characterize American educational processes as
    I. relied upon too heavily by the public
    II. a means of transmitting cultural heritage
    III. inconsistent with other institutions
    IV. consistent with other institutions
    V. a primary means of socialization
    The CORRECT answer is:

    A. I, II, IV, V
    B. I, II, III
    C. II, III, IV
    D. II, IV, V
    E. I, III, V

28. The primary school is sometimes criticized because its curriculum
    I. is antiseptic, portraying reality idealistically
    II. is practically nonexistent
    III. may be nonessential, i.e., the knowledge is useless
    IV. may be eclectic and random
    V. may be remote and not relevant to students' lives
    The CORRECT answer is:

    A. I, III, V
    B. II, IV
    C. II, III, IV
    D. I, IV, V
    E. II, IV, V

29. Education has become problematic in recent times because
    I. of the rapid population growth after World War II
    II. people have lost faith in education in general
    III. too many people are too educated for their own good
    IV. not enough people are equipped to function efficiently in society
    V. urbanization has decreased the sense of community
    The CORRECT answer is:

    A. I, II
    B. III only
    C. II, III
    D. I, V
    E. none of the above

30. The function of school today is
    I. that of moral guardian
    II. that of social and economic gatekeeper
    III. difficult for anyone to determine
    IV. that of babysitter
    V. to prepare children for complex adult roles
    The CORRECT answer is:

    A. I, V
    B. II, V
    C. III, IV, V
    D. IV only
    E. I, III, V

31. Compulsory education is ambiguous in that
    I. it prepares students to become successful but can't guarantee it
    II. it both shelters students from adult life and prepares them for it
    III. its teachers don't believe in the principles they practice
    IV. the students are disenchanted with the system
    V. it violates individual rights
    The CORRECT answer is:

    A. I, V
    B. III, IV
    C. II, III, IV
    D. II, V
    E. II only

32. According to Margaret Mead, the problem with education is that
    I. vertical transmission is insufficient in modern technological society
    II. transmitting tried and true knowledge cannot be achieved any more
    III. lateral transmission of knowledge is not being used
    IV. current information is not focused upon
    V. it is compulsory
    The CORRECT answer is:

    A. I, V
    B. I, III
    C. I, II, III, IV
    D. II, IV
    E. all of the above

33. Critics of compulsory education claim that
    I. schools are more agents of socialization than learning centers
    II. universal literacy only perpetuates a corrupt system
    III. schools ought to have better teachers
    IV. schools should have better textbooks
    V. schools should be better administered
    The CORRECT answer is:

    A. I, V
    B. I, II
    C. III, IV
    D. I, III, V
    E. II, IV

34. Technology influences education in that
    I. labor demands have shifted to more skilled positions
    II. service industries are growing faster than production industries
    III. mobility is increasing
    IV. the place where someone is educated will not be where he/she works
    V. long courses of training reduce a student's possibilities
    The CORRECT answer is:

    A. I, III
    B. II, IV
    C. I, II
    D. III only
    E. all of the above

35. Education has become *more* varied, in part, because
    I. of an increased tendency for people to want knowledge for its own sake
    II. anti-intellectualism is on the wane
    III. child labor laws have displaced children from factories to the schools
    IV. mass advertising has increased mass consumption
    V. machines can now perform simple mechanical tasks
    The CORRECT answer is:

    A. I, II B. III, IV C. III, IV, V
    D. I, IV E. I, III, V

36. Technologically advanced educational techniques
    I. are used increasingly
    II. are used less and less
    III. have advantages and disadvantages
    IV. include TV and language laboratories
    V. include self-help textbooks
    The CORRECT answer is:

    A. I, V B. II, III C. I, III
    D. I, III, IV E. I, III, IV, V

37. Innovative technological methodologies in education are helpful in that they
    I. free teachers for other work
    II. help students learn faster
    III. help students learn at their own rates
    IV. lower the cost of higher education
    V. lower the cost of primary education
    The CORRECT answer is:

    A. I, II, III B. II, III C. I, IV
    D. III, IV E. IV, V

38. Innovative technological methodologies in education are NOT helpful in that they
    I. lack sound psychological principles
    II. introduce new subject matters
    III. fail to adapt curricular content to new technology
    IV. increase student alienation
    V. frequently break down
    The CORRECT answer is:

    A. I, V B. II, III C. I, III, IV
    D. I, IV E. II, III, IV, V

39. External sources of problems for educational institutions include
    I. fragmented school districts and localities
    II. urban sprawl and suburbanization
    III. fragmentation of local governments
    IV. lack of optimism in the future
    V. decreased enjoyment of intellectual pursuits
    The CORRECT answer is:

    A. I, V B. I, II, III C. I, IV
    D. II, IV E. III, V

40. A MAJOR problem facing institutionalized education today is

   A. decreasing population of future students
   B. lack of funding for current programs
   C. truancy
   D. discipline problems
   E. lack of qualified teachers

41. Major factors involved in creating problems for American education include
   I. Americans' faith in education as a social panacea
   II. a decrease in native abilities of students
   III. the tradition of using schools as a means of Americanizing immigrants
   IV. the diversity of immigrant ethnic groups
   V. the exodus of the middle class to the suburbs

   The CORRECT answer is:

   A. I, III   B. II, IV   C. I, III, IV, V
   D. III, IV, V   E. I, III, IV

42. Local control of education has caused
   I. a homogeneous school system
   II. a heterogeneous school system
   III. organizational chaos
   IV. organizational symmetry
   V. insufficient tax bases

   The CORRECT answer is:

   A. I, IV   B. II, III   C. I, II
   D. III, IV   E. II, III, V

43. Sociologically, schools function as institutions that can
   I. reform society if they choose
   II. maintain the status quo if they choose
   III. process people as products, rather than goods
   IV. provide social continuity
   V. create social instability

   The CORRECT answer is:

   A. I, III   B. II, IV   C. I, II
   D. III, IV   E. all of the above

44. Primary goals of schools include
   I. increasing an individual's chances in life
   II. helping produce cogs for the industrial machine
   III. maintaining the health of the electorate in a democracy
   IV. keeping children and adolescents occupied
   V. providing babysitting services to parents

   The CORRECT answer is:

   A. II, V   B. I only   C. II only
   D. I, III   E. I, IV, V

45. Traditional responsibilities of American educational institutions include
    I. creating knowledgeable citizens
    II. keeping children busy
    III. instilling values of thrift, industriousness and moral virtue
    IV. creating a sense of community and togetherness
    V. creating independence and autonomy
    The CORRECT answer is:

    A. I, III, V   B. II, IV   C. II, III
    D. III, IV   E. I, V

46. Problems are created in educational institutions because
    I. educators are agents of cultural indoctrination
    II. a social elite arises if some receive poor education
    III. of social and economic inequalities
    IV. lack of physical maintenance can damage facilities
    V. juvenile delinquency is a fact of life
    The CORRECT answer is:

    A. I, V   B. I, II, III   C. I, III, IV
    D. IV, V   E. II, III

47. Educational reforms achieved by educational institutions
    I. may effectively shut out older people from jobs
    II. may divert resources from other worthwhile projects
    III. include urban community schools
    IV. include neighborhood schools
    V. include family schools
    The CORRECT answer is:

    A. I, II   B. I, II, III   C. II, IV, V
    D. III, IV   E. I, V

48. Approaches to educational organization include
    I. the family school
    II. the urban community school
    III. neighborhood schools
    IV. corporation schools
    V. factory schools
    The CORRECT answer is:

    A. I, III   B. II, IV   C. I, II, III
    D. III, IV, V   E. all of the above

49. The primary difference(s) between urban community schools and neighborhood schools is that
    I. the former is socially active and the latter is not
    II. the latter is socially active and the former is not
    III. the former takes on social responsibility for reform
    IV. the latter takes on social responsibility for reform
    V. geographical differences are significant
    The CORRECT answer is:

    A. I, III, V   B. II, IV   C. II, IV, V
    D. III, IV, V   E. I, II, III

50. Traditionally, equality of educational opportunity has been measured by
    I. an assessment of physical and economic factors
    II. taking in-depth surveys of students
    III. investigating student achievements later in life
    IV. evaluating laboratory facilities
    V. teacher-pupil ratios and per-pupil expenditures

The CORRECT answer is:

A. I, III
B. I, II
C. I, IV, V
D. III, IV, V
E. all of the above

KEY (CORRECT ANSWERS)

1. B	11. E	21. A	31. E	41. C
2. D	12. B	22. D	32. C	42. E
3. C	13. C	23. E	33. B	43. E
4. D	14. A	24. D	34. E	44. D
5. E	15. B	25. B	35. C	45. A
6. C	16. C	26. C	36. D	46. B
7. E	17. E	27. A	37. A	47. B
8. B	18. D	28. A	38. C	48. E
9. E	19. E	29. D	39. B	49. A
10. A	20. C	30. B	40. A	50. C

TEST 2

DIRECTIONS: Each question or incomplete statement is followed by several suggested answers or completions. Select the one that BEST answers the question or completes the statement. *PRINT THE LETTER OF THE CORRECT ANSWER IN THE SPACE AT THE RIGHT.*

1. The "Coleman Report" found
    I. later achievements of students are not related to expenditures
    II. physical facilities are not highly correlated with quality in schools
    III. family background is not important for student achievement
    IV. family background is very important for student achievement
    V. disadvantaged students benefit from integrated schools
    The CORRECT answer is:

    A. I, III   B. II, III, IV, V   C. I, II, IV
    D. I, III, IV   E. I, II, IV, V

2. Accepted conceptions of the American family find it to be
    I. a refuge for the weary
    II. a sacred institution
    III. corrupt and sexist
    IV. decadent and patriarchal
    V. ruined by promiscuity
    The CORRECT answer is:

    A. I, III   B. II, V   C. III, IV
    D. I, III, V   E. all of the above

3. The family is a fundamental social institution because
    I. it determines to a great extent the individual's life chances
    II. it provides the initial resources for the child
    III. it creates the child's personality
    IV. family responsibilities can be delegated to others
    V. family responsibilities cannot be delegated to others
    The CORRECT answer is:

    A. I, II, III, V   B. I, II, III   C. III, IV
    D. I, III, V   E. II, III, IV

4. The nuclear family in America is
    I. increasing in number
    II. comprised of an intimate sexual and emotional union
    III. comprised of husbands and wives
    IV. comprised of husbands and wives and their children
    V. comprised of husbands, wives, their children, and siblings
    The CORRECT answer is:

    A. I, V   B. II, III   C. II, IV
    D. I, II, IV   E. I, II, V

5. The extended family in America is
    I. increasing in number
    II. comprised of an intimate sexual and emotional union
    III. comprised of husbands and wives
    IV. comprised of husbands and wives and their children
    V. comprised of husbands, wives, their children, siblings, and parents
   The CORRECT answer is:

   A. I, V   B. II, V   C. I, III
   D. IV only   E. V only

6. For the sociologist, marriage is considered to be
    I. a matter of biological necessity
    II. evolutionary activity
    III. conducive to psychological health
    IV. a mating arrangement involving norms of sex behavior
    V. connected to responsibilities of adult mates
   The CORRECT answer is:

   A. I, II   B. III only   C. IV, V
   D. I, IV   E. I, III, V

7. A kinship system is
    I. a set of statuses made of geneological relationships
    II. a set of rights, privileges and obligations
    III. a system setting authorities
    IV. relatively important in American social life
    V. relatively unimportant in American social life
   The CORRECT answer is:

   A. I, II, IV   B. I, II, III, IV   C. I, II, V
   D. I, II, III, V E. II, V

8. Functions of the family institution include
    I. protective and educational functions
    II. economic functions
    III. socialization and social control functions
    IV. recreational and affectional functions
    V. reproductive functions
   The CORRECT answer is:

   A. I, V   B. II, III   C. I, III
   D. IV, V   E. all of the above

9. Fallacious views of the family include those that
    I. blame it for social problems
    II. condemn parents for problem children
    III. consider the family a passive social force
    IV. oversimplify and moralize about it
    V. consider it integrally related to other social institutions
   The CORRECT answer is:

   A. I, II, IV   B. I, II   C. III only
   D. II, V   E. I, V

10. A family crisis is a condition in which
    I. an event shocks a family unexpectedly
    II. the situation extends beyond the range of the family's solutions
    III. role performance is affected
    IV. hostilities emerge
    V. arguments take place
    The CORRECT answer is:

    A. I, II
    B. I, II, III
    C. III, IV, V
    D. IV, V
    E. all of the above

11. Family crises include:
    I. Dismemberment through death of a member
    II. Demoralization
    III. Accession, as in unwanted pregnancy or live-in relative
    IV. Lack of internal structure
    V. Disorganized role patterns
    The CORRECT answer is:

    A. I, II
    B. I, II, III
    C. III, IV, V
    D. IV, V
    E. all of the above

12. Working-class families differ from middle-class families in that the
    I. former are more, egalitarian
    II. latter are more egalitarian
    III. former are oriented toward order and obedience
    IV. latter are oriented toward order and obedience
    V. latter are more permissive in feeding infants
    The CORRECT answer is:

    A. I, IV, V
    B. II, III, IV
    C. II, III, V
    D. I, III, V
    E. II, IV, V

13. A source of debate among sociologists concerning the family is whether
    I. the family is disintegrating
    II. the nuclear family created industrialization
    III. industrialization created the nuclear family
    IV. families are isolated
    V. real families exist any more
    The CORRECT answer is:

    A. I, II
    B. III, IV
    C. I, II, III
    D. I, II, III, IV
    E. all of the above

14. Sources of family discord include
    I. the generation gap
    II. longer periods of adolescence
    III. vagueness attached to the role of adolescents
    IV. changing mores
    V. isolation of adolescents
    The CORRECT answer is:

    A. I, IV
    B. II, III, V
    C. II, IV
    D. I, III, IV
    E. all of the above

15. Parental roles in the American family
    I. are different for each parent
    II. more heavily involve mothers than fathers
    III. bridge the public and private spheres
    IV. are clear and well-defined
    V. are practically non-existent
    The CORRECT answer is:

    A. I, IV
    B. II only
    C. I, II, III
    D. IV only
    E. all of the above

16. A MAJOR factor affecting parental roles and responsibilities is
    A. the increasing number of wives who work
    B. the rate of divorce
    C. the spread of venereal disease
    D. mass propaganda
    E. media advertisement

17. Divorce in America has
    I. steadily increased since 1860
    II. exceeds the rates among the larger nations
    III. been more common in the upper-middle class than lower classes
    IV. been more common in the lower classes than upper-middle classes
    V. been less common among childless couples
    The CORRECT answer is:

    A. I, V
    B. II, III
    C. I, II, IV
    D. II, V
    E. I, II, III, V

18. A misconception concerning older people is that
    I. they are abandoned by their children
    II. they prefer to live independently
    III. they prefer to be dependent upon their children
    IV. families expect the government to help with their care
    V. families do not expect the government to help with their care
    The CORRECT answer is:

    A. I, III
    B. I, III, V
    C. II, IV, V
    D. I, III, IV
    E. II, III, IV

19. Problems associated with people who retire from work include
    I. trauma over the rite of passage
    II. worsened conditions as poor and unemployed old people
    III. learning to confront unusual amounts of leisure time
    IV. lessened responsibilities
    V. increased responsibilities
    The CORRECT answer is:

    A. I, V
    B. II, III
    C. I, IV, V
    D. I, II, III, IV
    E. all of the above

20. Considerations affecting the lower prestige accorded to old Americans include:
    I. Consumerism is based on youth markets
    II. Lack of respect for elders in this country
    III. Rapidly changing society makes their knowledge obsolete
    IV. Their existence is considered of little importance in the dynamic society
    V. Modern production requires the strength of young people
    The CORRECT answer is:

    A. I, II, III, IV   B. II, III, IV   C. I, III, V
    D. IV, V   E. V only

21. A major source of role re-definition is apparent in

    A. the women's movement
    B. industrial needs
    C. world population
    D. mass media
    E. current educational devices

22. Sex roles are
    I. determined by religious norms
    II. biologically determined
    III. strictly tied to genes
    IV. social and economically structures
    V. private and personally determined
    The CORRECT answer is:

    A. V only   B. I only   C. II, III
    D. I, IV   E. IV only

23. Shifts in attitude about sex have occured because
    I. women's functions have been socially undervalued
    II. the family has ceased to function as the central unit of society
    III. men have become disenchanted with monogamy
    IV. women have become disenchanted with the isolation of home life
    V. housework is a difficult, but necessary, occupation
    The CORRECT answer is:

    A. I, III   B. II, IV   C. I, III, IV
    D. I, II, IV, V E. all of the above

24. Human sexuality differs from animal sexuality in that
    I. the former are controlled by instinct
    II. the latter are controlled by instinct
    III. only the latter is necessarily linked to reproduction
    IV. only the former have sex for reasons other than reproduction
    V. only the former are monogamous
    The CORRECT answer is:

    A. I, V   B. II, IV   C. II, III, IV
    D. II, III, IV, V   E. I, III, V

25. The sexual revolution in America
    I. has been overrated
    II. has been underrated
    III. makes Americans more sexually permissive than Europeans
    IV. makes Americans less sexually permissive than Europeans
    V. has been confined to college age women
   The CORRECT answer is:

   A. I, V
   B. I, IV, V
   C. II, IV, V
   D. II, III, IV
   E. I, III

26. Sex roles are changing in America partly because
    I. concepts of femininity and masculinity have been challenged
    II. modern industrialization values intelligence over brawn
    III. laws have changed
    IV. legislation has required attitude change
    V. women want them to
   The CORRECT answer is:

   A. I, V
   B. I, II
   C. III, IV
   D. IV only
   E. V only

27. The double standard in sexual matters can be simply explained as
    I. some things women can do, men ought not to do
    II. everything women can do, men can do better
    III. certain things should be done by women, not by men
    IV. certain things should be done by men, not by women
    V. women can barely do anything well
   The CORRECT answer is:

   A. I, V
   B. V only
   C. II only
   D. I, III, IV
   E. III, IV

28. Reaction against equality for women can be explained by
    I. its affect on labor legislation
    II. its affect on family roles
    III. the superior sexual endurance of women
    IV. husbands feeling obligated to provide sexual pleasure
    V. mass media advertising by ultra-conservatives
   The CORRECT answer is:

   A. I, III
   B. II, IV
   C. II, III, IV
   D. I, III, V
   E. all of the above

29. Feminist sociologists claim that
    I. women's roles have been gradually overtaken by men
    II. women used to be valued more in previous societies
    III. women's biology rules out their equal participation in production
    IV. only by participating in production can women become equal
    V. capitalism is responsible for sexism
   The CORRECT answer is:

   A. I, V
   B. I, II, V
   C. I, II
   D. II, III, IV
   E. V only

30. Since 1970, women's salaries as compared with men's
    I. is about 52¢ to the man's $1.00
    II. is about 64¢ to the man's $1.00
    III. has increased in proportion to men's
    IV. has decreased in proportion to men's
    V. has become exactly the same as men's
    The CORRECT answer is:

    A. V only   B. II, IV   C. I, III
    D. II, IV, V   E. I, III, IV

31. The "feminine mystique" refers to the sociological phenomenon of
    I. women being subservient to men
    II. women not having sexual desires as men do
    III. the ideology that women's fulfillment is through motherhood
    IV. allures of women's secondary sex characteristics
    V. the manipulative sexuality of women
    The CORRECT answer is:

    A. I, II, III   B. II, IV   C. IV, V
    D. III, IV, V   E. I, III, V

32. A MAJOR factor bearing on new sex roles for women is
    I. technological advances in birth control
    II. medical progress in reducing infant mortality rates
    III. medical progress in reducing childbirth mortalities
    IV. men's historical abuse of women
    V. media propaganda against men
    The CORRECT answer is:

    A. I, II   B. I, II, III   C. III, IV
    D. IV, V   E. all of the above

33. Women's problems are frequently made analogous to those of
    I. political fringe groups
    II. foreign born nationals
    III. blacks
    IV. Jews
    V. poor people
    The CORRECT answer is:

    A. I only   B. I, III   C. II, III, IV
    D. II, III, IV, V E. all of the above

34. A patrilineal society is one in which
    I. kinship is determined through fathers
    II. kinship is determined through mothers
    III. family authority is centered on fathers
    IV. property is inherited by the oldest son
    V. social power is confined to men and fathers
    The CORRECT answer is:

    A. I, V   B. II, IV   C. I only
    D. IV only   E. III only

35. A matrilineal society is one in which
    I. kinship is determined through fathers
    II. kinship is determined through mothers
    III. family authority is centered on fathers
    IV. property is inherited by the oldest son
    V. social power is confined to women and mothers
    The CORRECT answer is:

    A. I, V   B. II only   C. II, V
    D. III, IV   E. III only

36. A patriarchal society is one in which
    I. kinship is determined through fathers
    II. kinship is determined through mothers
    III. family authority is centered on fathers
    IV. property is inherited by the oldest son
    V. social power is confined to men and fathers
    The CORRECT answer is:

    A. I, III   B. I only   C. III only
    D. III, IV   E. I, III, V

37. A matriarchal society is one in which
    I. kinship is determined through fathers
    II. kinship is determined through mothers
    III. family authority is centered on fathers
    IV. property is inherited by the oldest son
    V. social power is confined to women and mothers
    The CORRECT answer is:

    A. I, V   B. V only   C. III only
    D. II, IV   E. II, V

38. Primogeniture is an institution in which
    I. kinship is determined through fathers
    II. kinship is determined through mothers
    III. family authority is centered on fathers
    IV. property is inherited by the oldest son
    V. social power is confined to women and mothers
    The CORRECT answer is:

    A. IV only   B. I, IV   C. II, IV
    D. II, V   E. I, III, IV

39. Social taboos in almost all societies include those on
    I. murder
    II. incest
    III. adultery
    IV. promiscuity
    V. cannibalism
    The CORRECT answer is:

    A. I, II   B. II, III   C. II, V
    D. II, IV, V   E. all of the above

40. POLYGYNY is a marriage institution in which
    I. husbands may have more than one wife
    II. wives may have more than one husband
    III. husbands may have only one wife
    IV. wives may have only one husband
    V. both husbands and wives may have only one spouse
    The CORRECT answer is:

    A. I only   B. III, IV, V   C. IV only
    D. II only   E. I, V

41. POLYGAMY is a marraige institution in which
    I. husbands may have more than one wife
    II. wives may have more than one husband
    III. both husbands and wives may have more than one spouse
    IV. wives may have only one husband
    V. both husbands and wives may have only one spouse
    The CORRECT answer is:

    A. I only   B. I, III   C. III only
    D. II, V   E. III, IV

42. POLYANDRY is a marriage institution in which
    I. husbands may have more than one wife
    II. wives may have more than one husband
    III. both husbands and wives may have more than one spouse
    IV. wives may have only one husband
    V. both husbands and wives may have only one spouse
    The CORRECT answer is:

    A. I only   B. II only   C. III, IV
    D. II, III, IV   E. V only

43. MONOGAMY is a marriage institution in which
    I. husbands may have more than one wife
    II. wives may have more than one husband
    III. both husbands and wives may have more than one spouse
    IV. wives may have only one husband
    V. both husbands and wives may have only one spouse
    The CORRECT answer is:

    A. I, III   B. II only   C. III, IV
    D. V only   E. IV only

44. Historically speaking, monogamy in marriage has presented social problems because
    I. some societies do not allow divorce
    II. women have been more bound by monogamy than men
    III. men have been more bound by monogamy than women
    IV. inheritance lines have been too vague
    V. inheritance lines have been clear
    The CORRECT answer is:

    A. I, V   B. II only   C. I, II
    D. III, IV   E. III, V

45. Sociologically, homosexuality is
    I. a mental illness
    II. a sociopathic condition
    III. a condition of psychosexual propensity towards others of the same sex
    IV. a condition of psychosexual propensity towards others of the opposite sex
    V. difficult to characterize as a social problem
    The CORRECT answer is:

    A. I only
    B. I, II
    C. II, III
    D. II, IV
    E. III, V

46. Myths concerning homosexuality include claims that all
    I. male homosexuals are effeminate
    II. female homosexuals are effeminate
    III. female homosexuals are "butch"
    IV. female homosexuals are feminine
    V. homosexuals are emotionally unstable
    The CORRECT answer is:

    A. I, III, V
    B. II, III
    C. III, IV
    D. I, III, V
    E. all of the above

47. Marxists sociologists tend to explain kinship ties by referring to
    I. religious and philosophical ideologies
    II. economic conditions
    III. substructure relationships
    IV. superstructure justifications
    V. individual preference
    The CORRECT answer is:

    A. I, V
    B. II only
    C. I, III
    D. II, III, IV
    E. all of the above

48. Positivist sociologists explain social phenomena as
    I. scientifically objective
    II. economically and politically neutral
    III. individual incidences
    IV. inductive generalizations arising from observation
    V. independent of human choice
    The CORRECT answer is:

    A. I, II
    B. I, II, III
    C. IV, V
    D. I, III, V
    E. all of the above

49. Sociologically speaking, laws against some types of sexual behavior
    I. misplace social control as a substitute for morality
    II. place in the public realm what ought to be private
    III. enforce obligations rather than establishing norms
    IV. misunderstand social deviance
    V. are ill-worded and enforced whimsically
    The CORRECT answer is:

    A. I, V
    B. I, II, IV
    C. I, II, III, IV
    D. II, III, V
    E. all of the above

50. Paternalistic behavior is that which
    I. allows each individual freedom of choice
    II. coerces another to please oneself
    III. coerces another for his own good
    IV. coerces another to maintain social stability
    V. is well-intentioned

The CORRECT answer is:

A. I only
B. II only
C. III, V
D. II, IV
E. IV, V

KEY (CORRECT ANSWERS)

1. E	11. B	21. A	31. A	41. C
2. E	12. C	22. E	32. B	42. B
3. A	13. D	23. D	33. D	43. D
4. D	14. E	24. C	34. C	44. C
5. E	15. C	25. B	35. B	45. E
6. C	16. A	26. B	36. E	46. A
7. D	17. C	27. E	37. B	47. B
8. E	18. B	28. E	38. A	48. E
9. A	19. D	29. C	39. C	49. C
10. B	20. A	30. B	40. A	50. C

CAREERS IN SOCIOLOGY

Sociology is the study of social life and the social causes and consequences of human behavior. Sociology's subject matter ranges from the intimate family to the hostile mob, from crime to religion, from the divisions of race and social class to the shared beliefs of a common culture, from the sociology of work to the sociology of sport. In fact, few fields have such broad scope and relevance. Because sociology seems to offer something for everyone, it may seem surprising that its career potential is just beginning to be tapped.

Twenty years ago, there was really only one career in sociology. To be a sociologist was to be a professor, or at least a teacher of some sort. But as the title of this booklet indicates, there are now a number of possible careers for sociologists. Although teaching remains the dominant activity among the more than fifteen thousand professional sociologists today, other forms of employment are growing in both numbers and significance. Not all of these jobs are reserved exclusively for sociologists; in some sectors, sociologists are joined by economists, social workers, psychologists and others. All of this represents a growing appreciation of sociology's potential contribution.

And yet, career pay-offs are not the only reason for studying sociology. Its subject matter holds considerable interest for its own sake. Certainly, sociology offers valuable preparation for other sorts of careers. Sociology is a popular major for students planning futures in such professions as law, business, education, architecture, and even medicine—not to mention social work, politics, and public administration. Sociology provides a rich fund of knowledge directly concerning each of these fields. Sociology also provides many distinctive ways of looking at the world so as to generate new ideas and assess the old. Finally, sociology offers a range of research techniques which can be applied in many specific arenas—whether one's concern is with crime and criminal justice, client satisfaction in a business firm, the provision of medical care, problems of poverty and welfare, etc. Although sociology is valuable quite apart from a sociological career, our main purpose here is to consider sociological careers.

This booklet is organized into two major sections. The first section describes some of the various careers available in sociology. It provides a series of vignettes illustrating kinds of skills and routines involved, describing the nature of the working environment and discussing the prospects for advancement. These vignettes will provide examples of the uses of sociology at various levels of education. The examples will raise questions for which answers will be given in later sections. This section is intended to provide an initial understanding of the scope of sociology and its areas of specialization.

The second section explains the progression of educational preparation in sociology and offers some advice about the choice between major career options, particularly the steps which lead to a doctoral degree.

Finally, the booklet contains a brief statement about the American Sociological Association and other sociological societies.

This booklet is primarily written to inform and to clarify what further questions need to be asked. This booklet does not judge any career in sociology as being better than any other. As the following pages will convey, sociology is a discipline with expanding opportunities and choices.

Sociological Careers: Selected Vignettes and Basic Options

The following ten vignettes describe what ten different types of sociologists actually do. Of course, these career profiles are over-simplifications, and they represent only a few of the total careers in sociology. Nevertheless, they focus on some of the basic options available. The vignettes are listed in no particular order. The names are all fictitious, as one can quickly gather.

- ***Teaching Sociology in a State Community College***: Francis F_____ teaches in a two-year community college located fifty miles from the university where he did his undergraduate work and then completed an MA degree before deciding not to go on to the PhD. Francis enjoys teaching, which is good because he does a great deal of it. He teaches five classes a semester, and while these generally include at least two which are separate sections of the same course, the burden is heavy. This was particularly true when Francis was a new faculty member and starting from scratch without having taught any of the courses before. However, courses become less demanding as they are repeated from semester to semester, even though it is important to continually seek out new and up-to-date materials and teaching techniques. Although many people think that a teacher's work consists primarily of his or her time in class, this is often only a fraction of the responsibilities outside of the classroom. Such responsibilities include preparing for courses, serving on college committees, and meeting with individual students. These students not only have questions about the courses they are taking, but about the course they should take and their longer-range educational and occupational futures. Student counseling often goes beyond the formal rounds of regular office hours. Meanwhile, Francis also must devote time to reading so that he can keep up on those new developments in sociology and related fields. In fact, he is a member of the Behavioral Sciences Department, and his colleagues include anthropologists, economists, political scientists, and psychologists. The salary which Francis receives is quite competitive with that of other state workers and with that of sociologists who teach in four-year colleges. This represents a fairly recent improvement in the salaries at two-year community (or junior) colleges. After several years of adequate service, Francis should receive "tenure"—or almost a guarantee of continued employment. Francis is a member of a union which represents all community college teachers in bargaining with the state for cost-of-living raises and step increases with greater seniority. Actually many of today's community colleges are now re-evaluating their future missions and programs. For example, as traditional college-age populations have begun to decline, many colleges are now serving a new sort of student by emphasizing continuing education programs among their community's adults.

- ***Sociologists in a Health Center:*** Howard H_____ has a faculty position in the state-supported Health Science Center which includes Schools of Nursing, Medicine, Dentistry, Public Health and allied health professions. He and six other social scientists form a unit in the Department of Community Health. Howard's responsibilities include teaching students in every one of these schools. He and his colleagues teach future physicians, nurses and other health workers about sociological aspects of health care and health care organizations. Howard also works with the health services agencies as a sociological consultant providing data about the population groups to be served and about sociological aspects of the distribution of disease and health needs. He and his colleagues are used as resources by the staff of hospitals and clinics who turn to Howard to seek advice about a number of problems which they encounter with patients. Howard serves on the Medical School Admissions Committee, and serves on other committees in various health center schools. He also conducts research and currently is studying how patients with heart disease fare in their family and in their work after release from a hospital. Howard is rather well paid, but works in an environment in which he still has to convince some health professionals about the relevance of sociology to health care.

- **Staff Member of a Federal Agency**: Linda L_____ has only recently joined the staff of the U.S. Department of Justice where she serves as a staff member of a program which administers and monitors grants given to researchers throughout the country. After graduating from a small, predominantly black college in the South, Linda received a fellowship for graduate work at a private university in the North. Following some initial difficulties, she progressed quickly, choosing to specialize in criminology and deviance. While completing her PhD (or "doctoral") dissertation, she had a job with a large regional prison where she participated in evaluating the effects of treatment programs. In her new job, she discusses research plans with applicants for grants. These applications come from many disciplines. Linda has also been assigned a number of current projects which she supervises through communication with the project directors. Linda has been surprised to find many sociologists in federal departments in Washington. As in her own case, job titles do not always indicate who the sociologists are. In fact, there are many more opportunities for sociologists in government than strict job titles might indicate. Some sociologists work as "statisticians", "welfare workers", "economists", etc. Linda's salary is determined by the U.S. Civil Service scale. It provides her with a good income, even though Washington is a very expensive city in which to live.

- **Faculty Member of a Liberal Arts College**: While working on his doctoral dissertation, Clyde C_____ received an invitation to join the faculty of a liberal arts college located in a small town where it is the dominant institution. Since Clyde considered teaching his major goal in life, he accepted the position, despite some warnings from his advisor that he might find it difficult to complete his dissertation and his PhD. It took him two hard years to do so in addition to his regular duties. But now that Clyde has been at the college for six years, he has been promoted to Associate Professor and given tenure. This is an important source of security for Clyde, since it means that the college has virtually guaranteed his job (unless he were to commit some major moral offense or the college were to suffer a major economic catastrophe). Tenure is important in any educational institution as a safeguard of the teacher's academic freedom. Clyde's major activity is teaching, usually four courses each semester, which amounts to 12 hours per week. Occasionally he may teach during the summer for additional pay. His teaching is primarily oriented to students for whom sociology is part of their education for citizenship and he helps them in making choices among various occupational goals. He spends a lot of time with students in various campus activities and is active in community programs. Since college programs emphasize general liberal education, Clyde works with faculty members from other disciplines. He has learned to work with other social scientists and with the faculty in the biological and physical sciences. He knows that his salary may continue to be lower than that of his colleagues in universities or in some state institutions. But he also knows that life in this college town is relatively inexpensive and he is doing what he really enjoys in working closely and informally with young people.

- ***Planning Staff in a State Department of Transportation***: Paula P.____ has worked for five years in the State Department of Transportation and has now risen to the title of Assistant Director in the Office of Long-Range Forecasting. The job involves considerable sociological knowledge and skill, especially in projecting population shifts into and out of the state's major urban areas and suburban spinoffs. Here Paula is asked not only to commission research on her own, but to keep up with a growing research literature published in a wide variety of sources. While Paula does relatively little research herself, her work is particularly important since she keeps informed about relevant studies wherever they may be conducted and prepares frequent reports and analyses based on new findings. She serves as a bridge to outside research experts working on contracts with the department. In addition, Paula has taken on administrative responsibility for a growing staff working under her supervision. Her PhD in Sociology is a good preparation for many of her functions. However, she was never really trained to work with budgets, make personnel decisions, or allocate staff work assignments. These tasks all have their own challenges. In addition to making a good living, Paula is contributing to some critical decisions concerning the state's future transportation system. Without the research and professional judgment of such people, decisions concerning the routing of highways through urban areas, environmental conservation sectors, or suburban shopping tracts might be made with little regard for important social factors, that is, either haphazardly or on political grounds alone.

- ***Personnel Manager in a Small Manufacturing Firm***: Chris C_____ is viewed by most of his friends as a business executive rather than a sociologist. Nevertheless, he owes his start in the firm to his background in industrial sociology and social psychology. Starting as a lower-level assistant in the Personnel Department, Chris now has a post with considerable control over the company's personnel policies in general—that is, strategies and programs for hiring, training, supervising, promoting, etc. Ultimately, Chris may be either promoted to a higher executive position within the firm or seek advancement by joining another organization. He received a BA in sociology and did not go on to graduate school. In fact, he has not really kept up with sociological research for the past ten years, and he now thinks of himself more as a practitioner than a scholar. However, he does read specialized publications on organizational behavior, industrial and business practices, and here his sociological training is especially helpful. While the company does not consider his position as that of a "sociologist", it is one among many firms which is coming to realize that sociological training is worthwhile for administrators and executives.

- **Professor in a University Department of Sociology**: Shelly S_____ is an Assistant Professor of Sociology in a large university. Her department teaches both undergraduate and graduate students; it offers the MA and the PhD degrees, as well as the BA. Shelly recently received her own PhD from a similar department in a different region of the country. In fact, she began her teaching career there, serving as an Instructor before her PhD dissertation was actually finished. During her first year in her new job, she worked on her doctoral project evenings, weekends, and every other spare moment. Shelly has ample company and stimulation from her new faculty colleagues. After all, the department has twenty-five faculty members in order to handle the department's 400 undergraduate majors and 75 graduate students. Five of these faculty members are also assistant professors. In one sense, they are competing with Shelly for promotion to associate professor and the award of tenure. Shelly teaches five, sometimes six, courses a year, including two advanced seminars for graduate students. As important as teaching is to Shelly, research and writing may be even more important to her career development. In fact, at the graduate level, she teaches largely through her research. She has hired two graduate students as research assistants on a study financed by a grant from a federal research agency located in Washington. Shelly's tenure decision will be made in her sixth year at the university, and her chances will be improved considerably if she is able to publish a number of scholarly articles and perhaps a book before then. But these are the kinds of activities that attracted Shelly into sociology and academic life in the first place. Although her salary does not compete with the financial opportunities in the business world, it is more than adequate, especially when combined with that of her husband who teaches in the Physics Department of the same university. Shelly has avoided summer school teaching supplements to work on a book which could produce some additional income in the form of royalties. But she knows that scholarly books rarely make much money for anyone. In fact, only a few of the basic textbooks sell well in a highly competitive market.

- **Staff Member of a Research Institute**: Marion M_____ is a member of the staff of a private research institute which does sociological studies on specific problems of interest to Government agencies, business concerns, and political groups. The institute is located in a large metropolitan center and many of the studies concentrate on the city and the surrounding region. Marion began the job with a BA in sociology. She had focused her studies around courses in research methods and statistics. Since joining the institute she has gone back to graduate school for an MS degree and has had considerable on-the-job training. During her first several years, she was a "research assistant", but she is now an "associate project director" with more responsibility for developing new research projects as well as supervising the actual research process. She has developed a sense of how clients' problems can be met by appropriate research studies. She is learning to write research proposals and then to follow them through discussion and revision to actual funding. Her work schedule is basically 9 to 6. But she sometimes puts in considerable evening and weekend work, especially when she is conducting interviews, supervising an interviewing staff, or doing the statistical analysis and writing necessary for a final report to a client. Her salary is now somewhat above average for those in her graduating class. With success in obtaining contracts and advising clients, her income will probably increase considerably in a short period of time. Marion may stay here or move to another research firm, or consider starting her own agency. Some research agencies are run on a non-profit basis and are associated with an educational or governmental institution. If Marion were to open a research firm for profit, she would be facing the same substantial risks involved in launching any new business.

- **Staff Administrator in a Public Assistance Agency**: Throughout his studies, Wally W_____ was interested in using his knowledge to serve people. Unlike many students who go into sociology to become teachers or researchers, Wally saw sociology as a field which could be used to provide services. He now works for the city's Department of Social Service as a program coordinator. In this position, he draws on his studies in such areas as the family, social stratification, urban communities and group dynamics. His work includes routine processing of reports and legal forms, but it also involves much contact with agency clients and direct confrontation with the problems of the poor, disabled, aged and minorities. He also works with other employees, most of whom are professional social workers who work with individual families and clients. Actually, many people blur the distinction between social workers and sociologists. However, Wally brings a unique perspective and special resources to his job. He has mixed feelings about the possibility of taking on more administrative responsibility, since this would mean less time available to work with families directly. He often serves as a kind of trouble shooter by providing help in the personal crises of his clients. This, in turn, requires him to maintain contacts with various other public and private agencies that affect the lives of the poor. For example, one of his fellow undergraduate majors is now working on the staff of a large community mental health center, and another is involved in supervising rehabilitation for state penitentiary inmates. Like Wally, these two are using their undergraduate sociology as a basis for social service positions. All three receive satisfaction from being able to experience day to day accomplishments in their work. Their salaries are commensurate with the wage scales of public agencies generally. Wally could progress through Civil Service channels to a career of relative security. However, he still thinks about going back to school to earn a graduate degree, which would give him a considerable boost along the way.

- *Travelling Representative for a Publisher*. Terry T_____ works for one of the country's leading book publishers. She serves as a regional representative with responsibility for colleges and universities in a three state area. Her job has two major aspects. She is expected to establish and maintain contact with faculty members who are teaching courses in which the publisher's texts can be adopted—here sales are her principal concern. She is also required to seek out those professors who are likely prospects to write new books for her firm—here she serves as an editor and talent scout. Terry's sociology BA was one reason why she was hired, and it continues to be important to her duties. Although she has responsibility for all of the social sciences, including psychology, anthropology, political science, and economics as well, sociology was a good preparation for her responsibilities. Moreover, Terry may have a future opportunity to specialize in sociology. One avenue of advancement might involve promotion to "sociology editor" in the firm's New York headquarters. Here she would be less involved in sales and more involved in the choice of materials to be published and the form and schedule of publication. Alternatively, Terry could also be promoted within the sales division, and this too could lead to the New York office. Meanwhile, she enjoys the continued contact with campus life and the opportunity to interact with faculty members in community colleges, four-year colleges and universities. The heavy travel associated with her job has reduced her appetite for restaurant food and is sometimes exhausting; but she realizes that her current duties are a necessary first step in the occupational world of college text publishing. Her salary is competitive with most junior executive trainees in the business world and all expenses are paid. She even enjoys a free book now and then.

So much for a few of the things that sociologists do. It should be especially clear by now that there are various careers available, and the options are increasing. But it is important to underscore what lies beneath all of these vignettes; namely, sociology itself. Scratch a sociologist and you will find someone concerned with understanding human behavior and human relationships in various kinds of groups and social settings. Of course, sociologists pursue this concern in different ways. Quite apart from pursuing different career lines, sociologists pursue different specialty subjects within the very broad range of the field as a whole. Thus, sociologists may specialize in the family, the urban community, education, health, old age, occupations, environmental issues, sex roles, sports, the operation of government, the military, law enforcement, and any other area in which human behaviors are organized to pursue social functions.

Apart from such specific specialties, there are other types of specialization which cross-cut these interests and apply to them all. For example, that aspect of sociology which focuses primarily on the interaction between individuals and the behavior of small groups is usually referred to as "social psychology". On the other hand, a specialization in "social organization" involves studying characteristics of larger social institutions, agencies, occupations, and associations. "Human ecology" is that branch of sociology which looks at the spatial distribution of social behavior with reference to its environment. "Demographers" are primarily concerned with population processes; they study birth and death rates, migration and mobility, and the changing distribution of age, sex, marital statuses, etc. As a last important example, it is possible to specialize in the methods of sociological research as a subject in its own right. The "methodologist" is generally concerned with designing and assessing new research procedures. This often involves considerable quantitative or statistical know-how, but there are also experts on qualitative research concerned with techniques of depth interviewing, careful observation, and the use of historical documents.

Actually, any social phenomenon can be examined from a variety of sociological standpoints, i.e., from the perspective of social psychology, social organization, ecology or demography. Moreover, sociologists are as interested in that which is typical and "normal" as they are in topics defined as unusual or "deviant". Studies of bizarre phenomena may yield more publicity, but the bulk of sociological research seeks to explain the prevailing patterns of social behavior. But let us return to our main subject: sociological careers. We have already seen ten varied examples of what sociologists do, and have noted the increasing variety of job opportunities available. But many of those careers are not as different from each other as they may seem. Regardless of one's particular employer and one's special interest, there are some basic activities which overlap. Let's review a few of these activities in more detail, particularly "teaching", "research", and what might be called "policy administration".

Teaching.. Despite the changes that are occurring in the field, the fact remains that almost eight out of ten practicing sociologists teach in one setting or another, whether high schools, two year colleges, four year colleges or university graduate departments. Sociology is a rewarding field to convey to others. It combines the importance of social relevance with the rigor of a scientific discipline. It includes a broad range of subject matter, since all forms of social behavior are potential objects of sociological study. Sociology is not only being taught to future sociologists and to undergraduate students as part of their liberal arts or vocational education, but is also included in the programs of many professions, such as law, education, medicine, engineering, social work, nursing, etc. In addition to the standard college and university courses, sociology courses are popular with adult and continuing education programs and are increasingly prominent in the nation's high schools.

Teaching sociology is not the same in every setting. It is one thing to give a general introduction to a class of high school students and quite another to give a specialized course to college seniors. Both of these differ from leading an advanced research seminar for graduate students who are well along toward the PhD. In each case there are rewards and frustrations. For many persons, teaching seems a desirable occupation which provides considerable job security and the satisfaction of providing knowledge and stimulation to students who respond with respect and appreciation. But if this is teaching at its best, there are moments when even the best teachers are disappointed. It is not easy to communicate material to students of unequal and uneven capacities. Invariably, some students will be more turned on than others. And no matter how much work the teacher puts into a particular presentation, there is almost always a student who not only keeps looking at his or her watch, but actually listens to see if it is running!

It is also important to be realistic about job security as a teacher. Over the next decade, the demand for teachers will decline because there will be fewer students to be taught. Although population experts (often sociologists who specialize in "demography") now foresee a time in the late 1980s and 1990s when the number of students will increase and the demand for teachers rise again, the crystal ball remains a bit cloudy. Recent data suggest that in this general atmosphere of uncertainty, sociology is doing better than many other disciplines. However, anyone who launches a teaching career over the next decade or so must be prepared for considerable uncertainty and competition in the academic employment market.

Research: Teaching is one of the two most common career options within sociology and research is the other. Note, however, that there is not necessarily a choice *between* teaching and research. Many teaching positions, particularly in universities, require research activities. This is the basis for the academic cliches: "Publish or perish." Like most cliches, this one has some truth and a good deal of distortion. It is certainly true that publishing scholarly articles or books is the foremost route to job security, promotion and salary increases in most universities. But this applies to only a relatively small number of faculty members in those settings where original scholarship is highly prized and supported. In other schools, there is much less pressure to publish. In fact, some secondary schools, community colleges, and four-year colleges actively discourage research and writing activities because they are assumed to get in the way of teaching.

Certainly, one should enjoy research and writing if one seeks a career in the more advanced academic settings. In these institutions, research as well as teaching is expected. As the vignettes indicated, other kinds of jobs also feature sociological research and some of them are exclusively research positions. In fact, the number of full time researchers whose jobs require no teaching at all is increasing fairly rapidly. One can do research in a variety of employment settings, whether a public agency at the federal, state, or local level, a business or industrial firm, or as a staff member of a research institute.

Just as there are various settings in which to conduct research, there are various types of research to conduct. There are as many research specializations as there are methods of sociological inquiry. Methods range from questionnaire and interview surveys to working with census materials, from analysis of historical documents to actual experiments, whether in laboratory simulation or out in society. One form which is becoming especially important is "evaluation research". Here the investigator uses a variety of sociological methods to assess the impacts of a particular policy or program. Ideally, such evaluation involves careful experiments designed before a policy trial goes into effect. It may also involve opinion surveys of individuals directly or indirectly affected, or organizational analyses of a policy's implications for changes in the agency responsible. Frequently, evaluation research may be focused on the conduct and organization of the program itself in an attempt to explore unintended and unanticipated consequences of a social policy. Evaluation research is a response to the growing recognition that it is not enough to launch a new policy and hope for the best. Policies must be continually assessed to see if they are doing what was intended. New legislation often requires some kind of evaluation. For example, the law now requires studies of the environmental impact of large-scale federal projects and installations.

All of this is related to a fundamental change that has occurred in sociology in recent years. There once was a rigid distinction between what was called "basic" (or "pure") research, on the one hand, and "applied" (or "policy") research, on the other. The latter presumably uses the former to shed light on particular problems needing solutions; the former expands sociology itself on "purely" scholarly grounds without regard for relevance. Of course, the distinction still holds to some extent; some studies are inevitably more oriented toward specific problems and applications than others. But most sociologists now realize that these two types of research complement each other rather than compete. No longer is "basic" research reserved for the universities, while applied research is shunted off to non-academic settings. Some of the most important basic research findings of recent years have come from people working outside of universities. Conversely, university faculty members have produced some of the most pertinent, policy-oriented, applied research dealing with matters ranging from population growth to juvenile delinquency; from alternatives to the current welfare system to problems of racial integration and education. The ivory tower is tumbling, and this is a good thing for those within as well as for those on the outside. Here is one more factor which is expanding the career possibilities in sociology.

Policy Making and Administration: As a last set of career activities, consider one that is just beginning to develop. There are increasing opportunities for sociologists who can use their basic sociological training to make more informed policy decisions and administer programs more effectively and more imaginatively. This kind of career option is quite new, but it may well become increasingly prominent. Activities here do not involve teaching of the conventional sort, but they often involve research—at least in the sense of research consumption, if not production. A skilled policy administrator would normally not do research of his own (perhaps having done it at an earlier career stage). But he or she would be expected to read the research literature, to imagine useful research projects which might be commissioned, to interact with full time researchers who are either on the staff or who serve as outside consultants, and to apply the developing knowledge of sociology and the social sciences to the problems at hand. Of course, these problems would vary depending upon the particular employment setting—they might involve transportation, education, business personnel matters, community relations, corporate marketing strategies, health, law enforcement, or other areas of societal concerns.

Regardless of the area, this kind of career also involves working closely with others, ultimately as a supervisor, administrator or as a staff specialist. Of course, it is unlikely that younger persons will be hired directly into such positions. Typically, they work their way up from lower level staff positions. For example, it is not at all uncommon for young sociologists to be hired as staff members in a government social welfare agency and then follow a career which involves increased policy influence and administrative responsibility.
Competent administration often involves good sociological principles, although there are still very few administrative positions for which sociological training is a formal requirement.

A special type of policy making role for sociologists is the opportunity to incorporate sociological knowledge into planning and policy making in areas primarily dominated by practicing professions. At this time, this is primarily true in the field of health where sociologists serve with health planning boards and health services agencies. This also applies to the fields of education, law enforcement, and government. Sociologists have contributed their knowledge effectively in each of these areas, though it is true that sociologists themselves may disagree in such sensitive areas as school busing, crime control, or community planning.

This concludes our review of the various career patterns and job activities which sociologists pursue. The options range widely, especially since we have included not only the traditional academic occupations, but some of the non-traditional and non-academic careers which should begin to loom larger in the future than they do now. Having presented some of the employment prospects, let's turn now to the question of preparation. How does one prepare for a career in sociology? What do different sociology degrees prepare you for? What is graduate school really like, and how do you pick from among the many available?

Career Preparation

Success in most careers depends upon both long term career preparation and short term responses to changing circumstances. It is virtually impossible for anyone to fully anticipate what lies five years ahead, much less ten, twenty, or forty. Still, it remains true that some kinds of training are more appropriate than others for a given career. Even within sociology, different career options may require different types of career preparation. But many people put it the other way around and ask what kinds of careers are possible with a given type of preparation.

Job Prospects for the BA: One of the most frequent questions asked of any sociology teacher is, "What can I do with a sociology BA?" Actually, there are several answers. Certainly a BA in sociology is at least as good as any other BA degree in preparing the student for future graduate work or for general employment. On the other hand, if the question concerns professional employment specifically as a sociologist, the only honest answer continues to be "very little". There are still very few employers who are looking for sociology BA's in the same sense in which they might look for BA's in engineering, nursing, accounting, etc. Sociology BA's will often find themselves competing with other liberal arts students who have majored in English, history, psychology, etc. Here, a strong undergraduate program in sociology can conceivably produce a competitive advantage. For example, students interested in business careers after the BA might emphasize courses in industrial sociology and complex organization; students seeking work with public welfare agencies might concentrate their course work in areas such as stratification, race and ethnic relations, sociology of the family, and urban sociology.

Regardless of one's special interests, many students would do well to emphasize research methods and statistics. It is precisely these courses that are cited as most valuable by persons already employed in non-academic jobs who are asked to reconsider their education with the wisdom of hindsight. Statistics is not as difficult as many students fear and it often provides the most valuable and marketable career skills. This is especially true for the student who plans to stop with the BA.

And yet, even the most thorough BA degree is limited in the kinds of employment for which it prepares the student. Most professional work requires graduate education. Under graduate sociology majors frequently go on to graduate work in other areas such as social work, education, public health, business administration, and urban planning, not to mention law, medicine, and divinity school. A sociology major offers good training for them all, though many have additional prerequisites. These various degrees take different lengths of time and lead to different types of activities, opportunities, and economic and social rewards. For example, many law schools offer a professional degree after three years of study; a Masters of Business Administration will likely take two years, and a Masters of Education can be achieved in only one year in some schools. By all means, consult your local campus counselors for further information on such programs.

Graduate Training in Sociology: What about graduate work in sociology itself? Certainly this is necessary for a career in academic sociology, at least beyond the secondary school level. It is also important for many non-academic careers—or to put it another way, it is hard to imagine any career for which no graduate training is preferable to some. But how much training, of what sort, and where?

There are two basic graduate degrees available in sociology, the "doctorate" and the "masters" degree. The Doctorate in Philosophy (PhD) is typically the highest degree awarded in sociology. The Master's degree may be either an MA (Master of Arts) or an MS (Master of Science), depending upon the educational institution or the preference of either the department or, in some cases, the individual student. The PhD requires at least four or five years of study beyond the BA or BS and signifies competence for original research and scholarship as evidenced by the completion of a book length research study called a "dissertation". The Master's degree can be either a step toward the PhD or an end in its own right. It generally signifies sophisticated knowledge of the field's perspectives and methods, but does not necessarily indicate that any original research has been conducted. The Masters may take anywhere from one to three years, depending upon the particular department, whether or not a thesis is required, and the speed of the students.

There are some jobs and careers for which a Masters alone is adequate. A sociology MA or MS is sufficient for teaching at the secondary school or two-year college level and for work with public agencies and private businesses. However, there are few situations in which a PhD would not be preferable to a Master's degree. A PhD is usually required for teaching and research at the university level and for high-level employment with good promotion prospects in non-academic research institutes, private industry, and government agencies.

Most graduate schools which offer the PhD also offer a Master's degree as part of the program. However, there are a number of schools which offer the Master's only, and a few which are exclusively devoted to the PhD. The following describes a typical PhD program in somewhat more detail.

We have already noted that the PhD generally requires at least four or five years of study beyond the BA, and that it often involves completion of an MA degree as the first major step along the way. Few students move at an uninterrupted pace through the PhD program. While some have been awarded fellowships or use private means to allow full time study, many must work part time to support themselves. Fortunately, work is often available as part of the learning experience itself as a teaching assistant or research assistant. The typical "TA" helps a faculty member by grading exams, meeting with students who need extra help, and perhaps leading regular discussion sections. In some universities, advanced graduate students actually serve as instructors and teach their own separate courses under faculty supervision. "RAs" or research assistants are generally hired by faculty members who have received grants or have other financial support for specific research projects. Both TAs and RAs are generally expected to work about 20 hours each week and receive a stipend which may be combined with tuition reduction or waiver.

In most cases, new graduate students begin with courses quite similar in content to their advanced undergraduate courses, although the work is more demanding and sophisticated. At this level, courses typically focus on basic theoretical issues, research methods, and statistics. Many entering PhD students will not have majored in sociology as undergraduates and some may not have even taken a course; hence this work may be new to them. A year or so of such courses is usually followed by some form of examination and perhaps by the awarding of the Master's degree. At this point, training generally shifts more to *doing* sociology than learning it. Here lecture courses give way to seminars as advanced students begin to conduct individual research in their developing areas of specialization.

As these research activities proceed, students are exposed to the wide variety of methods which sociologists have at their disposal. These include computer skills, mathematical modeling, depth interviewing, participant observation, use of census materials and historical demography, questionnaires, surveys, and field observation. Besides such skills, the advanced graduate student is expected to develop enriched perspectives on the general core concerns of sociology by exploring specific problems of personal interest. At the same time, many departments require a demonstration of reading competence in one or two foreign languages; some of these schools permit a substitution of other skills, for example, "computer language".

At this point, the student is typically ready for a set of PhD examinations. These take very different forms in different departments. They range from long, written exams to relatively brief orals; they may include the presentation of a research paper in a colloquium setting, lengthy essays reviewing the sociological literature in a particular area, or any of a myriad of other tests of professional competence.

The final PhD hurdle is the dissertation. Although it must be an original piece of scholarship, it can take many forms and be somewhat brief or very long indeed. It is hoped that the dissertation will make a substantial contribution to existing scientific knowledge. Most departments require a formal proposal beforehand that must be approved by the student's committee of faculty advisors. This same committee often presides over the student's oral defense of the dissertation once it is completed. This defense is frequently a ritual which marks the end of the student's training and the beginning of a career as an autonomous scholar. However, the ritual is frequently an anticlimax since many students have already taken their first jobs and have been working full time while completing their dissertations during their free time.

Choosing a Graduate School: There are now slightly more than 130 universities in the U.S. which offer the PhD in sociology; most of these also offer the MA or MS, and there are over 150 additional schools which offer only a Master's degree. Clearly the prospective graduate student has ample room for choice. In fact, the choice is particularly important because even those schools which offer the same formal degrees will differ greatly in their strengths and weaknesses, the nature of their curriculum, and various special programs and opportunities.

To illustrate such differences, some graduate programs are geared particularly to prepare students for non-academic careers in business or government. Some of these departments feature student internships in agency offices rather than the teaching or research assistantships which are traditional in the more academically oriented departments. Some departments have highly structured curricula with a great many requirements, while others are relatively unstructured, leaving a good deal of the selection of courses to the individual student working autonomously. Departments continue to differ on such matters as whether they require foreign language skills and, if so, how many; whether they require statistics, and, if so, how advanced; whether they require a Master's degree en route to the PhD, and, if so, whether a Master's thesis is required or whether course work alone is sufficient.

Last, but probably most important, some departments will be strong in your particular area of interest, and others will be weak. In fact, a weaker department overall may be better in your area—whether criminology, demography, family and sex roles, Third World sociology and modernization, etc. Here you must obviously weigh the importance of your specific interests versus the value of more solid training in general.

In the midst of all these issues, how does anyone reach a decision? Fortunately, there is plenty of help available. For one thing, many of the above differences are summarized in a volume put out each year by the American Sociological Association. Called the Guide to Graduate Departments of Sociology, it contains critical information on over 200 programs in the U.S. and Canada. It includes degrees awarded, rosters of individual faculty and their interests, special programs, tuition and fees, the availability of fellowships and assistantships, deadlines for applications, and the names, addresses, and telephone numbers to contact for further information and application forms. College libraries should have a copy of the Guide (even last year's copy will do). Otherwise, one can be ordered directly from the American Sociological Association for a fee (write to 1722 N Street, N.W., Washington, D.C. 20036).

By all means consult with others. This should include undergraduate sociology teachers who know your strengths and weaknesses as well as your special interests. Encourage these teachers to be as candid as possible in counselling you toward a realistic choice. Make sure, too, that you are exploring several options, not just one, or not just the graduate school closest to home. Most sociology teachers have friends and colleagues in various departments around the country. Even if they do not know anyone personally in a particular department, they should be able to help you make a decision.

Early in your senior year or in the year before entering graduate school, you should begin to make contact with the schools you wish to consider. Most departments require you to fill out a rather extensive application form. This will often include a personal statement on why you want to pursue graduate work, why you chose sociology and that particular school. In addition, you will probably be asked to supply a transcript of your undergraduate record and several letters of reference. Many departments require applicants to take the nationally administered Graduate Record Examinations. This involves a battery of exams on verbal and quantitative skills, and sociology itself. Note that these examinations are administered on a fixed schedule in designated locations. You must apply to take these examinations several months in advance and your college should have all the appropriate information and forms. Finally, take advantage of the opportunity to visit the sociology departments you are considering. However departments differ in other ways, they also differ in tone and style and in the environment which they will provide the student. You are considering not just a set of sociology courses, but a larger learning context and a town and region in which you may be living for the next several years. Don't be misled by superficial differences, but it is probably just as silly for a surfing nut to go to the upper Midwest as it is for a student interested in 19th Century sociological theory to enroll in a department whose major emphasis is on mathematical models.

"When you choose a career, you bet your life"—this is how an earlier edition of this booklet began. Perhaps the statement is a bit too dramatic. People often change their careers; some change them several times during the course of their lives, and many who do not, should. It is not at all unusual for young adults to explore more than one career option before settling on one in particular. In fact, it is important for any young adult to embark on any career with full realization that the choice may be wrong. It is sad to see a person in his first job or a graduate student in his first year who is simply going through the motions. It is sadder still to project this over a lifetime.

All of this also underscores the importance of solid training as a basis for flexible career development. The better the training you have had and the more skills you have acquired, the better you will be able to take advantage of new opportunities. This is especially important in sociology because of the changes occurring within the discipline. Sociology is beginning to change from simply another academic subject to the source of sound judgments and possible solutions in confronting major social issues. Many sociologists predict that the next quarter-century will be the most exciting and most critical period in the field's 150-year history. If such estimates are correct, some of the best employment prospects will be outside of education and primarily in government circles; the real pay-offs will come not just in teaching and basic research, but also in policy research and administration.

But much of this is speculation, and its confirmation depends partly on the opportunities which develop and the skills of those responding. After all, society knows it needs medicine and routinely interrupts MDs for emergency services. Perhaps sociology will not really have arrived until you hear over the stadium loudspeaker: "Will sociologist number 26 please report to Community X for emergency consultation."

www.ingramcontent.com/pod-product-compliance
Lightning Source LLC
Chambersburg PA
CBHW082033300426
44117CB00015B/2469